Freedom

Freedom: An Introduction with Readings is an introduction to the arguments about individual freedom. It presupposes no prior knowledge of philosophy or political thought and is ideal for anyone coming to the topic for the first time.

With the beginner firmly in mind, Nigel Warburton carefully introduces and assesses the key arguments for and against individual freedom. Each chapter considers a fundamental argument about the scope of individual freedom, including the concepts of negative and positive freedom, freedom of belief, the Harm Principle, and freedom of speech and expression. Each argument is then clearly linked to a reading from one of the following key thinkers: Isaiah Berlin, Jeremy Waldron, Jonathan Wolff, Bernard Williams, Ronald Dworkin, H.L.A. Hart and Charles Taylor.

Freedom: An Introduction with Readings is a superb introduction to thinking clearly about the arguments for and against individual freedom and toleration. It will be of interest to students of philosophy, politics and critical thinking.

Nigel Warburton is lecturer in philosophy at the Open University. He is author of the bestsellers *Philosophy: The Basics*, *Thinking from A to Z*, *Philosophy: The Classics* and *Philosophy: Basic Readings*, all available from Routledge.

Freedom

An Introduction with Readings

Nigel Warburton

London and New York

First published 2001
by Routledge
11 New Fetter Lane, London EC4P 4EE

Simultaneously published in the USA and Canada
by Routledge
29 West 35th Street, New York, NY 10001

Routledge is an imprint of the Taylor & Francis Group

Typeset in Perpetua and Grotesque Monotype by Taylor & Francis Books Ltd
Printed and bound in Great Britain by TJ International Ltd, Padstow, Cornwall

British Library Cataloguing in Publication Data
A catalogue record for this book is available from the British Library

Library of Congress Cataloging in Publication Data
Warburton, Nigel, 1962–
    Freedom: An Introduction with Readings / Nigel Warburton.
    1. Liberty. I. Title.
    B824.4 .W36 2000
    323.44–00-031135

ISBN 0–415–21245–6 (hbk)
ISBN 0–415–21246–4 (pbk)

Contents

Preface

ACKNOWLEDGEMENTS

This book was originally written as part of the Open University course A211, 'Philosophy and the Human Situation'. I am grateful to members of the A211 Course Team and to Michael Clark, Shirley Coulson, Nicola Durbridge and Joanna Kerr for helpful comments. Peter Wright's editorial input significantly improved this book.

Grateful acknowledgement is made to the following sources for permission to reproduce readings: Isaiah Berlin (1969), 'Two Concepts of Liberty', taken from *The Proper Study of Mankind*, Pimlico, 1998, reproduced with permission of Curtis Brown Ltd, on behalf of The Isaiah Berlin Literary Trust, © Isaiah Berlin 1958, 1969; J. Waldron (1988), 'Locke: Toleration and the Rationality of Persecution' in S. Mendus (ed.), *Justifying Toleration: Conceptual and Historical Perspectives*, Cambridge University Press, also with permission of Professor Jeremy Waldron; J. Wolff (1996), *An Introduction to Political Philosophy*, Oxford University Press, by permission of Oxford University Press; B. Williams *et al.* (1981), *Obscenity and Film Censorship*, Cambridge University Press, © Crown Copyright 1979, 1981: Crown copyright is reproduced with the permission of the Controller of Her Majesty's Stationery Office; R. Dworkin (1991), 'Liberty and Pornography', *New York Review of Books*, by permission of the *New York Review of Books* and the author; H.L.A. Hart (1971), 'Immorality and Treason' in R.A. Wasserstrom (ed.), *Morality and the Law*, Wadsworth Publishing Co. Inc.; The Law Commission Consultation Paper 139, *Consent in the Criminal Law*, © Crown Copyright 1995: Crown copyright is reproduced with the permission of the Controller of Her Majesty's Stationery Office; Charles M. Taylor (1979), 'What's wrong with negative liberty' in A. Ryan (ed.), *The Idea of Freedom*, Oxford University Press, by permission of the author.

HOW TO USE THIS BOOK

This book consists of six chapters, each of which, together with the accompanying readings, was designed to provide a week's independent part-time study. Three of the six chapters concentrate on John Stuart Mill's classic defence of freedom, *On Liberty*, substantial extracts from which are included in the main text. Although this is an introduction to the topic of political freedom, it can also serve as an introduction to the study of philosophy in general and has been written assuming no prior knowledge of the subject on the part of the reader.

I have included exercises throughout. These are an integral part of the book. Answers and explanations are provided at the back of the book, or in some cases immediately after the exercise, but you will only get the full benefit of the exercises if you attempt them before checking to see what I have written there. As with most areas of philosophy, there is some scope for disagreement with the answers I have provided. These are intended for guidance; if you can make a good case for a different answer to any question, you should not be unduly worried if your answer differs from the one I have given, provided that you understand why I have given that answer.

Throughout the book there is an emphasis on the structure of arguments and on critical reasoning techniques. Those who have not studied philosophy before may want to begin by reading the Appendix 'Reasoning', which provides an introduction to the analysis of arguments and some general comments about the nature of philosophy. My book *Thinking from A to Z* (2000) goes further into reasoning techniques, providing an alphabetically arranged glossary of key terms and techniques. For those wanting a more general introduction to philosophy, my *Philosophy: The Basics* (1999), *Philosophy: The Classics* (1998) and *Philosophy: Basic Readings* (1999) may all be useful.

By the end of this book you should:

- have a good knowledge and understanding of some of the most important philosophical arguments for political freedom; in particular, you should have a detailed knowledge of Mill's arguments in *On Liberty*
- be able to offer arguments for and against the main positions discussed
- have had practice in a range of reasoning techniques
- have broadened your philosophical vocabulary
- have gained confidence in your ability to read long extracts from philosophical texts

1   Two concepts of freedom

OBJECTIVES

By the end of this chapter and its associated reading you should:

- be able to distinguish between negative and positive concepts of freedom
- have a good knowledge of the main points in Isaiah Berlin's article 'Two Concepts of Liberty'
- be able to recognize emotive language, to distinguish between necessary truths and contingent facts, and to appreciate what is involved in refutation by counter-example

---

INTRODUCTION

What are the limits of individual freedom in a civilized society? Should we tolerate unlimited freedom of speech, no matter how offensive the views expressed? Can the state ever be justified in interfering with what consenting adults choose to do in private? When, if ever, is coercion acceptable? Are all laws obstacles to freedom, or are they the very condition of achieving it? Should we sometimes force people to be free, or is that a contradiction in terms? These are serious questions. They're not merely abstract puzzles for philosophers to ponder in comfortable armchairs. They are the sorts of issues that people are prepared to die for.

Even if you choose to ignore them, the way other people answer these questions will impinge on your life. Philosophers at least since Plato's time have put forward answers to them. Here we'll be examining the arguments some of them have used. However, this won't just be a survey of some interesting thoughts on the subject. The point is to engage with the arguments — to examine their structure and content to see if they really support their conclusions. You needn't agree with these conclusions. As long as you think critically about the concept of freedom and are capable of arguing your case rather than simply stating your prejudices, you will be reading this book in the spirit in which it is intended.

To live in a society requires all kinds of co-operation. Usually this means curbing some of our more selfish desires in order to accommodate other people's interests. That is an element of the human situation. Given that our desires often conflict, it would be impossible for us to live in a society which imposed no limits whatsoever on what we do. It would be absurd to argue that we should all have complete licence to do whatever takes our fancy, no matter who is affected by our actions. I shouldn't be allowed to walk into your house and help myself to your stereo and television. Hardly anyone would argue that I should be free to steal your possessions simply because I want them; but deciding where to set the limits on individual freedom in less extreme cases is no easy task.

THE WORD 'FREEDOM'

The word 'freedom' can have powerful emotive force, that is, the power to arouse strong emotions. Its connotations are almost exclusively positive. If you describe a group as 'freedom fighters' this suggests that you approve of the cause for which they are fighting; call them 'terrorists' and you make clear your disapproval.

EXERCISE 1.1

EMOTIVE WORDS

The following statements all use language calculated to arouse emotion. Circle the words which are particularly emotive.

1   Meat is murder.
2   The workers in this factory are little more than beasts of burden driven on by an evil capitalist master.
3   I am firm, you are obstinate, he is pigheaded.
4   Television is entertainment for philistines.
5   Britons never, never, never shall be slaves.

Check your answers against the ones at the back of the book before reading on.

'Freedom' is not usually a neutral term. Freedom seems noble and worthy. It is hard to imagine anyone declaring that they are fundamentally opposed to it. Many people have laid down their lives in the name of freedom, or of liberty (like most writers on the subject, I'll be using the words 'freedom' and 'liberty' interchangeably here); yet we should not lose sight of the fact that 'freedom' is used to mean many different and sometimes incompatible things. Just because one word (or two, if you count 'liberty') is used, it does not follow that there is one thing to which it refers. A quick perusal of the philosophical writing about freedom will reveal the wide variety of approaches to political life which have been defended in the name of freedom.

The arguments we'll be examining are arguments for *political* or *social* freedom: the freedom of the individual in relation to other people and to the state. The aim is to explain and unravel some arguments for this kind of freedom. In the process we'll be examining some of the classic philosophical defences of particular types of freedom. The stress will always be on the arguments used rather than on the detailed historical context in which the views were originally expressed. Many of the central arguments transfer readily to the contemporary situation, if you make appropriate changes. They contribute to the pressing debates about the limits of individual freedom that affect us today.

You might think that the meaning of 'freedom' is straightforward: at an individual level it means not being imprisoned. If I'm imprisoned then, obviously, I'm not free. I can't choose to go out for a stroll, eat a pizza, go to the cinema and so on. But on the other hand, even as a prisoner, I am likely to be free in many respects. I am free to think about whatever I want to think about. In all but the cruellest prison regimes I will be free to pace around my cell, do a few push-ups or stare blankly at the wall; I'll also be free to write a letter to my family, perhaps even to study for a qualification, and so on. However, this may be a sentimental view of what prison life is actually like for most prisoners. Several of the activities I have described, particularly studying, require a certain amount of concentration. For most of us concentration requires relative quiet. Here is one prisoner's account of trying to study:

> One of the main problems is that of noise. Jail is a very noisy place and it is rarely quiet. The quietest periods are after 8.30 at night and the normal lock-up times. At other times it is very hard to concentrate with all the noise. I can't study during communal periods because of the loudness of the TV. Noise is a major problem.
>
> (Ashley *et al.* (1994), p. 12)

So is this prisoner really free to study? Although the prison authorities don't actively prevent him from doing so, the noise in the prison at some times of the day does. A prisoner's freedom may be curtailed in many ways beyond preventing him or her leaving the prison, and not all of those curtailments of freedom are necessarily a result of someone *deliberately* imposing restrictions on behaviour. Nevertheless, most prisoners have considerably more freedom in most respects than did Gulliver, in Swift's novel *Gulliver's Travels* (1726), when he woke up after being shipwrecked on the shore of Lilliput:

> I attempted to rise, but was not able to stir: for as I happened to lie on my back, I found my arms and legs were strongly fastened on each side to the ground; and my hair, which was long and thick, tied down in the same manner. I likewise felt several slender ligatures across my body, from my armpits to my thighs. I could only look upwards, the sun began to grow hot, and the light offended my eyes. I heard a confused noise about me, but in the posture I lay, could see nothing except the sky.
>
> (Swift 1985 edn, p. 55)

In this condition, Gulliver had virtually no freedom of movement. Even physical freedom is not a matter of all or nothing, but rather of degree. You may be imprisoned, but there are still further freedoms that you can lose.

For a nation, 'freedom' may mean not being occupied. France during most of the Second World War was not a free country in this sense as it was occupied by the Nazis or controlled by the Vichy government. The Resistance saw themselves as *freedom* fighters, risking their lives to liberate France. Their aim was quite simply a free France, which meant a France which was free from Nazi occupation. Yet when France was liberated it did not miraculously become free in every respect; nor were the French completely constrained in what they could do while the Nazis were in occupation.

However, 'a free nation' or 'a free state' may also mean one that is not totalitarian. A totalitarian state is one in which the state authorities, in principle at least, exercise control over most aspects of subjects' lives. Totalitarianism may take many different forms. Its essence, in its most extreme form, is captured in George Orwell's novel *Nineteen Eighty-Four*: because the state authorities want to have complete control over individuals' lives, there is an elaborate mechanism for surveillance, summed up in the slogan 'Big Brother is Watching You':

> A Party Member lives from birth to death under the eye of the Thought Police. Even when he is alone he can never be sure that he is alone. Wherever he may be, asleep or awake, working or resting, in his bath or in bed, he can be inspected without warning and without knowing that he is being inspected. Nothing that he does is indifferent. His friendships, his relaxations, his behaviour towards his wife and children, the expression of his face when he is alone, the words he mutters in sleep, even the characteristic movements of his body, are all jealously scrutinised. Not only any actual misdemeanour, but any eccentricity, however small, any change of habits, any nervous mannerism that could possibly be the symptom of an inner struggle, is certain to be detected. He has no freedom of choice in any direction whatever.
>
> (Orwell 1989 edn, p. 219)

In such a totalitarian state there is no significant private realm in which individuals can exercise free choice: every area of life is subject to control by the state authorities. Here, then, is another sense in which a state or nation can lack freedom.

What these examples show is that freedom isn't a matter of all or nothing. You can be free in some respects and not in others (usually the context in which freedom is being discussed makes clear what kind of freedom is at stake). And you can have a greater or lesser degree of a particular freedom.

When philosophers ask 'What is political freedom?' they are not asking for a dictionary definition. 'Political freedom', unlike, say, 'aardvark', isn't the sort of phrase that a dictionary definition is likely to shed much light upon. There is, as far as I know, no controversy about what an aardvark is. It is a species of animal; my dictionary says 'the ant bear, a South African edentate'. If I were unsure whether or not the animal in front of me was an aardvark, a competent zoologist could easily set me straight. There are established criteria for determining which animals are aardvarks; if an animal meets these criteria, then it must be an aardvark. But political freedom is a notion that has been argued about for centuries: there is no uncontroversial way of defining it. The definition you give usually implies a particular view about human beings and about the things we do or should value most. In this respect it is more like 'art' than like 'aardvark'. There are numerous, conflicting definitions of what art is. Similarly there are many different views about what political freedom is, and in particular about where its limits should be set.

ISAIAH BERLIN'S 'TWO CONCEPTS OF LIBERTY' (1958)

In a ground-breaking lecture, the philosopher and historian of ideas Isaiah Berlin (1909–97) argued that there are two basic types of freedom which have been defended by philosophers and political theorists: negative freedom and positive freedom. Within each category there is scope for a wide range of positions; but most theories of freedom fit quite comfortably into one category or the other.

Berlin's article is important for three reasons. First, it provides a useful distinction between these two types of freedom. Second, it makes a case for the view that theories of positive freedom have often been used as instruments of oppression. Third, by describing the incompatibility of various fundamental human aims in life, it suggests a reason why we put such a high value on freedom. For our purposes, the most important feature is the first, the distinction between the two types of freedom: negative and positive.

NEGATIVE FREEDOM

The concept of negative freedom centres on _freedom from_ interference. This type of account of freedom is usually put forward in response to the following sort of question: 'What is the area within which the subject – a person or group of persons – is or should be left to do or be what he is able to do or be, without interference by other persons?' (Berlin 1969, pp. 121–2; see Reading 1, p. 127). Or, more simply, 'Over what area am I master?' (Berlin 1969, p. xliii). Theories of negative freedom spell out the acceptable limits of interference in individuals' lives. You restrict my negative freedom when you restrict the number of choices I can make about my life. The extent of my negative freedom is determined by how many possible choices lie open to me, or, to use one of Berlin's metaphors, how many doors are unlocked. It is also determined by the types of choices that are available. Clearly not every sort of choice should be given equal status: some choices are of greater importance than others. For most of us having freedom of speech, even if we don't take advantage of this opportunity, is a more important freedom than the freedom to choose between ten different sorts of washing powder. This is how Berlin puts it: 'The extent of a man's negative liberty is, as it were, a function of what doors, and how many are open to him;[1] upon what prospects they open; and how open they are' (Berlin 1969, p. xlviii).

It doesn't matter whether or not I actually take advantage of the opportunities open to me: I am still free to the extent that I could, if I chose, take advantage of them:

The freedom of which I speak is opportunity for action, rather than action itself. If, although I enjoy the right to walk through open doors, I prefer not to do so, but to sit still and vegetate, I am not thereby rendered less free. Freedom is the opportunity to act, not action itself.

(Berlin 1969, p. xlii)

So, if you park your car across my drive, thereby preventing me from getting my car out, you restrict my freedom; and this is true even if I choose to stay in bed listening to my CDs all day, and would have done so even if you hadn't parked there. Or, if the state prevents me from going on strike by making my actions illegal, even if I don't have anything to strike about, and even if I don't ever intend to strike, my freedom is still curtailed. Negative freedom is a matter of the doors open to me, not of whether I happen to choose to go through them.

However, not all restrictions on my possible choices are infringements of my negative freedom. Berlin states that 'only restrictions imposed by other people affect my freedom.' Colloquially, we might say that because we are human we aren't free to jump ten feet in the air or free to understand what an obscure passage in a book by the notoriously difficult philosopher Hegel means. But when discussing political freedom, the sort we are interested in here, these sorts of restrictions on what we can do aren't counted as obstacles to freedom, however distressing they may be. Other people limit our freedom by what they do.

Limitations on our action brought about by the nature of the universe or the human body aren't relevant to the discussion of political freedom. Political freedom is a matter of the relations of power which hold between individuals and between individuals and the state.

The clearest cases in which freedom is restricted are when someone forces you to do something. You might be forced to join the army, for instance, if you live in a country which has compulsory military service. The law might force you to wear a crash helmet every time you ride your motorcycle. Your partner might force you to stay in rather than go out to the cinema, or to tidy up the kitchen rather than do another hour's study.

Read the following extract from Berlin's article. Then do the exercise below.

I am normally said to be free to the degree to which no man or body of men interferes with my activity. Political liberty in this sense is simply the area within which a man can act unobstructed by others. If I am prevented by others from doing what I could otherwise do, I am to that degree unfree; and if this area is contracted by other men beyond a certain minimum, I can be described as being coerced, or, it may be, enslaved. Coercion is not, however, a term that covers every form of inability. If I say that I am unable to jump more than ten feet in the air, or cannot read because I am blind, or cannot understand the darker pages of Hegel, it would be eccentric to say that I am to that degree enslaved or coerced. Coercion implies the deliberate interference of other human beings within the area in which I could otherwise act. You lack political liberty or freedom only if you are prevented from attaining a goal by human beings. Mere incapacity to attain a goal is not lack of political freedom. [The philosopher Helvétius (1715–71) made this point very clearly: 'The free man is the man who is not in irons, nor imprisoned in a gaol, nor terrorized like a slave by the fear

of punishment ... it is not lack of freedom not to fly like an eagle or swim like a whale'
(Berlin's note).]

(Berlin 1969, p. 122; see Reading 1, p. 128)

EXERCISE 1.2

NEGATIVE FREEDOM

Which of the following involve limitations on an individual's negative freedom in
the sense outlined by Berlin above? Not all the cases are clear-cut.

1   The state prevents you from purchasing certain kinds of pornography.
2   You aren't tall enough to pick quinces from the tree in your garden.
3   You aren't tall enough to join the police force.
4   You aren't rich enough to buy a private island.
5   You aren't permitted to own a handgun.
6   The law forces you to wear a seatbelt when driving.
7   No one has ever selected you to play football for your country.
8   You are forced to study philosophy against your will.
9   Someone has handcuffed you to a lamp-post.
10 You can't read because you are blind. Officers of an evil totalitarian regime
    blinded you to prevent you reading and writing subversive literature. You are
    denied access to braille books and audio tapes.
11 You are too poor to buy a loaf of bread because you've spent all your money on
    champagne.
12 You are simply too poor to buy a loaf of bread, not through any fault of your
    own.

Compare your answers with the answers and explanations at the back of the book
before reading on. Don't worry if your answers differ from the ones I have given,
provided that you can give good reasons to back up your position and can see why
I have given the answers I have done.

It might have seemed to follow from Berlin's account of negative freedom that
poverty couldn't count as a limitation on individual freedom. True, poverty effectively locks many doors. But these doors aren't necessarily locked by other
people's actions; poverty may have other, non-human, causes. It may be due to
the effects of freak weather conditions leading to famine; or perhaps to sudden
illness or accident. Whether or not poverty is to count as a limitation of negative
freedom depends entirely on your view of the *causes* of the poverty in question.
This becomes clear in the following passage from Berlin's essay:

It is argued, very plausibly, that if a man is too poor to afford something on which there is no
legal ban – a loaf of bread, a journey round the world, recourse to the law courts – he is as
little free to have it as he would be if it were forbidden him by law. If my poverty were a kind

of disease, which prevented me from buying bread, or paying for the journey round the world or getting my case heard, as lameness prevents me from running, this inability would not naturally be described as a lack of freedom, least of all political freedom. It is only because I believe that my inability to get a given thing is due to the fact that other human beings have made arrangements whereby I am, whereas others are not, prevented from having enough money with which to pay for it, that I think myself a victim of coercion or slavery.

[...]

'The nature of things does not madden us, only ill will does', said Rousseau. The criterion of oppression is the part that I believe to be played by other human beings, directly or indirectly with or without the intention of doing so, in frustrating my wishes. By being free in this sense I mean not being interfered with by others. The wider the area of non-interference the wider my freedom.

(Berlin 1969, pp. 122–3; Reading 1, p. 128)

If the man described above is too poor to buy a loaf of bread as a consequence of other people's actions, then, whether these other people intended this effect or not, his freedom has been curtailed. But if his poverty is a result of non-human causes, such as a drought-induced famine, or some natural disaster, terrible as his plight might be, it would not limit his negative freedom.

POSITIVE FREEDOM

Positive freedom is a more difficult notion to grasp than negative. Put simply it is *freedom to* do something rather than *freedom from* interference. Negative freedom is simply a matter of the number and kind of options that lie open for you and their relevance for your life; it is a matter of what you aren't prevented from doing; the doors that lie unlocked. Positive freedom, in contrast, is a matter of what you can actually do. All sorts of doors may be open, giving you a large amount of negative freedom, and yet you might find that there are still obstacles to taking full advantage of your opportunities. Berlin sometimes talks of positive liberty in terms of the question 'Who is master?' I want to be in control of my life, but there may, for example, be internal obstacles to my living the way I really want to. Here we might talk of my increasing my freedom (in the positive sense) by overcoming my less rational desires.

This is easier to understand if you consider some examples. I might recognize the value of study for making my life go well, but keep getting sidetracked by less important, immediately gratifying activities, such as going out for a drink, or staying in and spending the whole evening watching 'soaps' on television. I know that studying is important to me, and will increase my control over my life. But I really enjoy going out for a drink and I really enjoy watching television 'soaps'. So the short-term gratifications tend to seduce me away from activities which are better for me in the long term. My positive freedom would be increased if my 'higher' rational side could overcome my 'lower' tendency to be sidetracked. It is not a question of having more, or more significant, opportunities: the opportunity for me to study is there now. Rather it is a question of being able to take advantage of the opportunity by being in control of my life. Positive freedom in this example is a matter of my having the capacity to take the rational option as well as having the opportunity; whereas, according to a concept of negative freedom, the opportunities that I have alone determine the extent of my freedom. I am free to study in the negative sense since no one is preventing me from doing it; no one has locked away my books, or hidden my pen and paper; no one has dragged me out of the door to go to the pub, or chained me to my armchair in front of the television. However, I am not free in the positive sense; I am not truly free, because I am a slave to my tendency to be sidetracked. True positive freedom would involve seizing control of my life and making rational choices for myself. Those who defend positive freedom believe that just because no one is preventing you from doing something, it does not follow that you are genuinely free. Positive freedom is a matter of achieving your potential, not just having potential.

Consider another example, a real one this time. James Boswell, the eighteenth-century diarist and biographer of Dr Johnson, included the following in his journal for Sunday 31 March 1776. It describes how he spent a night in London following a dinner with friends:

> I behaved pretty decently. But when I got into the street, the whoring rage came upon me. I thought I would devote a night to it. I was weary at the same time that I was tumultuous. I went to Charing Cross Bagnio with a wholesome-looking, bouncing wench, stripped, and went to bed with her. But after my desires were satiated by repeated indulgence, I could not rest; so I parted from her after she had honestly delivered to me my watch and ring and handkerchief, which I should not have missed I was so drunk. I took a hackney-coach and was set down in Berkeley Square, and went home cold and disturbed and dreary and vexed, with remorse rising like a black cloud without any distinct form; for in truth my moral principle as to chastity was absolutely eclipsed for a time. I was in the miserable state of those whom the Apostle represents as working all uncleanness with greediness. I thought of my valuable spouse with the highest regard and warmest affection, but had a confused notion that my corporeal connection with whores did not interfere with my love for her. Yet I considered that I might injure my health, which there could be no doubt was an injury to her. This is an exact state of my mind at the time. It shocks me to review it.
>
> (Boswell 1992 edn, p. 295)

Here Boswell's confession reveals clearly the tension between two sides of his character. In his sober reflection he can see the foolishness of his having spent the night with a prostitute. Even soon after the event he is stricken with remorse, which he attempts to dispel by means of the transparent rationalization that somehow, despite breaking his principle of chastity, his infidelity does not interfere with his love for his wife. Yet he can't hide behind self-serving justifications for long, when he realizes that he has risked catching a venereal disease, something that undoubtedly has the potential to harm her. His higher self endorses a principle of chastity and fidelity; his lower self succumbs to temptations of the flesh. According to some theories of positive freedom, Boswell's 'true' freedom could only be realized by achieving a greater degree of self-mastery. To achieve 'true' freedom, your higher self must have control over the impulses of the lower self. Otherwise, you are simply a slave to passing emotions and desires; lusts in this case. Sober, Boswell is shocked by his actions of the previous night. Perhaps the only way he could have achieved 'true' freedom in the circumstances, given his lustful nature, would be to have been forced to go straight home to bed after dining with his friends. This would certainly have infringed his negative liberty in the sense of reducing his opportunities, but it would have allowed him to do what at some level he felt was best for him, and thereby to enjoy positive freedom in this respect.

From this it should be clear that the notion of positive liberty may rely on the belief that the self can be split into a higher and a lower self, and that the higher or rational self's priorities should be encouraged to overcome the lower, less rational self's inclinations – the passing desires that, if acted on, can so upset a life-plan. The higher self has desires for what will make the individual's life go well; it wishes to pursue worthwhile and noble goals. The lower self is easily led astray, often by irrational appetites. Consequently, advocates of positive liberty argue, we need to be protected against our own lower selves in order to realize the goals of our higher, 'true' selves. In many cases this can only be achieved by coercing us to behave in ways which seem to go against our desires; in fact this coercion is necessary to allow us to fulfil our rational higher desires, desires which we may even be unaware of having. On this view, the freedom which is self-mastery, or positive freedom, may only be achievable if our lower selves are constrained in their actions. By preventing me from going out for a drink or from watching television all night, you may help me to realize my 'true' freedom which is achievable only if I spend a significant portion of my available time studying. This is what I would have wanted had I been truly free. If Boswell had been forced to go home straight after dinner rather than given the opportunity to spend the night with a prostitute, his positive freedom might have been significantly extended.

This is Berlin's description of positive liberty and its origins:

> The 'positive' sense of the word 'liberty' derives from the wish on the part of the individual to be his own master. I wish my life and decisions to depend on myself, not on external forces of whatever kind. I wish to be the instrument of my own, not of other men's acts of will. I wish to be a subject, not an object; to be moved by reasons, by conscious purposes which are my own, not by causes which affect me, as it were, from outside. I wish to be somebody, not nobody; a doer – deciding, not being decided for, self-directed and not acted upon by external nature or by other men as if I were a thing, or an animal, or a slave incapable of playing a human role – that is, of conceiving goals and policies of my own and realizing them. This is at least part of what I mean when I say that I am rational, and that it is my reason that distinguishes me as a human being from the rest of the world. I wish, above all, to be conscious of myself as a thinking, willing, active being, bearing responsibility for his choices and able to explain them by reference to his own ideas and purposes. I feel free to the degree that I believe this to be true, and enslaved to the degree that I am made to realize that it is not.
>
> (Berlin 1969, p. 131; see Reading 1, p. 133)

It is important to realize that Berlin's notion of positive liberty doesn't just apply to self-mastery at the individual level; it also encompasses theories of freedom which emphasize collective control over common life. So, for example, when someone calls a society a free society because its members play an active role in controlling it through their participation in democratic institutions, they are appealing to a notion of positive freedom rather than of negative freedom. In this example the people as a whole are free because they, collectively, have mastery over the life of their society. A free society based upon the concept of negative freedom would typically be one in which state interference in individual lives is kept to a minimum. This would not necessarily be a democratic society, since a benevolent dictator might be concerned to provide an extensive realm of individual negative freedom for each of his or her subjects.

EXERCISE 1.3

POSITIVE AND NEGATIVE FREEDOM

Which sort of conception of freedom, positive or negative, is appealed to in each case? Bear in mind that not all the answers are clear-cut.

1   The state intervenes to prevent an alcoholic drinking himself to death on the grounds that this is what, in his sober and rational moments, he would clearly desire and so is a basic condition of his gaining true freedom.
2   The state protects an alcoholic's freedom to consume huge amounts of whisky in the privacy of his or her own home.
3   I cease to be free when I follow my baser sensual appetites: I am in thrall to mere passing desire.
4   It is an infringement on my freedom to prevent me from engaging in consensual sado-masochism in the privacy of my own dungeon.
5   I don't need the nanny state forcing me to have fluoride in my drinking water for my own good: that infringes my freedom.
6   You can only really be free in a well-governed state with harsh but well-chosen laws which shape your life in a rational way, thereby encouraging you to flourish. Increasing your opportunities to make a mess of your life doesn't increase your freedom in any meaningful sense.

Turn to the back of the book and compare your answers with the answers there before reading on.

Berlin's distinction between negative and positive freedom remains a useful one, and much of this book is structured around it. However, his aim in the paper was not simply to make the distinction, but rather to make a claim about the ways in which theories of positive freedom have been misused.

THE MISUSE OF THE CONCEPT OF POSITIVE LIBERTY

One of the main claims that Berlin makes in 'Two Concepts of Liberty' is a historical one. It is that positive theories of freedom, or perversions of them, have been more frequently used as instruments of oppression than have negative ones. These positive theories typically rely on a split between a 'higher' and a 'lower' self, or between a 'rational' and an 'empirical' self, as Berlin sometimes puts it. Coercion is justified on the grounds that it leads to a realization of the aims of the higher or rational self, even if the lower, everyday, empirical self opposes the coercion with all its might. The final humiliation in such a situation is to be told that, despite appearances, what is going on is not coercion, since it actually increases your freedom. In other words, Berlin believes that positive theories of freedom have historically been used to justify some kinds of oppression and that it is a relatively short step from saying that freedom involves self-mastery to the justification of all kinds of state interference in the lives of individuals on the grounds that, in Rousseau's words, it can, in some circumstances, be right to be 'forced to be free'.

Read the following extract from Berlin's article (1969, pp. 131–4; see Reading 1, pp. 133–5), and then answer the questions below.

> The freedom which consists in being one's own master, and the freedom which consists in not being prevented from choosing as I do by other men, may, on the face of it, seem concepts at no great logical distance from each other – no more than negative and positive ways of saying much the same thing. Yet the 'positive' and 'negative' notions of freedom historically developed in divergent directions not always by logically reputable steps, until, in the end, they came into direct conflict with each other.
>
> One way of making this clear is in terms of the independent momentum which the, initially perhaps quite harmless, metaphor of self-mastery acquired. 'I am my own master'; 'I am slave to no man'; but may I not (as Platonists or Hegelians tend to say) be a slave to nature? Or to my own 'unbridled' passions? Are these not so many species of the identical genus 'slave' – some political or legal, others moral or spiritual? Have not men had the experience of liberating themselves from spiritual slavery, or slavery to nature, and do they not in the course of it become aware, on the one hand, of a self which dominates, and, on the other, of something in them which is brought to heel? This dominant self is then variously identified with reason, with my 'higher nature', with the self which calculates and aims at what will satisfy it in the long run, with my 'real', or 'ideal', or 'autonomous' self, or with my self 'at its best'; which is then contrasted with irrational impulse, uncontrolled desires, my 'lower' nature, the pursuit of immediate pleasures, my 'empirical' or 'heteronomous' self, swept by every gust of desire and passion, needing to be rigidly disciplined if it is ever to rise to the full height of its 'real' nature. Presently the two selves may be represented as divided by an even larger gap: the real self may be conceived as something wider than the individual (as the term is normally understood), as a social 'whole' of which the individual is an element or aspect: a tribe, a race, a church, a state, the great society of the living and the dead and the yet unborn. This entity is then identified as being the 'true' self which, by imposing its collective, or 'organic', single will upon its recalcitrant 'members', achieves its own, and therefore their, 'higher' freedom. The perils of using organic metaphors to justify the coercion of some men by others in order to raise them to a 'higher' level of freedom have often been pointed out. But what gives such plausibility as it has to this kind of language is that we recognize that it is possible, and at times justifiable, to coerce men in the name of some goal (let us say, justice or public health) which they would, if they were more enlightened, themselves pursue, but do not, because they are blind or ignorant or corrupt. This renders it easy for me to conceive of myself as coercing others for their own

sake, in their, not my, interest. I am then claiming that I know what they truly need better than they know it themselves. What, at most, this entails is that they would not resist me if they were rational and as wise as I and understood their interests as I do. But I may go on to claim a good deal more than this. I may declare that they are actually aiming at what in their benighted state they consciously resist, because there exists within them an occult entity – their latent rational will, or their 'true' purpose – and that this entity, although it is belied by all that they overtly feel and do and say, is their 'real' self, of which the poor empirical self in space and time may know nothing or little; and that this inner spirit is the only self that deserves to have its wishes taken into account. Once I take this view, I am in a position to ignore the actual wishes of men or societies, to bully, oppress, torture them in the name, and on behalf, of their 'real' selves, in the secure knowledge that whatever is the true goal of man (happiness, performance of duty, wisdom, a just society, self-fulfilment) must be identical with his freedom – the free choice of his 'true', albeit often submerged and inarticulate, self.

This paradox has been often exposed. It is one thing to say that I know what is good for X, while he himself does not; and even to ignore his wishes for its – and his – sake; and a very different one to say that he has *eo ipso* chosen it, not indeed consciously, not as he seems in everyday life, but in his role as a rational self which his empirical self may not know – the 'real' self which discerns the good, and cannot help choosing it once it is revealed. This monstrous impersonation, which consists in equating what X would choose if he were something he is not, or at least not yet, with what X actually seeks and chooses, is at the heart of all political theories of self-realization. It is one thing to say that I may be coerced for my own good which I am too blind to see: this may, on occasion, be for my benefit; indeed it may enlarge the scope of my liberty. It is another to say that if it is my good, then I am not being coerced, for I have willed it, whether I know this or not, and am free (or 'truly' free) even while my poor earthly body and foolish mind bitterly reject it, and struggle against those who seek however benevolently to impose it, with the greatest desperation.

EXERCISE 1.4

COMPREHENSION

1   Lines 1–2. Which of the following two phrases describes the concept of positive freedom and which the concept of negative freedom?

   (a)   'The freedom which consists in being one's own master.'
   (b)   'The freedom which consists in not being prevented from choosing as I do by other men.'

2   Lines 8–30. Put the main point of these lines in your own words. You should not use more than fifty words to do this.
3   Lines 16–30. Why has Berlin put the words 'real' and 'higher' in such phrases as ' "real" nature' and ' "higher" freedom' in quotes?
4   Berlin (lines 31–41) says that coercing people for their own sake is sometimes

justifiable. What, then, is the 'good deal more than this' which advocates of positive liberty sometimes go on to claim (lines 42–53)?

5 A paradox is a situation which yields an apparent contradiction. What is the paradox that Berlin refers to in line 54?

Compare your answers with those at the back of the book. Then re-read the whole passage before reading on. You should find that your understanding of the main points made in the passage has increased significantly.

Although Berlin doesn't actually use the term, in the passage you have just read Berlin contrasts paternalism with a particular way in which the concept of positive freedom has frequently been misused. Paternalism is coercing people for their own sake. An example of paternalism is putting fluoride in drinking water, whether or not the population wants it there, on the grounds that it will significantly reduce the incidence of tooth decay, and thus improve the health of the population. The fluoride is added for the good of the people who drink the water, whether they realize that it will do them good or not. Misuse of positive freedom differs from this in that it involves the claim that the coercion is something the people coerced have, in a sense, chosen: they have 'chosen' it as rational selves, but not in the everyday sense of 'chosen'. Though it might not seem like it to them, they are, allegedly, freer as a result of the coercion. In other words, this misuse of positive freedom rests on the belief that it can be acceptable to force people to be free. Indeed, in some cases this seems to be the only way in which, according to the theory, some individuals will ever attain 'true' freedom. This move from positive liberty to forcing people to be 'free' has, in recent history, led to oppression on a massive scale. It has been the source of much misery and many ruined lives.

It is important to realize that Berlin is *not* saying that only the concept of positive liberty can be misused. In fact it is obvious that versions of the negative concept can also be used to justify some terrible states of affairs. In some situations, preserving individuals' freedom from interference might be tantamount to encouraging the strong to thrive at the expense of the weak. As it has been memorably put, 'Freedom for the pike is death for the minnows.' The pike might think it an excellent idea to allow fish to go about their business unimpeded by rules or interventions. The minnows, who stand to be his lunch, will no doubt see the limitations of a negative theory of liberty which allowed them to be eaten on the grounds that otherwise the pike's freedom would have been seriously curtailed.

However, although theories based on a concept of negative liberty can lead to unsatisfactory situations, Berlin's point is that historically this is not usually what has happened. It is the theories of positive liberty which have led to human tragedy on a massive scale. The terrible irony is that the justification for oppression has so often been that coercion actually increases the 'real' or 'true' freedom of the coerced.

Berlin has sometimes been interpreted as saying that all theories of positive freedom are bad, and that the only type of theory worth defending is one based on the concept of negative freedom – freedom from interference. But this is a misinterpretation which he has been at pains to dispel. For instance, he has written:

> 'Positive' liberty, conceived as the answer to the question, 'By whom am I to be governed?', is a valid universal goal. I do not know why I should have been held to doubt this … I can only repeat that the perversion of the notion of positive liberty into its opposite – the apotheosis of authority – did occur, and has for a long while been one of the most familiar and depressing phenomena of our time. For whatever reason or cause, the notion of 'negative' liberty (conceived as the answer to the question 'How much am I governed?'), however disastrous the consequences of its unbridled forms, has not historically been twisted by its theorists as often or as effectively into anything so darkly metaphysical or socially sinister or remote from its original meaning as its 'positive' counterpart. The first can be turned into its opposite and still exploit the favourable associations of its innocent origins. The second has, much more frequently, been seen, for better and for worse, for what it was; there has been no lack of emphasis, in the last hundred years, upon its more disastrous implications. Hence, the greater need, it seems to me, to expose the aberrations of positive liberty than those of its negative brother.
>
> (Berlin 1969, p. xlvii)

He has also expanded on this topic in an interview:

> The only reason for which I have been suspected of defending negative liberty against positive and saying that it is more civilized, is because I do think that the concept of positive liberty, which is of course essential to a decent existence, has been more often abused or perverted than that of negative liberty. Both are genuine questions; both are inescapable … Both these concepts have been politically and morally twisted into their opposites. George Orwell is excellent on this. People say 'I express your real wishes. You may think that you know what you want, but I, the Führer, we the Party Central Committee, know you better than you know yourself, and provide you with what you would ask for if you recognised your "real" needs.' Negative liberty is twisted when I am told that liberty must be equal for the tigers and for the sheep and that this cannot be avoided even if it enables the former to eat the latter if coercion by the state is not to be used. Of course unlimited liberty for capitalists destroys the liberty of the workers, unlimited liberty for factory-owners or parents will allow children to be employed in the coal-mines. Certainly the weak must be protected against the strong, and liberty to that extent be curtailed. Negative liberty must be curtailed if positive liberty is to be sufficiently realised; there must be a balance between the two, about which no clear principles can be enunciated. Positive and negative liberty are both perfectly valid concepts, but it seems to me that historically more damage has been done by pseudo-positive than by pseudo-negative liberty in the modern world.
>
> (Jahanbegloo 1993, p. 41)

As can be seen from the mention of the Führer and of the Party Central Committee, Berlin believes that in the twentieth century both Nazism and communism have perverted the notion of positive freedom and that both Nazi and communist states have coerced their citizens, often against their will, to realize what their coercers believe to be their 'true' freedom, or the 'true' freedom of their nation state.

Berlin is making a generalization about the concept of positive freedom on the basis of his observation of history, some of it first hand (as a boy, he witnessed the Russian revolutions of 1917). This is a historical thesis rather than a philosophical one: it is a thesis about what has actually happened. In the part of his paper where he puts forward this thesis, Berlin is writing more as a historian of ideas than as a philosopher pure and simple. In Berlin's case his activity as a historian and as a philosopher are intimately entwined. However, it is important to realize that philosophers don't primarily put forward empirical hypotheses: their main concerns are the analysis of concepts (such as Berlin engages in, in his examination of the nature of the two types of freedom); and the analysis of arguments. (For more on the nature of philosophy, see the Appendix 'Reasoning', especially pages 227–32.)

The argument Berlin has presented about past perversions of the concept of positive freedom is based on empirical evidence; that is, its truth or falsity depends on facts, facts which are ultimately discovered by observation. It is not a logically necessary consequence of the intrinsic nature of the concept of positive freedom that it is prone to this sort of misuse. It is a *contingent* fact: this is just how it is, but it could have been otherwise. This distinction between what is logically necessary and what is contingent is an important one. If something is logically necessary you can't deny it without contradicting yourself. For example, it is logically necessary that all vertebrates have backbones; it is true by definition since 'vertebrate' just means 'creature with a backbone'. Similarly it is necessarily true that if someone is dead they are no longer living – that just follows from the meaning of 'dead'. Saying 'I've found a vertebrate with no backbone', or 'My uncle is dead but he's still alive' (unless you are giving a new meaning to 'vertebrate' or 'alive', in which case you would be guilty of equivocation) involves a contradiction. It would be like saying 'Here is a creature which both has and does not have a backbone', or 'My uncle both is and is not alive.' In contrast contingent facts need not be as they are; as a consequence we usually have to make some sort of observation or conduct some sort of experiment to discover what they are. So, for example, it could have turned out historically that a concept of negative freedom was more often used as an excuse for oppression than a positive one. It is a contingent fact that, at least according to Berlin, things are the other way round. The way Berlin arrived at his conclusion was by considering the evidence of recent history.

EXERCISE 1.5

NECESSARY TRUTHS AND CONTINGENT STATEMENTS

Which of the following are logically necessary truths, and which contingent statements?

1   All aardvarks are animals.

2   All heads of industry are overpaid.

3   Many philosophers wear glasses.

4   Some politicians are corrupt.

5   Nothing that is red all over is turquoise.

6   Everyone who is over 18 is over 16.

7   The concept of negative freedom has rarely been invoked to justify oppression.

Check your answers against those at the back of the book before reading on.

THE NOTION OF A FINAL SOLUTION

Motivating much of Berlin's essay on the two concepts of liberty is a pair of related beliefs. First he believes that the notion of a so-called 'final solution', the belief that ultimately all human differences of goal can be reconciled, has led to terrible consequences, often to atrocities. Secondly, he believes that there is not, in principle, any way of resolving the widely different goals that human beings have. There can, then, be no simple panacea to cure all the problems that arise as a result of conflicting aims. This second belief goes some way to explaining why we place such a high value on negative freedom.

Here is his account of the consequences of attempting a final solution (a term which he presumably chose for its emotive force, given that it is the term which is usually used for Hitler's attempt to exterminate the Jewish people):

> One belief, more than any other, is responsible for the slaughter of individuals on the altars of the great historical ideals – justice or progress or the happiness of future generations, or the sacred mission or emancipation of a nation or race or class, or even liberty itself, which demands the sacrifice of individuals for the freedom of society. This is the belief that somewhere, in the past or in the future, in divine revelation or in the mind of an individual thinker, in the pronouncements of history or science, or in the simple heart of an uncorrupted good man, there is a final solution. This ancient faith rests on the conviction that all the positive values in which men have believed must, in the end, be compatible, and perhaps even entail one another …
>
> It is a commonplace that neither political equality nor efficient organisation nor social justice is compatible with more than a modicum of individual liberty, and certainly not with unrestricted *laissez-faire*; that justice and generosity, public and private loyalties, the demands of genius and the claims of society, can conflict violently with each other. And it is no great way from that to the generalisation that not all good things are compatible, still less all the ideals of mankind. But somewhere, we shall be told and in some way, it must be possible for all these values to live together, for unless this is so, the universe is not a cosmos, not a harmony; unless this is so, conflicts of value may be an intrinsic irremovable element in human life. To admit that the fulfilment of some of our ideals may in principle make the fulfilment of others impossible is to say that the notion of total human fulfilment is a formal contradiction, a metaphysical chimera.

(Berlin 1969, pp. 167–8)

The central point here, like the argument about past misuses of the notion of positive liberty discussed in the previous section, is a historical claim, a pessimistic one. Berlin is saying that historically the belief in a 'final solution', a way of harmonizing all the different goals that human beings have, has had disastrous consequences for those whose goals don't happen to have fitted neatly into the master plan.

However, towards the end of this quotation he introduces a different idea, namely that the different goals may in principle be irreconcilable: perhaps there just can't be a way of harmonizing all the different goals (such as justice, equality and the cultivation of geniuses), that people have and do consider worthwhile. If this thesis is true, then it follows that 'the notion of total human fulfilment is a formal contradiction.'

What this means is that the notion of total human fulfilment embodies an unachievable goal. If it is a necessary feature of human goals that they can't all simultaneously be achieved, then it follows that any theory that says they can is self-contradictory: it will end up implying both that human goals cannot all be fulfilled and that they can, which is a logical absurdity. In other words, Berlin is suggesting that the notion of human goals carries within it the implication that not all human goals can be fulfilled. But what is his evidence for this pessimistic conclusion?

He considers two possibilities: first that there might be some *a priori* guarantee of the notion that the goals different people have can actually be harmonized. By '*a priori* guarantee' he means an argument that doesn't rely on empirical observation, but rather provides a logically secure proof of the point independently of any evidence. We can, for instance, know that all aardvarks are animals independently of conducting any experiments on actual aardvarks; this is because it is true by definition that all aardvarks are animals. You can know *a priori* that if you have in your sack something that isn't an animal, then it certainly isn't an aardvark. So, returning to Berlin's discussion: he suggests that there is no *a priori* guarantee that human goals can all in fact be achieved. He assumes this, rather than providing any argument to show that it is true. If we accept this point (which is reasonable enough since it is unclear how we could know *a priori* that all human goals could in principle be harmonized), we must fall back on observation. Do we, then, have any empirical evidence that all human goals might in fact be fulfilled? Or, to put it another way, has human history provided us with any evidence that would suggest the fundamental compatibility of the diverse goals that different human beings seek and value? Berlin's answer to these questions is a straight 'No':

> But if we are not armed with an *a priori* guarantee of the proposition that a total harmony of true values is somewhere to be found – perhaps in some ideal realm the characteristics of which we can, in our finite state, not so much as conceive – we must fall back on the ordinary resources of empirical observation and ordinary human knowledge. And these certainly give us no warrant for supposing (or even understanding what would be meant by saying) that all good things, or all bad things for that matter, are reconcilable with each other. The world that we encounter in ordinary experience is one in which we are faced with choices between ends equally ultimate, and claims equally absolute, the realisation of some

of which must inevitably involve the sacrifice of others. Indeed, it is because this is their situation that men place such immense value upon the freedom to choose; for if they had assurance that in some perfect state, realisable by men on earth, no ends pursued by them would ever be in conflict, the necessity and agony of choice would disappear, and with it the central importance of the freedom to choose. Any method of bringing this final state nearer would then seem fully justified, no matter how much freedom were sacrificed to forward its advance. It is, I have no doubt, some such dogmatic certainty that has been responsible for the deep, serene, unshakeable conviction in the minds of some of the most merciless tyrants and persecutors in history that what they did was fully justified by its purpose. I do not say that the ideal of self-perfection – whether for individuals or nations or churches or classes – is to be condemned in itself, or that the language which was used in its defence was in all cases the result of a confused or fraudulent use of words, or of moral or intellectual perversity. Indeed, I have tried to show that it is the notion of freedom in its 'positive' sense that is at the heart of the demands for national or social self-direction which animate the most powerful and morally just public movements of our time, and that not to recognise this is to misunderstand the most vital facts and ideas of our age. But equally it seems to me that the belief that some single formula can in principle be found whereby all the diverse ends of men can be harmoniously realised is demonstrably false. If, as I believe, the ends of men are many and not all of them are in principle compatible with each other, then the possibility of conflict – and of tragedy – can never wholly be eliminated from human life, either personal or social. The necessity of choosing between absolute claims is then an inescapable characteristic of the human condition.

(Berlin 1969, pp. 168–9)

If Berlin is right that it is a fundamental and inescapable feature of being human that we have to choose between incompatible alternatives (both as individuals and as members of a society), in a sense creating ourselves through our choices, then this helps to explain why freedom is so important to us. It is through our freely made choices that we make ourselves what we are, whether as individuals or societies. If there were some true 'final solution', then it wouldn't matter whether we made the choices, or someone else made the right ones for us: one simple concept of positive freedom would be sufficient, and coercion might be justified on the basis of it. But, since, as Berlin believes, no final solution is in principle ever going to harmonize the different aims that human beings have, and since there are numerous incompatible, worthwhile ways of living (a view some-times known as pluralism), a combination of negative and positive freedom is a precondition of a satisfactory life. Take away the guarantee of some basic negative freedoms for all adults, and the result will be misery for those whose aims in life do not conveniently harmonize with the dominant view in that society.

BERLIN CRITICIZED: ONE CONCEPT OF FREEDOM?

I've already mentioned that the most important feature of Berlin's article for our purposes is his distinction between negative and positive concepts of freedom: freedom from constraint, and the freedom that results from self-mastery or self-realization. Most discussion of Berlin's article has also focused on this distinction.

Now I want to consider a criticism of the distinction between two types of freedom.

The whole article rests on the assumption that we can make a meaningful distinction between negative and positive concepts of freedom. Gerald MacCallum challenged this view in an article, 'Negative and Positive Freedom', in which he claimed that there is just one concept of freedom, not two, and that the idea that there are two concepts introduces confusion about what is really at stake. MacCallum summarizes his position on the distinction between negative and positive concepts of freedom:

> the distinction between them has never been made sufficiently clear, is based in part upon a serious confusion, and has drawn attention away from precisely what needs examining if the differences separating philosophers, ideologies, and social movements concerned with freedom are to be understood. The corrective advised is to regard freedom as always one and the same triadic relation, but recognise that various contending parties disagree with each other in what they understand to be the ranges of the term variables. To view the matter in this way is to release oneself from a prevalent but unrewarding concentration on 'kinds' of freedom, and to turn attention toward the truly important issues in this area of social and political philosophy.
>
> (MacCallum, in Miller 1991, p. 100)

The single concept of freedom that MacCallum puts forward as a replacement for Berlin's two concepts is 'triadic'. All this means is that it has three parts. The three parts are as follows: freedom is always freedom for someone; it is also freedom from some possible constraint; and it is freedom to do (or not do) something. MacCallum believes that in any discussion of freedom, we should be able to fill in the details for each of the three parts. When one of the parts seems to be missing this is simply because it is implicit in the context. So, for example, any discussion of freedom of speech will, implicitly or explicitly, refer to some person or persons who are or are not constrained to make some sort of public statement.

What MacCallum is doing is arguing that there is a simpler and more useful concept of freedom available than the two concepts set out by Berlin. This simpler concept embodies aspects of both the negative and the positive concepts of freedom described by Berlin. However, Berlin has responded to this criticism by pointing out that there are important cases in which freedom is at issue which cannot be fitted into this three-part concept of freedom. Here is Berlin's response:

> It has been suggested that liberty is always a triadic relation: one can only seek to be free from X to do or be Y; hence 'all liberty' is at once negative and positive or, better still, neither ... This seems to me an error. A man struggling against his chains or a people against enslavement need not consciously aim at any definite further state. A man need not know how he will use his freedom; he just wants to remove the yoke. So do classes and nations.
>
> (Berlin 1969, footnote, p. xliii)

Put simply, what Berlin has done here is to provide several counter-examples to

MacCallum's general claim that all discussions of freedom can be resolved into a single triadic concept of freedom with varying content. To MacCallum's claim that freedom must always include an explicit or implicit view about what it is freedom to do or be, Berlin has presented some cases in which this does not appear to be so. Any general claim, such as one that begins 'All ... are ... ' (e.g. all aardvarks have long tongues) can be refuted by a single counter-example (e.g. in this case, a short-tongued aardvark). If someone claims that all mammals live on land, you only need to cite the single counter-example of dolphins to make clear that the generalization is false. Similarly, if someone claims that no one ever lived over the age of one hundred and twenty, you only need to produce evidence that one person has lived to be one hundred and twenty-one to refute their claim. (Notice that the word 'refute' means 'demonstrate to be false'; it shouldn't be confused with the word 'repudiate' which simply means 'deny'.) Counter-examples provide a powerful way of undermining a generalization.

EXERCISE 1.6

GENERALIZATIONS REFUTED BY COUNTER-EXAMPLE

Which of the following pairs of statements consist of a generalization followed by a refutation by counter-example?

1   No one has ever returned from the dead.
No one will ever return from the dead.

2   All cats like eating tuna fish.
My cat detests tuna fish and won't touch it.

3   All bachelors of arts have degrees.
My aunt is a bachelor of arts.

4   No self-respecting intellectual would enjoy watching television 'soap operas'.
A.J. Ayer was a self-respecting intellectual and he enjoyed watching television 'soap operas'.

5   Everyone who has written about freedom has maintained that there are at least two concepts of freedom.
MacCallum has written about freedom maintaining that there is just one basic concept of freedom.

Compare your answers with those at the back of the book before reading on.

If any of Berlin's examples are accurate descriptions of possible states of affairs, then it follows that he has refuted MacCallum's notion that all meaningful senses of freedom can be captured within a single triadic concept. It *does* seem reasonable to say that someone struggling for freedom may just seek to 'remove the yoke'. Indeed this seems to be a basic sense in which we use the word 'freedom', one that is not captured by MacCallum's triadic concept.

Reading
p. 127

READING

When you have finished this chapter, try reading through the long extract from Berlin's 'Two Concepts of Liberty' (Reading 1). It concentrates on the distinction between negative and positive liberty and doesn't cover the issues raised in the second half of this chapter. Don't worry if you can't follow every point; Berlin refers to a wide range of thinkers in passing, most of whose work you probably won't know. Also, like many philosophers, he writes at quite an abstract level. However, much of this essay should already be familiar to you from the long quotations included in this book. The discussion of Mill's *On Liberty* (pp. 130–3) should give you a succinct introduction to the book we'll be looking at closely in Chapters 3 and 4.

CONCLUSION

This chapter has introduced Berlin's two concepts of freedom. This provides a framework for understanding the various arguments for freedom that we'll be examining in subsequent chapters. In the next chapter we will examine an argument for a specific kind of negative freedom, namely freedom from coercion in matters of religion.

CHAPTER SUMMARY

'Freedom' can mean many different things; the word can have a powerful emotive force. We're concerned here with political freedom. Isaiah Berlin distinguished between a concept of negative freedom and a concept of positive freedom. Negative freedom is freedom from interference, it is a matter of the opportunities that lie open to you. Positive freedom is the capability of doing what you really want to do. Historically, according to Berlin, the concept of positive freedom has been used to justify various kinds of oppression. Berlin also believes that there is no 'final solution', no simple way of reconciling the different goals that different people have. Berlin's view, that there are two concepts of freedom, has been attacked by Gerald MacCallum, who thinks there is only one concept. Berlin has provided several counter-examples to MacCallum's point.

FURTHER READING

The complete text of Isaiah Berlin's essay 'Two Concepts of Liberty' is contained in his *Four Essays on Liberty* (Oxford University Press, 1969). This book also contains an essay on John Stuart Mill's theory of liberty; this would provide useful background material for Chapters 3–5 of this book. A more wide-ranging selection of Berlin's essays is *The Proper Study of Mankind* (Pimlico, 1998). This also includes the full text of 'Two Concepts of Liberty'. The best commentary on Berlin's writings is *Isaiah Berlin* (Fontana, 1995) by John Gray. Although quite difficult in places, this book extracts the main philosophical themes from Berlin's work.

NOTE

1   It is worth bearing in mind when reading extracts from Berlin's article that it was written in the late 1950s when there was little concern about the apparent sexism of using the word 'man' to mean 'human', i.e. man or woman. He certainly does not intend to imply that only men can be free, or that only men can limit another's freedom. For 'man' read 'human being' or 'person'.

2 Freedom and belief

JOHN LOCKE'S *A LETTER CONCERNING TOLERATION* (1689)

Should the state allow its members to follow the religion of their choice, or should they be coerced into orthodoxy? What limits should be set on religious toleration? These were particularly pressing questions in seventeenth-century Europe, as they still are in many parts of the world today. In that period religion was the unquestioned centre of most people's lives and religious persecution was rife. For example, in France, following the revocation of the Edict of Nantes, there was widespread persecution of Huguenots, who were Protestants, by Roman Catholics. Maurice Cranston has written of this:

> I think it is not generally remembered today how cruel and barbarous was the repression of the Huguenots in France in 1685. Protestants who refused to convert, under orders of Louis

XIV, were beaten, pillaged, dragooned, their children were taken from them; men were sent to the galleys or driven into exile.

(Horton and Mendus 1991, p. 82)

In England, during the same period, many Catholics and non-conformists such as Quakers were treated as ruthlessly. If you openly maintained that the Pope had a higher status than the King, you risked having your possessions confiscated, and even being executed. If you failed to attend Anglican worship you could forfeit two-thirds of your estate.

John Locke's *A Letter Concerning Toleration*, first published in 1689 but probably written in 1685 during Locke's self-imposed exile in Holland, addresses the question of religious toleration, giving interesting and original justifications for the state refraining from intervening in matters of individual conscience. Within *A Letter Concerning Toleration* Locke includes an important argument as to why the state should tolerate religious diversity. Here Locke argues that intolerance by Christians isn't just unchristian; it is irrational. This is an argument for a specific kind of negative freedom – freedom from interference in matters of personal religion. In this chapter we will be focusing on this argument and determining whether or not it supports the conclusion that the state should not intervene in matters of individual religious conscience.

Toleration will almost certainly be necessary in any situation in which individual freedom is at issue, at least when freedom is understood in the negative sense. Toleration does not imply that you approve of the activity in question, only that you don't intervene to prevent it occurring. You may think that those who exercise their particular freedoms are misguided, or even mad, but if you tolerate them, then you allow them to pursue their chosen way of life without harassment or intervention. All theories of negative freedom advocate toleration in some respect. Toleration of a wide range of religious views is a hallmark of liberalism, a political philosophy which puts a high value on the preservation of various negative liberties.

In Locke's case, the toleration in question is toleration by the state of those who do not subscribe to the orthodox religion of that state. Locke argued that the state should tolerate a wide range of religious beliefs (though, as we shall see, with a few notable exclusions). He argued for preserving individual freedom of religious belief in the face of possible oppression by the state. Like many arguments for freedom, Locke's defends freedom in one specific respect rather than freedom in a wide range of areas. It provides a marked contrast with the classic defence of negative freedom, John Stuart Mill's *On Liberty* (the subject of the following three chapters). Mill wanted to preserve a wide range of negative liberties, most of which fall into the broad categories of freedom of speech and freedom of lifestyle. In contrast, Locke, in his *A Letter Concerning Toleration*, was concerned exclusively with defending freedom of religious belief within the context of a Christian society.

Locke's *Letter* retains its relevance in the twentieth century, not just as a historical document, but because it makes a case for religious toleration on the basis of philosophical principles. Locke doesn't simply state his opinions, but rather puts forward principles which he backs up with reasons. He argues for his conclusion.

The fact that he argues his case and the type of argument that he uses make this a contribution to philosophy, rather than simply a manifesto for a particular change in attitude and law.

Locke uses a number of other arguments to make his case, some of which we will also be examining in this chapter. But, for our purposes, the argument that religious intolerance is irrational is the most important feature of the *Letter*. We'll examine the structure of this argument and consider whether or not, with minor adaptations, it could be relevant to present-day disputes about religious freedom.

Locke's argument is unusual amongst arguments for negative freedom. These typically focus either on the harmful effects of curtailing liberties (for those whose liberty is curtailed, or perhaps for society at large), or else on what makes curtailing other people's liberties intrinsically wrong, regardless of the consequences.

REINTERPRETING LOCKE FOR TODAY

Considering Locke's *Letter* as a possible contribution to our present-day understanding of the concept of freedom inevitably involves ignoring parts of the text. It also involves extracting Locke's principles from their original context and examining them more or less as if they were put forward yesterday. Some historians of ideas take exception to this sort of use of classic philosophical texts; they believe that we can only understand such works in the full detail of their original context. This point has some force, since there is great value in a historically informed reading of a seventeenth-century text such as Locke's. Yet, philosophy, if it is to remain a living subject, must also concern itself with living questions. We want to know if Locke's argument has any relevance for us now, not just what its relevance was to his contemporaries.

So, what was the basis of Locke's argument, and will it stand up to scrutiny? Before examining his main argument, the one I have labelled his 'Irrationality Argument', let's consider two further arguments he offers in support of religious toleration: the 'Unchristian Argument' and the 'Inconsistency Argument'.

THE UNCHRISTIAN ARGUMENT

Locke suggests that lack of religious toleration can be unchristian, citing the example of the 'Prince of Peace' (i.e. Jesus) who did not resort to violence and coercion against those who did not follow him. As Locke puts it: 'If the gospel and apostle may be credited [i.e. believed] no man can be a Christian without charity, and without that faith which works, not by force, but by love' (Horton and Mendus 1991, p. 14).

The structure of the implied argument, is simple:

Premise 1	No one can be a true Christian unless they are charitable.
Premise 2	Religious persecutors aren't charitable.
Conclusion	Therefore religious persecutors aren't true Christians.

This is a valid argument: if the premises are true, then the conclusion must also be true. In other words the structure of the argument is a reliable one. The premises appear to be true. So it seems that this provides a knock-down argument against lack of toleration by Christians. However, it might be argued that the whole argument turns on the question of what 'charitable' means. Those Christians who persecuted religious dissenters on the grounds that this would probably save the souls of those they persecuted from eternal damnation would no doubt have seen themselves as acting charitably. If they were genuinely acting out of charity, then they would be immune to Locke's Unchristian Argument. In other words, the persecutors might be able to sustain their position by showing that Premise 2 was false. If this premise really were false, then the conclusion that religious persecutors were unchristian might or might not be true.

However, Locke offers a second, related type of argument which they could still fall foul of – his Inconsistency Argument.

THE INCONSISTENCY ARGUMENT

Early on in the *Letter* Locke accuses Christian champions of religious intolerance of inconsistency. Their professed aim is to save souls. However, he points out that if this really were their aim, then they would be at least concerned to stamp out the activities of a whole range of sinners, many of whose sins are far more serious than those of the typical religious dissenter:

> For if it be out of a principle of charity, as they pretend, and love to men's souls, that they deprive them of their estates, maim them with corporal punishments, starve and torment them in noisome prisons, and in the end even take away their lives; I say, if all this be done merely to make men Christians, and procure their salvation, why then do they suffer [i.e. endure] 'whoredom, fraud, malice, and such like enormities' which, according to the apostle, Rom.i [New Testament, St Paul's Letter to the Romans 1] manifestly relish of heathenish corruption, to predominate so much and abound amongst their flocks and people? These, and such like things, are certainly more contrary to the glory of God to the purity of the church, and to the salvation of souls, than any conscientious dissent from ecclesiastical decision, or separation from public worship, whilst accompanied with innocence of life. Why then does this burning zeal for God, for the church and for the salvation of souls; burning, I say, literally with fire and faggot [i.e. by burning heretics at the stake]; pass by those moral vices and wickednesses, without any chastisement, which are acknowledged by all men to be diametrically opposite to the profession of Christianity, and bend all its nerves either to the introducing of ceremonies, or to the establishment of opinions, which for the most part are about nice [i.e. 'fine', as in 'fine distinction'] and intricate matters, that exceed the capacity of ordinary understandings?
>
> (Horton and Mendus 1991, p. 15)

Locke's argument here is this. Christians who persecute others on religious grounds claim that their motive is saving souls from eternal damnation by forcing their victims to adopt the true religion which they, the persecutors, believe is their victims' only chance of avoiding eternal damnation.

However, if these Christian persecutors are sincere, they should concentrate their energies on conspicuous sinners whose religious shortcomings are far more serious than those of most dissenters. They don't do this, so the suggestion is that they are insincere. The difference between an orthodox believer and a dissenter is typically slight, and usually turns on subtle points of doctrine. In contrast, those who practise 'whoredom, fraud and malice' very obviously defy the explicit teaching of the New Testament, and more seriously jeopardize their chances of salvation. So Christian persecutors, if they really want to save souls, should focus their persecutory zeal on sinners rather than dissenters. This is what consistent application of a principle of saving souls implies.

Implicit in this passage is the idea that Christian persecutors of dissenters, although they claim to be acting from charity and have the interests of dissenters at heart, are really acting from some other motive. The claim to be acting for the salvation of souls is then a rationalization, a self-serving justification which disguises the underlying motive. Locke is hinting strongly at the hypocrisy of such persecutors: they don't really practise what they preach. The suggestion is that they are exacting some kind of vicious revenge on dissenters – an obviously unchristian motive for action.

Both the Unchristian Argument and the Inconsistency Argument in the form Locke gives them have relevance for only certain sorts of Christian persecutors, though with some appropriate alterations, they might provide a case against persecution by members of some other religions too (for instance, a Buddhist persecutor might be guilty of unbuddhist behaviour inasmuch as he or she failed to exhibit genuine compassion). However, Locke provides a further and poten- tially far more powerful argument against any attempt whatsoever to force people into particular religious beliefs. This, his Irrationality Argument, is the most interesting aspect of his *Letter* from a philosophical viewpoint, and is the main focus of this chapter. It is the argument that there is something irrational about trying to coerce people into religious views since it is an impossible goal to achieve. To attempt the impossible is, in most cases where you have a choice in the matter, an irrational thing to do.

THE IRRATIONALITY ARGUMENT

Locke believed that responsibility for salvation lay with the individual, as he put it: 'The care of each man's soul, and of the things of heaven … is left entirely to every man's self' (Horton and Mendus 1991, p. 44). No one else's possibility of salvation is affected by an individual's religious beliefs, so this is a matter for individual conscience. This is an unquestioned assumption. It is not a view that he argues for, but rather it is something that he takes for granted. But it is no trivial matter since your chances of eternal bliss or eternal damnation are at stake.

The state is capable of forcing its members to behave in particular ways by means of laws. Locke speaks of the powers of magistrates, by which he means those whose duty it is to create and enforce laws for the good of the state. These laws are enforced by the threat of penalties. 'It is the magistrate's province to give orders by decrees and compel with the sword' (Horton and Mendus 1991, p. 19).

In Locke's day, the methods of law enforcement could legitimately include severe torture. But powerful as such methods might be, Locke argues, they can never bring about the requisite change in religious belief:

> The care of souls cannot belong to the civil magistrate, because his power consists only in outward force: but true and saving religion consists in the inward persuasion of the mind, without which nothing can be acceptable to God. And such is the nature of the understanding that it cannot be compelled to the belief of anything by outward force.
>
> (Horton and Mendus 1991, p. 18)

If you try to persuade a devout religious Jew of the truth of the New Testament, for example, then no matter how horrible the tortures you are capable of inflicting, you will not be able to change his or her belief. You might extort a verbal retraction of faith, but the mere utterance of words does not in itself constitute a genuine religious belief. It doesn't amount to 'the inward persuasion of the mind'. Locke assumes that the purpose of religious persecution is to convert people to the true religion. His argument is that the nature of religious belief makes this an impossible goal:

> Neither the profession of any articles of faith, nor the conformity to any outward form of worship … can be available to the salvation of souls, unless the truth of the one and the acceptableness of the other unto God, be thoroughly believed by those that so profess and practise. But penalties are no ways capable to produce such belief. It is only light and evidence that can work a change in men's opinions; and that light can in no way proceed from corporal sufferings, or any other outward penalties.
>
> (Horton and Mendus 1991, p. 19)

You can't simply decide to believe that Christ was the son of God just because this would conveniently persuade your torturer to put down the red-hot pincers. And without genuine belief, prayers and religious ceremonies are just empty words and insincere actions. Beliefs are not the sort of thing that you can simply adopt at will. This is just how the human mind, or 'the understanding' as Locke calls it, works. Torture can make you dearly *want* to believe something; but it can't actually make you believe it. As Locke points out: 'To believe this or that to be true is not within the scope of the will' (Horton and Mendus, p. 41).

Much the same point about belief has been put forcefully by the present-day philosopher Bernard Williams:

> it is not a contingent fact that I cannot bring it about, just like that, that I believe something, as it is a contingent fact that I cannot bring it about, just like that, that I'm blushing. Why is this? One reason is connected with the characteristic of beliefs that they aim at truth. If I could acquire a belief at will, I could acquire it whether it was true or not; moreover I would know that I could acquire it whether it was true or not. If in full consciousness I could will to acquire a 'belief' irrespective of its truth, it is unclear that before the event I could seriously think of it as a belief, i.e. as something purporting to represent reality.
>
> (Williams 1973, p. 148)

What Williams is saying here is that the concept of belief implies that beliefs cannot be adopted at will; if they could, then the conceptual link between belief and reality would be severed. Beliefs aim to represent reality. If you believe, for example, that the Houses of Parliament are in London, then this means that you take it to be true that that is where Parliament is based. If you have this belief, then you can't simply for fun acquire the belief that Parliament is based in Sidcup. You can exercise your imagination, thinking, perhaps, 'What would it be like if Parliament were based in Sidcup?' but that is very different from believing that it *is* based there. Similarly, if you believe that only one God exists this means that you believe that it is true that only one God exists. To talk of a belief that didn't aim at truth (one that was simply adopted for convenience, say) would be like talking of a bachelor who was married or a vertebrate that didn't have a spine.

If beliefs cannot be adopted at will, even under threat of torture, then, Locke suggests, there is no point in trying to force anyone to adopt a religious belief. This argument, if sound, would completely undermine the justification given for a great deal of religious persecution. This has been implemented in order to force its victims either to jettison their deepest religious beliefs, or else sincerely to affirm the basic principles of the religion of their persecutors. For example, when Miles Phillips, an English member of a slave-trading party, was captured by the Spanish in Mexico in 1568, he and his companions were imprisoned and tortured by the Spanish Inquisition. The Inquisitors seemed to want the captives to declare their beliefs in the main Catholic orthodoxies:

> we were conveyed and sent as prisoners to the city of Mexico; and there committed to prison, in sundry dark dungeons, where we could not see but by candle light; and were never past two together in one place: so that we saw not one another, neither could one of us tell what was become of another.
>
> Thus we remained close imprisoned for the space of a year and a half ... During which time of our imprisonment, at the first beginning, we were often called before the Inquisitors alone; and there severely examined of our faith; and commanded to say the *Pater noster*, the *Ave Maria*, and the *Creed* in Latin: which, God knoweth! a great number of us could not say otherwise than in the English tongue ... Then did they proceed to demand of us, upon our oaths, 'What we did believe of the Sacrament?' and 'Whether there did remain any bread or wine, after the words of consecration, Yea or No?' and 'Whether we did not believe that the Host of bread which the priest did hold up over his head and the wine that was in the chalice, was the very true and perfect body and blood of our Saviour Christ, Yea or No?'
>
> (Phillips, in Carey 1987, p. 112)

Quite simply, the Inquisitors wanted their captives to declare, on pain of death, that they believed that the consecrated Host (the bread) was transubstantiated (i.e. literally became Christ's body) as the priest raised it above his head, and the wine in the chalice became Christ's blood during Communion. The issue of whether or not such transubstantiation occurred was the fundamental area of disagreement between Roman Catholics and Protestants during the Reformation. The threat of death, and no doubt further tortures, had a powerful effect on what the prisoners said. They were willing to say whatever their captors wanted them to say, if it would save their lives. Very few people would be resolute in such a situation after a year and a half of confinement underground.

With the constant threat of torture implicit in the Inquisitors' questioning, they had very good reasons to lie about what they believed (assuming, as is likely, that they didn't actually believe in transubstantiation). However, Locke's point is that no threat or torture could actually change what the prisoners believed: you can't just change your belief because it is convenient to do so; and saying that you believe something is not the same as actually believing it. Even if the prisoners wanted to change their beliefs, this alone wouldn't be enough actually to change them; they would have to believe that the Catholic doctrine was true. This is because beliefs aim at truth. That's just part of the meaning of 'belief'. If you believe something, you must believe that it is true. And believing that something is true is just not a matter of our willing it. If you don't believe that the bread becomes Christ's flesh during Mass, then no amount of willing yourself to believe that it does will make you actually believe that it does. You can, of course, lie about your beliefs. There is nothing in Miles Phillips's testimony of his experiences at the hands of the Inquisition to suggest that he or any of his companions actually changed their religious beliefs as a result of their treatment, though they certainly told their captors whatever they believed they wanted to hear.

Locke maintains that only 'light and evidence' can work this sort of change on your opinions. 'Light' presumably is intended as in the metaphor 'seeing the light': you have to see the truth of the matter for yourself, or else have persuasive evidence before you can change your mind about something so fundamental as a religious belief. You can adopt the outward appearance of religious belief, mouth the appropriate words, take part in religious ceremonies such as Mass, and so on, but Locke takes it for granted that this does not amount to genuine religious belief and so will not guarantee you salvation:

> It is in vain for an unbeliever to take up the outward show of another man's profession. Faith only, and inward sincerity, are the things that procure acceptance with God … In vain, therefore, do princes compel their subjects to come into their church communion, under pretence of saving their souls. If they believe, they will come of their own accord; if they believe not, their coming will nothing avail them.
>
> (Horton and Mendus 1991, p. 32)

The absurdity of commanding people to say prayers and go through the motions of religious ceremonies should be obvious to anyone who has been coerced into mouthing the Lord's Prayer and into singing hymns during school assemblies. Outward shows of religion involve simply going through the motions; what matters is inward sincerity.

THE STRUCTURE OF LOCKE'S IRRATIONALITY ARGUMENT

Let's pause at this point and review Locke's argument. In essence he is saying this:

Premise 1	Magistrates' only sanction is physical force.
Premise 2	Physical force cannot alter religious beliefs.
Conclusion	So magistrates cannot alter religious beliefs.

Locke's argument as outlined above is a valid one: if the premises are true, then the conclusion must be true. You would be contradicting yourself to assert the premises and deny the conclusion.

If his premises are indeed true, then Locke has discovered an extremely powerful argument against attempts at religious coercion: since all such attempts are necessarily doomed to failure, no rational agent of the state should propose them. Because magistrates cannot alter religious beliefs, it would be irrational for them to attempt to do so. Consequently religious toleration is justified.

EXERCISE 2.1

CONTRADICTION

Which of the following statements involve a contradiction, either explicit or implicit?

1   No one is immortal. However, I will live forever.
2   All fish live in water. Whales aren't fish.
3   Religious beliefs can never be coerced. The Spanish Inquisition sometimes managed to change their captives' religious beliefs through torture.
4   You can have some jam today, but you certainly can't have any tomorrow.
5   Some eminent philosophers are women. Some women are eminent philosophers.

Compare your answers with those at the back of the book before reading on.

EXERCISE 2.2

VALID/INVALID AND TRUE/FALSE

The following questions are about Locke's argument as I have summarized it below. If you are unsure about the meanings of 'valid' and 'invalid' then work through the Appendix, before doing these exercises.

Premise 1   Magistrates' only sanction is physical force.
Premise 2   Physical force cannot alter religious beliefs.
Conclusion   So magistrates cannot alter religious beliefs.

1   If Premise 1 turned out to be false, would the argument still be valid?
2   If both the premises and the conclusion were false, would it be invalid?
3   If both the premises turn out to be true, can the conclusion be false?
4   If it were true that physical force could sometimes alter religious beliefs, would the conclusion that attempting to coerce religious beliefs is irrational still follow?

Compare your answers with those at the back of the book before reading on.

It is worth bearing in mind that Locke's argument here is more restricted than it might at first appear. It only covers cases in which persecution is intended to change people's religious beliefs. It is neutral on the question of whether other sorts of religious persecution should be tolerated. For instance, historically much religious persecution has been concerned to stamp out practices which are abhorrent to orthodox believers. In the Christian context, idolaters (people who worship idols) have come in for particular persecution, not necessarily with a view to saving their souls, but rather to stop them performing public acts of idolatry which some devout Christians have found peculiarly offensive. Locke's Irrationality Argument provides no grounds for preventing such persecution. However, his Unchristian and Inconsistency Arguments could justify toleration in these sorts of circumstances.

It could be argued that if the persecutors don't realize that any attempt to coerce belief is doomed to failure, then there is nothing strictly irrational in their behaviour. They simply lack an important piece of knowledge about the nature of belief. If they possessed this knowledge, then their behaviour would certainly be irrational. Without this knowledge, their behaviour isn't strictly irrational since they are acting consistently on the best knowledge that they have. However, the justification for my labelling Locke's argument his Irrationality Argument is that he is making the point that from the perspective of someone who recognizes that beliefs can't be adopted at will, religious persecution of the sort he describes *is* irrational.

THE LIMITS OF TOLERATION

The extent of religious freedom that Locke argues for is in fact even smaller than the discussion so far might suggest. There are groups of people for whom, he maintains, toleration would be inappropriate despite the impossibility of changing their heartfelt beliefs. Anyone whose religious beliefs threaten society should not be tolerated. There are two important groups that he mentions in this context. The first is those whose religious belief might put them in thrall to a foreign power:

> That church can have no right to be tolerated by the magistrate, which is constituted upon such a bottom [i.e. such foundations], that all those who enter into it, do thereby, *ipso facto*, deliver themselves up to the protection and service of another prince. For by this means the magistrate would give way to the settling of a foreign jurisdiction in his own country, and suffer his own people to be listed, as it were, for soldiers against his own government.
>
> (Horton and Mendus 1991, p. 46)

Locke's point is that when the state is potentially threatened from within there are no grounds for tolerating the source of the threat. Those who put the security of the state at risk should not be free from interference. Although he doesn't actually name them here, his main target is certainly Roman Catholics, or at least those Catholics who had greater allegiance to the pope and to any other Catholic power than to the English sovereign (assuming the English sovereign wasn't a Catholic). Locke would have been particularly concerned about Jacobites, those who believed that the Catholic James 'the Pretender', son of King James II, should be instated as king; however, as the above passage makes clear, his worries extended to any member of any religion which by its nature would put them under the service of a foreign power. Despite this intolerance, his earlier argument would still hold: it still would not be possible (and hence not rational to attempt) to coerce their beliefs; only their behaviour should be controlled. In other words, he thinks that persecution, or at least intolerance, may be an appropriate reaction to some religious groups, but not so much because their religious beliefs were mistaken, rather on the grounds that they were a potential threat to the stability of the society in which they were living. This is revealed elsewhere in the *Letter*, when he explicitly states that beliefs about transubstantiation don't merit intolerance (i.e. just because Catholics believe in transubstantiation, this is no reason for being intolerant towards them, since the belief itself is a harmless one).

Locke also thought that the freedom of atheists should be curtailed. Atheists could not be trusted to keep their promises, and so, like religious believers in the power of a foreign prince, posed a threat to society: 'Promises, covenants, and oaths, which are the bonds of human society, can have no hold upon an atheist. The taking away of God, though but even in thought, dissolves all' (Horton and Mendus, p. 47).

His suggestion is that Christians would keep their promises because they believed that God would punish them (either in this world or the next) if they didn't. Atheists, on the other hand, would have no incentive for keeping promises when they could get away with breaking them, since they did not believe that they would be hauled up before a divine judge; all they had to worry about was human retribution, which is less than inevitable. Today, this justification for curtailing the freedom of atheists would find few sympathizers; the notion that atheists cannot be relied upon to honour their obligations is simply implausible.

WALDRON'S COUNTER-ARGUMENT

In a recent article, the philosopher Jeremy Waldron has challenged Locke's Irrationality Argument by questioning one of its premises. Locke was convinced that religious beliefs could never be changed by coercion – a view which, as we have seen, is plausible, at least at first sight. Waldron, by distinguishing between coercion by *direct* and *indirect* means, reveals that the situation is more complicated than Locke assumed, a point first made by Locke's contemporary Jonas Proast. Waldron agrees that religious beliefs cannot simply be adopted at will in the face of coercion; however, since we always acquire our religious beliefs as a result of our experience, there are other less direct ways in which a magistrate could have an effect on them, namely by restricting and directing our experience. Waldron invites us to consider an imaginary situation in order to make his position clear:

Suppose there are books and catechisms, gospels and treatises, capable of instructing men in the path of the true religion, if only they will read them. Then although the law cannot compel men coercively to believe this or that because it cannot compel the processes of the understanding, it can at least lead them to water and compel them to turn

their attention in the direction of this material. A man may be compelled to learn a catechism on pain of death or to read the gospels every day to avoid discrimination. The effect
of such threats and such discrimination may be to increase the number of people who eventually end up believing the orthodox faith. Since coercion may therefore be applied to
religious ends by this indirect means, it can no longer be condemned as in all circumstances irrational.

(Waldron, in Horton and Mendus 1991, p. 116)

In other words, there may be indirect ways in which religious beliefs can be
coerced. Even if the above example sounds implausible as a device for persuading
a devout non-believer to adopt the orthodoxy, Waldron suggests a second sort of
case which is closer to real life. He asks us to suppose that there are books which
are capable of shaking the faith of those who currently believe in the orthodoxy.
By banning these books, the magistrates could effectively reduce the risk of loss
of faith. Waldron's claim is that by curtailing individual freedom of speech, and
freedom to read what you want to read, the population's religious beliefs *could* be
controlled. Locke does not provide any argument against this sort of measure.

To return to the underlying argument outlined above:

Premise 1	Magistrates' only sanction is physical force.
Premise 2	Physical force cannot alter religious beliefs.
Conclusion	So magistrates cannot alter religious beliefs.

We can see that Waldron has cast doubt on the second premise. He has explained
how physical force can be used to alter religious beliefs. If he is correct, then
Locke's argument that religious persecution is irrational will fall apart. Only
attempts at direct coercion will be irrational; subtler, less direct kinds of coercion
would seem to be entirely appropriate techniques to use, given Locke's assumptions about religion. Locke seems to have made the assumption that the only way
that physical force can work on someone is by giving them a desire to change
their beliefs. That is why he stresses that belief is not subject to the will: it is not
sufficient to want to change your beliefs. You have to believe that they are true, or
else they don't count as beliefs at all. But Waldron's point about less direct means
of coercion is that these can work independently of what the person in question
wills. Of course, there might be further arguments which could reveal coercion
by indirect means as irrational; but Locke has not provided them. With the
second premise of the argument undermined we have no guarantee of the truth
of his conclusion. Waldron believes that he has exposed a 'fatal crack' in the
edifice of Locke's argument, one which reveals Locke's whole approach to have
been based on a 'radical and distorted simplification' of the complexity of religious belief. As such Waldron finds it inadequate as a defence of religious
toleration: according to him there is nothing to be salvaged from it. However, this
conclusion is too strong: Locke's argument does have value in that it provides an
argument against religious intolerance when the issue is one of *direct* coercion of
belief.

Waldron accepts Locke's point that beliefs can't be coerced directly by physical force. But this view can itself be challenged. Perhaps, in some circumstances,

some beliefs, even fundamental and apparently unalterable ones, can be changed. In the novel *Nineteen Eighty-Four*, George Orwell describes an imaginary case in which precisely this occurs. Of course, Orwell's is a work of fiction, but it reminds us that some kinds of brainwashing are possible.[1]

The central character, Winston Smith, lives in a future totalitarian society in which almost all his actions are observed and controlled. Access to truth is extremely difficult; the state has a complicated system which is constantly rewriting history in terms favourable to it. Smith is guilty of dissent. He has been caught and imprisoned in the ironically named Ministry of Love. His interrogator, O'Brien, tortures him. Not to make him recant his dissenting views. Not to change what he says he believes. But to change what he actually believes. The belief that two plus two equals five is symbolic; it is an apparently undeniable truth. O'Brien wants Smith to believe that two plus two equals five. Earlier, Smith had written in his notebook '*Freedom is the freedom to say that two plus two make four*' (Orwell 1949, p. 84). Now, gradually, through torture, O'Brien breaks down Smith's resistance to the idea that two plus two equals five:

> 'You are a slow learner, Winston', said O'Brien gently.
>
> 'How can I help it?' he blubbered. 'How can I help seeing what is in front of my eyes? Two and two are four.'
>
> 'Sometimes, Winston. Sometimes they are five. Sometimes they are three. Sometimes they are all of them at once. You must try harder. It is not easy to become sane.'
>
> (Orwell 1949, p. 263)

O'Brien tortures Smith, but still he can't help seeing that two fingers plus two fingers comes to four fingers when O'Brien holds them up in front of him. So far Orwell's novel corresponds to Locke's view of the nature of belief: it cannot be coerced; it can only lead people to change what they say about their beliefs, it can't change them directly. But, under intense torture, Winston Smith begins to believe that two plus two might equal five:

> O'Brien held up the fingers of his left hand, with the thumb concealed.
>
> 'There are five fingers there. Do you see five fingers?'
>
> 'Yes.'
>
> And he did see them, for a fleeting instant, before the scenery of his mind changed. He saw five fingers, and there was no deformity. But there had been a moment — he did not know how long, thirty seconds, perhaps — of luminous certainty, when each new suggestion of O'Brien had filled up a patch of emptiness and become absolute truth, and when two and two could have been three as easily as five, if that were what was needed.
>
> (Orwell 1949, pp. 270–1)

By the end of the novel Smith really does believe whatever O'Brien wants him to believe. There is little doubt that some kinds of brainwashing scientifically applied could produce precisely this effect, albeit at the price of the victim's mental health (this is perhaps Orwell's point when he has O'Brien say 'It is not easy to become sane'; in the topsy-turvy world of *Nineteen Eighty-Four* 'sane' means 'insane'). Changing such a fundamental belief as that two fingers plus two fingers comes to four fingers may only be achievable by destroying the personality and mental health of the person who holds the belief. Even so, Locke's assumption that physical force can't ever change beliefs might well be false. Waldron argued that physical force might change beliefs by indirect means, but cases of brainwashing would be ones in which beliefs are changed directly by force. This would only seem to strengthen Waldron's conclusion that Locke's Irrationality Argument doesn't provide a watertight defence of religious toleration.

However, Susan Mendus has introduced further arguments into the debate which could support Locke's general conclusions in the religious context.

MENDUS'S RESPONSE

While agreeing with the general thrust of Waldron's argument, Susan Mendus has made a case for the value of Locke's position. She tries to show that there may be something 'alive and important' in it. In the course of her discussion of Waldron's criticism of Locke, she makes two points that are intended to cast some doubt on his conclusion that the flaw he has discovered in Locke's reasoning is fatal.

Her first point is that, though coercion of the type Waldron mentions can certainly be achieved by attention to the ways in which beliefs are acquired rather than by a head-on assault on the belief in question, the beliefs coerced in this indirect fashion may yet be inappropriate simply because they were acquired in such a manner:

> the irrationality of coercing belief, even indirectly, is akin to the irrationality of brainwashing; it can certainly be done but it does not generate the right kind of belief or, more precisely, it does not generate a belief which is held in the right way.
>
> (Horton and Mendus 1991, p. 154)

Her suggestion, then, is that an indirectly induced religious belief won't be a genuine one, that it may be sincerely held, yet still not guarantee your salvation because, ultimately, you were pushed into acquiring it. The obvious conclusion to draw from this would be that if indirect coercion really doesn't furnish genuine religious belief, then it would be just as irrational to use it as direct coercion since it would similarly be attempting the impossible.

In his article, Waldron actually anticipates this line of argument based on how beliefs are caused. He has two responses. First, he questions why the free input of ideas (as opposed to the censored input of ideas allowed by the magistrate practising indirect coercion) should make any difference to the question of whether or not a belief is genuine. He likens the situation to being forced at the point of a bayonet to look at the colour of snow: the fact that you have been coerced to look at it does not affect your belief that the snow is white. The manner in which you are led to form your belief does not alter the content of that belief. There is, however, a simple response to this point, namely that religious beliefs are importantly different from most other beliefs in precisely this respect: how you come to have them *is* relevant to the question of whether they are genuine religious beliefs at all.

Waldron's second, and perhaps stronger response, employs what is sometimes known as the companions in guilt move. He suggests that indirectly coerced religious beliefs are very similar to most of our beliefs, and hence if we are to rule out the former as not genuine, then consistency will demand that we rule out the latter too, which would be absurd. As he points out: 'In most cases (not just a few), the selection of sensory input for our understanding is a matter of upbringing, influence, accident or constraint' (Waldron, in Horton and Mendus 1991, p. 118).

So, according to Waldron, there is rarely an important role for a wide and unconstrained range of input in the formation of our beliefs. The consequence of ruling out indirectly coerced beliefs as not genuine would seem to be that most of us are, by the same principle, incapable of genuine beliefs in other areas. Also, most people with sincere religious beliefs have acquired them in the first instance as a result of their upbringing, which, in many cases, won't have involved a free choice of what to believe, but rather will have consisted of a selective and possibly even coercive introduction to the fundamental religious beliefs of their family or culture.

Since Mendus's argument apparently leads to the absurd conclusion that many of our most cherished beliefs won't count as genuine by her criteria, it seems that she has set the standards for genuine belief too high. Waldron's conclusion is that there is no obvious reason why some indirectly coerced religious beliefs shouldn't be counted as genuine.

The companions in guilt move is the technique of attacking an argument or principle by showing that it has unpalatable implications if its conclusions are applied consistently in other contexts. It challenges the assumption that the case in question is a special case.

EXERCISE 2.3

COMPANIONS IN GUILT MOVE

Which of the following are examples of the companions in guilt move?

1   Boxing should be banned because it sometimes results in the death of participants. So rugby, mountaineering, all motor sports, horse racing and sea fishing should all also be banned because they all result in more deaths per year than does boxing.

2   Polytheists (people who believe in more than one god) should be burnt at the stake because they break one of the Old Testament Commandments. Adulterers and people who take God's name in vain should also be burnt at the stake for the same reason.

3   People should be encouraged to eat healthy food because it eases the strain on the National Health system. People who smoke and drink heavily must realize that they use a disproportionately large share of the nation's health resources.

Check your answers at the back of the book before reading on.

Mendus's further point about Waldron's approach is that he has underestimated the difficulty of changing firmly held beliefs, such as religious ones characteristically are. Waldron argues that they can be changed by indirect means; but Mendus points out that this may not be an easy task since religious beliefs typically affect every aspect of a believer's life and so are not easily separated out. Consequently, she believes: 'virtually everything will have to be dismantled if religious belief is to be stamped out or radically transformed' (Horton and Mendus 1991, p. 155).

She makes her point by contrasting indirect coercion of religious beliefs with indirect coercion towards healthier eating habits. It would be relatively simple to coerce a population indirectly into healthier eating habits by such measures as subsidizing the price of wholemeal bread and putting high taxes on refined sugar. In contrast, because religious beliefs pervade almost every aspect of a believer's life, it would be extremely difficult in practice to coerce religious beliefs by indirect means.

However, it is important to realize that, even if Mendus is correct about the difficulty of putting indirect coercion of religious beliefs into practice, this in no way undermines Waldron's criticism of Locke's position. As long as it is *possible* (even if difficult) to coerce religious beliefs by indirect means in some cases, then Locke's strong claim that it is *always* irrational to attempt to force people to adopt or renounce religious beliefs is no longer plausible. In some conceivable cases, given Locke's assumptions, it *would* be rational to attempt to coerce people in this respect. However, we might want to modify Locke's position in the light of this discussion to the claim that it is usually or, perhaps, often irrational to attempt to coerce religious beliefs.

The whole notion of forcing people to adopt a particular set of religious beliefs may seem alien to you if you are an atheist. However, the same sorts of arguments can be turned around. If you are completely convinced that all religions are founded on an erroneous belief that some god or gods exists, then you might feel that you have good grounds for creating a society in which everyone else comes to share your belief that no god or gods exist. In the face of the criticism that you wouldn't be able to force anyone to become an atheist (though you might be able to get them to *say* that they no longer believe in the existence of one or more gods), it would be possible to bring in Waldron's point that indirect coercion could be effective. Perhaps there are books which contain extremely persuasive arguments disproving the existence of god. If religious believers are forced to read these books, and to learn the arguments thoroughly, perhaps some of them will come to see the error of their ways, and genuinely be converted to atheism rather than simply paying it lip service.

 Reading
p. 137

Now read the extracts from Waldron's article (Reading 2), paying particular attention to his criticisms of Locke's Irrationality Argument.

CONCLUSION

Locke's *A Letter Concerning Toleration*, as we have seen, focuses exclusively on freedom from persecution in the area of religion; in contrast, John Stuart Mill's

On Liberty (the subject of the next three chapters) provides a wider justification for a range of negative freedoms, including freedom of speech and of lifestyle.

CHAPTER SUMMARY

In addition to the Unchristian and Inconsistency Arguments, Locke's *A Letter Concerning Toleration* contains an interesting argument with the conclusion that religious persecution is irrational: the state is powerless to bring about anything more than cosmetic changes in those who persist in unorthodox beliefs and so should not attempt to intervene. The argument is a valid one. But, as Waldron has demonstrated, it has a false premise, namely that physical force cannot alter religious beliefs. The premise is false because religious beliefs *can* be coerced by indirect means (and possibly even by direct ones).

Mendus has raised doubts about whether indirect coercion generates the appropriate sorts of beliefs, because of the way they have been caused they may be less than genuine. But, by the same principle, Waldron argues, most of our beliefs would turn out to be less than genuine; an unacceptable consequence of her view.

FURTHER READING

John Locke: A Letter Concerning Toleration *in Focus*, John Horton and Susan Mendus (eds), Routledge, 1991, includes the complete text of Locke's *Letter* together with several recent essays about it, including Waldron's 'Locke: Toleration and the Rationality of Persecution' and Mendus's 'Locke: Toleration, Morality and Rationality'.

Susan Mendus also discusses Locke on toleration in her book *Toleration and the Limits of Liberalism*, Macmillan, 1989.

NOTE

1   Bruno Bettelheim provides a more subtle and extended discussion of brainwashing based on his experiences in Nazi concentration camps in his book *The Informed Heart* (Penguin, 1986, see especially pp. 69–75).

3 The Harm Principle

OBJECTIVES

By the end of this chapter and associated reading you should:

■ understand the main features of Mill's argument for negative liberty
■ appreciate the sorts of criticism that can be levelled at the theory, and some counter-arguments to these criticisms
■ have a clear idea of what utilitarianism is
■ have improved your skills in reading longer passages of philosophy
■ be confident that you can distinguish vagueness from ambiguity

INTRODUCTION

John Stuart Mill's *On Liberty* is the classic defence of a concept of negative liberty. In places it seems also to rely on an implicit concept of positive liberty, but the main thrust of the argument is that, other things being equal, individuals should be left free from interference, either by the state or by other citizens. *On Liberty* was published in 1859 and was in part a reaction to what Mill perceived as an oppressive drive towards collective mediocrity in mid-Victorian Britain. Mill felt that not only laws, but also social pressures, resulted in many potentially great individuals leading cramped and stultifying lives. The sum of misery was being increased by laws and attitudes which were detrimental to the society which imposed them. One of Mill's main targets was what he called 'the tyranny of the majority': the oppressive effects of social pressure to conform. *On Liberty* provided a range of arguments as to why we should preserve a large area of individual freedom, including freedom to be eccentric and outspoken, even if our eccentricities might not be fruitful ones and our outspoken opinions false. As we shall see, not all the arguments in *On Liberty* are sound ones. It has nevertheless exerted and continues to exert a profound influence on decisions about the acceptable limits of negative freedom.

WHO WROTE IT?

Although *On Liberty* was published under Mill's name, this may be slightly misleading. In the dedication to the book he acknowledged the contribution made by his wife, Harriet Taylor, who died before it was completed: 'Like all that I have written for many years, it belongs as much to her as to me' (Mill 1985 edn, p. 58).

In his *Autobiography* (1873), he explained what this meant:

> When two persons have their thoughts and speculations completely in common; when all subjects of intellectual or moral interest are discussed between them in daily life, and probed to much greater depths than are usually or conveniently sounded in writings intended for general readers; when they set out from the same principles, and arrive at their conclusions by processes pursued jointly, it is of little consequence in respect to the question of originality, which of them holds the pen; the one who contributes least to the composition may contribute most to the thought; the writings which result are the joint product of both, and it must often be impossible to disentangle their respective parts, and affirm that this belongs to one and that to the other. In this wide sense, not only during the years of our married life, but during many of the years of confidential friendship which preceded, all my published writings were as much her work as mine; her share in them constantly increasing as years advanced.
>
> (Mill 1989 edn, pp. 183–4)

Mill is explicit that *On Liberty* was the result of such a collaborative approach to writing :

> The *Liberty* was more directly and literally our joint production than anything else which bears my name, for there was not a sentence of it that was not several times gone through by us together, turned over in many ways, and carefully weeded of any faults, either in thought or expression, that we detected in it. It is in consequence of this that, although it never underwent her final revision, it far surpasses, as a mere specimen of composition, anything which has proceeded from me either before or since. With regard to the thoughts, it is difficult to identify any particular part or element as being more hers than all the rest. The whole mode of thinking of which the book was the expression, was emphatically hers. But I also was so thoroughly imbued with it that the same thoughts naturally occurred to us both.
>
> (Mill 1989 edn, pp. 188–9)

Mill's commentators have debated the extent to which Harriet Taylor can really be considered the joint author of *On Liberty*, but the sincerity of Mill's estimate of her input is not in question. He certainly believed that the work was as much hers as his. Perhaps, though, a more appropriate gesture would have been to make the joint authorship apparent by including both authors' names on the title page.

ONE VERY SIMPLE PRINCIPLE

In his *Autobiography*, Mill described *On Liberty* as 'a kind of philosophic text-book of a single truth' (Mill 1989 edn, p. 189), and in the book itself he describes his aim as 'to assert one very simple principle'. This 'very simple principle' is now usually known as the Harm Principle, or sometimes as the Liberty Principle. Mill gives several formulations of it. For instance, he writes early on in the book:

> the only purpose for which power can be rightfully exercised over any member of a civilised community against his will, is to prevent harm to others. His own good, either physical or moral, is not a sufficient warrant.
>
> (Mill 1985 edn, p. 68)

The Harm Principle, at least at this stage in Mill's argument, relies on a concept of negative liberty. In the first instance, Mill wants to establish an area of freedom from constraint or interference for each member of a civilized society. The limit on that freedom is where the actions of one individual harm someone else. Only when there is a risk of harm to others is there any justification for intervention. Mill explicitly rules out paternalistic intervention, intervention for the good of the individual concerned. I should, according to the Harm Principle, be free to flail my arms about wildly up to the point where I risk hitting someone and thereby harming them; you shouldn't intervene to stop me flailing my arms, even if you think I risk harming myself by hitting various inanimate objects. You can reason with me, but you shouldn't act paternalistically and physically restrain me.

EXERCISE 3.1

COMPREHENSION

Read the questions below. Then read the passage which follows them and answer the questions. The reason for looking at the questions before reading the passage is to help you focus your reading of the passage. Finally, compare your answers with the ones given in the Discussion below. Resist the temptation to skip ahead to the Discussion. Part of the point of this exercise is to give you practice extracting the main points from a passage of philosophical writing. This aim will be thwarted if you don't try to answer the questions before looking at the answers I have given.

1   What two methods of coercion does Mill identify? Give an example of each.
2   Does Mill allow any grounds for coercing responsible adults in a civilized country, other than to prevent harm to others?
3   Although Mill rules out using force to prevent me from doing things which will physically harm myself, what methods of preventing me from harming myself does he allow?
4   Which three groups of people does Mill exempt from the Harm Principle?

5   What prerequisite does he stipulate must be met by a nation or a people
before his Harm Principle can be applied to them?

MILL *ON LIBERTY*

The object of this Essay is to assert one very simple principle, as entitled to
govern absolutely the dealings of society with the individual in the way of
compulsion and control, whether the means used be physical force in the
form of legal penalties or the moral coercion of public opinion. That principle
is that the sole end for which mankind are warranted, individually or collectively, in interfering with the liberty of action of any of their number is
self-protection. That the only purpose for which power can be rightfully exercised over any member of a civilized community, against his will, is to prevent
harm to others. His own good, either physical or moral, is not a sufficient
warrant. He cannot rightfully be compelled to do or forbear because it will be
better for him to do so, because it will make him happier, because, in the
opinions of others, to do so would be wise or even right. These are good
reasons for remonstrating with him, or reasoning with him, or persuading
him, or entreating him, but not for compelling him or visiting him with any evil
in case he do otherwise. To justify that, the conduct from which it is desired to
deter him must be calculated to produce evil to someone else. The only part
of the conduct of anyone for which he is amenable to society is that which
concerns others. In the part which merely concerns himself, his independence is, of right, absolute. Over himself, over his own body and mind, the
individual is sovereign.

It is, perhaps, hardly necessary to say that this doctrine is meant to apply
only to human beings in the maturity of their faculties. We are not speaking of
children or of young persons below the age which the law may fix as that of
manhood or womanhood. Those who are still in a state to require being taken
care of by others must be protected against their own actions as well as
against external injury. For the same reason we may leave out of consideration those backward states of society in which the race itself may be
considered as in its nonage. The early difficulties in the way of spontaneous
progress are so great that there is seldom any choice of means for overcoming them; and a ruler full of the spirit of improvement is warranted in the
use of any expedients that will attain an end perhaps otherwise unattainable.
Despotism is a legitimate mode of government in dealing with barbarians,
provided the end be their improvement and the means justified by actually
effecting that end. Liberty, as a principle, has no application to any state of
things anterior to the time when mankind have become capable of being
improved by free and equal discussion. Until then, there is nothing for them
but implicit obedience to an Akbar or a Charlemagne, if they are so fortunate
as to find one. But as soon as mankind have attained the capacity of being
guided to their own improvement by conviction or persuasion (a period long

since reached in all nations with whom we need here concern ourselves), compulsion, either in the direct form or in that of pains and penalties for noncompliance, is no longer admissible as a means to their own good, and justifiable only for the security of others.

(Mill 1989 edn, pp. 68–9)

DISCUSSION

1   Legal penalties and the moral coercion of public opinion. An example of coercion by means of legal penalties is the law that punishes murder with imprisonment. An example of moral coercion by public opinion is the way some homosexual couples have found it impossible to live together in some blocks of flats, because of the constant hostility of other tenants. In Britain there is no law against homosexual couples living together, but in some cases public opinion can have a coercive effect, making it practically impossible without deception.

2   No. This is the only grounds for coercing responsible adults in a civilized country. See the answer to (4) below for how Mill treats those who are not adults, not fully responsible or not members of a civilized country.

3   You can remonstrate with me, reason with me, persuade me, or entreat me, but you aren't justified in compelling me to abstain from an activity that only harms myself.

4   (a) Children and young people below a legal age of consent; (b) those who need to be cared for by others to protect themselves (he has in mind here, those people, such as the certified insane, who are not in a position to make decisions concerning their own safety and need to be protected against the consequences of their actions); (c) lastly, and most controversially, he believes that it is acceptable to coerce 'backward states of society'; if you intend to improve barbarians it is acceptable to use force against them, even against their will.

5   They must 'have become capable of being improved by free and equal discussion'. Mill's reasons for believing this should become clearer when we have examined his general arguments for preserving freedom of speech.

The passage we have been examining, which occurs early in *On Liberty*, offers Mill's main conclusions. Notice that, despite the fact that the word 'conclusions' suggests that they will come at the end of a piece of writing, in many instances people setting forward a case for a position (as Mill is here) begin by stating their main conclusions. Most of the rest of Mill's book is taken up with the arguments he gives to support these conclusions, and with some examples of how the Harm Principle is to be applied in particular cases.

EXERCISE 3.2

MILL'S HARM PRINCIPLE

Which of the following would Mill probably count as unacceptable infringements of individual liberty?

1   You forcibly prevent a young child from running across the road.
2   You are prevented from entering your home by a cordon of aggressive neighbours.
3   A police officer confiscates the kitchen knife that you are carrying because she believes, with good reason, that otherwise you will very likely injure someone with it.
4   Against your will, your partner handcuffs you to your chair 'for your own good', to prevent you going out and getting drunk.
5   A dangerous criminal is locked in a prison cell.
6   You are prevented from sunbathing nude on a private beach by a local by-law.
7   You are prevented from sunbathing nude on a private beach by a group of angry locals who dislike naturists.
8   You are prevented from seeing an '18' certificate film because you are only eleven.
9   You are prevented from keeping an unexploded bomb which you dug up in your back garden.
10 The law prevents you from driving on the right-hand side of the road in Britain.
11 You are forced to take regular exercise by your boss on the grounds that it is for your own good, and that you are leading an unhealthy lifestyle.

Check your answers against those at the back of the book before reading on.

A NATURAL RIGHT TO FREEDOM?

What sort of general argument does Mill give in support of the notion that we should preserve an area of non-interference for each responsible adult in a civilized society? You might be tempted to suppose that he believes that the kind of freedom he has described in the passage above is simply a natural right. Somehow, as adult human beings in what Mill would count as a civilized society, we just have this fundamental right to freedom from intervention by the state or by the moral coercion of public opinion. However, Mill rejects outright the notion that we have any natural rights. Like his mentor, Jeremy Bentham (1748–1832), he regarded talk about the existence of natural rights as 'nonsense on stilts'. For Mill, all meaningful talk about human rights is grounded on a more basic principle, known as the Greatest Happiness Principle. According to Mill, to say that you have a right to freedom means that a law preserving your freedom will tend to maximize happiness, or 'utility' as he calls it. In order to understand this, you need to understand Mill's utilitarianism, the moral philosophy which he thinks provides the ultimate answers to questions of how we should behave towards each other.

MILL'S UTILITARIANISM

As a utilitarian Mill believed that the morally right action in any circumstance was the one which would bring about the greatest total (or aggregate) happiness. This is the Greatest Happiness Principle, sometimes called the Principle of Utility. In other words, all moral questions boil down to the probable consequences of the various possible courses of action: 'actions are right in proportion as they tend to promote happiness, wrong as they tend to produce the reverse of happiness' (Mill 1991 edn, p. 137).

Because it focuses exclusively on the consequences of actions rather than on the motives of those who perform them, or on absolute rules about right and wrong regardless of consequences, utilitarianism is described as a 'consequentialist' theory. For utilitarians and other consequentialists the end (in this case, maximizing happiness) can justify the means. According to some other moral theories, such as that of Immanuel Kant (1724–1804), various actions are just right or wrong independently of consequences. For Mill, whichever action maximizes happiness is the morally right one to implement. Utilitarians use the word 'utility' in a technical sense to mean 'happiness'. So when, in *On Liberty*, Mill writes 'I regard utility as the ultimate appeal on all ethical questions', he doesn't mean 'usefulness' but rather 'tendency to maximize happiness'.

However, utilitarians differ considerably on the question of what 'happiness' or 'utility' is. Jeremy Bentham's was probably the simplest approach: what he meant by happiness was pleasure and the absence of pain. Happiness on this view is simply a blissful mental state. For Bentham it did not matter how this state was produced; he famously declared that, provided that they produce the same amount of pleasure, pushpin (a children's game) should count as highly as poetry. Mill, however, viewed happiness as more complex than this. He, for example, distinguished between types of happiness: he thought there were both higher and lower pleasures. The higher ones, which were the intellectual pleasures of thought, were always preferable to the lower sensual pleasures, such as the pleasures of eating, or the physical pleasures from sex. In his book *Utilitarianism* (published in 1863), he argued that the higher pleasures were always preferable to the lower ones, even if the lower ones were experienced with great intensity; as he put it:

> It is better to be a human being dissatisfied than a pig satisfied; better to be Socrates dissatisfied than a fool satisfied. And if the fool, or the pig, is of a different opinion, it is because they only know their own side of the question.
>
> (Mill 1991 edn, p. 140)

In *On Liberty* Mill makes it clear that the kind of liberty he proposes is justified on utilitarian grounds; that preserving this range of negative freedoms will maximize utility in the relevant sense. But we should not read into this the idea that preserving these freedoms would result in everyone walking around in a blissful mental state (Bentham's account of happiness). Mill's complex notion of happiness is grounded on 'the permanent interests of man as a progressive being'.

This phrase is somewhat vague. Some commentators have taken it to imply a positive sense of freedom. They believe that Mill's ultimate justification for guaranteeing a wide range of negative liberties is that this is the best way of ensuring the possibility of the development of humans as 'progressive' beings – a kind of self-realization, perhaps. Whether or not this is so, Mill's basic justification for preserving a wide range of negative freedoms is that this will have beneficial consequences for society. In other words, *On Liberty* presents a consequentialist justification for its stance. As Mill puts it: 'Mankind are greater gainers by suffering [i.e allowing] each other to live as seems good to themselves than by compelling each to live as seems good to the rest' (Mill 1985 edn, p. 72).

The benefits of allowing people to have a wide area of choice over their own lives far outweigh any benefits which would arise from coercing them into other ways of living, even if the coercion were applied for the good of the individuals concerned. Notice that this is an empirical claim: it is a claim about the probable consequences of various negative freedoms as compared with the consequences of various kinds of coercion. It is not a necessary truth that preserving an inviolable area of individual negative freedom will maximize utility: it isn't necessarily so. It is a contingent fact, if it is a fact at all (for the distinction between necessary and contingent see Chapter 1, pp. 16–17). It is one which requires research and evidence to corroborate it.

A SUFFICIENT CONDITION FOR INTERVENTION?

At first glance it might seem that Mill is saying that if an action causes or is likely to cause harm to someone else then the state should intervene to prevent this harm. However, he is explicit that this is not what he means. The fact that an action causes harm is not alone sufficient to warrant state intervention. There can be many cases of legitimate competition in which those who lose are certainly harmed. Mill mentions free trade and competitive competition in this respect. Yet his Harm Principle is not intended to justify intervention in such cases. What Mill does say, on the most plausible interpretation of *On Liberty*, is that an action's causing harm is only a necessary condition of intervention, that is, *only* if an action causes or is likely to cause harm does the state have grounds for intervention. However, the fact of its causing or being likely to cause harm need not always lead to intervention.

EXERCISE 3.3

NECESSARY AND SUFFICIENT CONDITIONS

Fill in the blanks with either 'necessary' or 'sufficient'.

1   You have to be over 18 to vote, so being over 18 is a _____ condition of

voting. It is not a _____ condition, however, because you also must be eligible to vote either by your nationality or residency.

2   If you've got a ticket you can go into the stadium. So having a ticket is a _____ condition of entry. Players don't need tickets. So being a player is a _____ condition. Having a ticket, then, isn't a _____ condition of entry.

3   Causing others harm is a _____ condition for state intervention. It is not a _____ condition because there are many cases in which harm to others inevitably occurs and yet in which state intervention is not justified.

Check your answers against those at the back of the book before reading on.

MILL'S GENERAL APPROACH CRITICIZED

From the time of its first publication up to the present day Mill's *On Liberty* has been discussed and criticized. Some of Mill's critics have concentrated on relatively minor details of the book; others, however, have identified problematic aspects of his theory as a whole. In this section we'll be looking at the major criticisms of Mill's whole approach. The three sorts of criticism can be summarized in the form of three questions:

1   What exactly does Mill mean by 'harm'?
2   Are there really any actions which don't affect other people?
3   Is the Harm Principle really utilitarian?

The first of these focuses on a key term in Mill's theory; the second questions an assumption that Mill makes, one on which the whole theory depends; the third asks whether the fundamental principle of the book is consistent with the general moral framework that Mill claims to endorse. We will consider each type of criticism in turn.

CRITICISM 1: HARM

Mill is often accused of being vague about his use of the word 'harm'. The Harm Principle stipulates that only when other people are at risk of being harmed is there any justification for coercing their behaviour. When the sole person who can be harmed is the person performing the act, we can only try to talk them out of it and are never justified in intervening forcibly to prevent them doing what they, as a responsible adult, have freely chosen to do (or for that matter, freely consented to have done to them). This seems at first glance straightforward enough. Yet in order to put this principle into practice, we need to have a clear notion of what sorts of thing count as harmful.

EXERCISE 3.4

VAGUENESS AND AMBIGUITY

Vagueness is lack of precision. This is not the same as ambiguity, which is when a word or phrase has two or more possible meanings.

Which of the following answers are vague, and which ambiguous? Which, if any, are neither vague nor ambiguous? Indicate what the possible meanings are for those you think are ambiguous.

1   'What are you doing later?' asked the heron?
     'I've got to go to the bank', the duck replied.

2   'Could you tell me how I get to Bank from Charing Cross station in a car?'
     'Oh, it's east of here.'

3   'If you want to take out life assurance I need to know how old you are.'
     'Fifty something.'

4   'I need financial help.'
     'You need to see our small business expert.'

5   Bank clerk: 'I'm sorry, I must have dozed off.'
     Customer: 'I hope you haven't been overworking yourself on my account.'

6   'What's your bank manager like?'
     'Oh he's very fair.'

Check your answers against those at the back of this book before reading on.

Although Mill's notion of harm draws on the common meaning of the term, it is clear that this doesn't coincide completely with what he intends. For example, some people think that various kinds of blasphemy harm everyone in the society in which this occurs; but Mill is clear that, unless it is an incitement to violence against these people, the fact that some people find some views offensive doesn't count as their having been harmed. Undoubtedly many Muslims are deeply offended when, in a Muslim country, someone chooses to eat pork (a meat forbidden them by their religion); but Mill states that this sort of taking of offence wouldn't justify a ban on pork-eating, even in a Muslim country. The religious offence, no matter that it is deep and genuine, wouldn't amount to a harm. Again, after watching a rugby match in which someone was seriously injured, we might be unlikely to think of the sport as 'harmless fun'. But for Mill, if the participants in a rugby match have given free and informed consent to play, then they cannot be harmed (in the relevant sense) by anything that occurs on the pitch, provided that their injuries occur within the rules of the game. For Mill, then, if you take offence at something it doesn't mean you've been harmed; and if you get physically injured as a result of a risky activity to which you have given your free and informed consent, then that doesn't amount to harm either.

But these refinements of the ordinary notion of 'harm' don't provide enough detail to overcome a range of difficulties. Some of these difficulties are summarized in the following list of questions about Mill's notion of harm given by the contemporary philosopher and political theorist John Gray:

> Does he intend the reader to understand 'harm' to refer only to physical harm, or must a class of moral harms to character be included in any application of the liberty principle? Must the harm that the restriction on liberty prevents be done directly to indentifiable individuals, or may it also relevantly be done to institutions, social practices and forms of life? Can serious offence to feelings count as harm so far as the restriction of liberty is concerned, or must the harm be done to interests, or to those interests the protection of which is to be accorded the status of a right? Can a failure to benefit someone, or to perform one's obligations to the public, be construed as a case in which harm has been done?
>
> (Gray 1996, p. 49)

Mill doesn't provide straightforward answers to any of these questions in *On Liberty*, and yet most of them are questions which need to be answered before we could put Mill's Harm Principle into practice. In some cases there would be no obvious way of telling whether or not an action conflicted with the Harm Principle.

In Mill's defence, it should be pointed out that he was aware of the need for sensitivity to the sort of case in question when applying the Harm Principle. The principle itself does not, and was not intended to, give a simple, easily applied answer to every difficulty about restricting negative liberties; rather it was meant to provide an explanation of the kinds of justification which were appropriate and acceptable.

Nevertheless, Mill is certainly vaguer than he might have been about what harm is. But how serious a criticism of Mill's whole approach is this? It does have serious implications for the confident application of the theory. However, the upshot of the criticism is that *On Liberty* is in an important sense incomplete, but not that it is incoherent. The book was intended for a wide general readership, and over-concern with the definition of 'harm' would have seriously detracted from its appeal. And in many cases covered by the Harm Principle there is no difficulty in establishing that harm to others has occurred. Since its publication philosophers sympathetic to Mill's approach have tried to give a more precise formulation of the notion of harm than he gave. For instance, the philosopher of law Joel Feinberg has provided a number of what he calls 'mediating maxims' to suggest how we might weight the relative importance of the variety of things which can be considered harms when attempting to apply the Harm Principle. Some of the most important of these are:

> *The magnitude of harm*: People can be assumed to share certain basic interests in continued life, health, sustenance, shelter, procreation, political liberty, etc. (the 'welfare

interests'*). Without these basic necessities people are precluded from doing whatever else they would like to do. Other things being equal, setbacks to these interests are the most serious. Conversely, it would never be right to invoke the cumbersome machinery of the criminal law in order to address very trivial harms, even if they are capable of setting back interests in extreme cases.

The probability of harm: Where a harmful consequence is not certain, risk is the gravity of harm multiplied by the probability of its occurring. Risk has to be balanced against social utility in order to decide whether conduct is too risky to be lawful and should therefore be proscribed.

The relative importance of harm: Where competitive interests make harm of someone inevitable, the relative importance of harm can be assessed according to:

- the vitality of the interest: how important is the interest to a person's network of interests and projects? How central is it to their life?
- the extent to which the interest is reinforced by related and overlapping interests, public and private.
- the moral value of the interest. Some interests are so manifestly morally repugnant (e.g. the sadist's interest in torturing children) that they should be ascribed no weight at all in calculating the balance of interests.

*These ... include 'the interests in one's own physical health and vigour, the integrity and normal functioning of one's body, the absence of absorbing pain and suffering or grotesque disfigurement ... '

(Feinberg, quoted in *Consent in the Criminal Law* [1995], p. 254)

Clearly such mediating maxims are potentially controversial. However, some such set of principles is needed if we are to put Mill's Harm Principle or its descendants into practice. But the fact that Mill's theory as expressed in *On Liberty* is incomplete in this respect does not necessarily undermine its value.

Let's turn now to the second sort of criticism levelled against Mill's general approach, namely that it relies on an untenable distinction between actions which affect other people and those which affect only the person performing the action.

CRITICISM 2: NO MAN IS AN ISLAND

Mill's Harm Principle states that the only acceptable justification for coercion of responsible adults in a civilized society is that they risk harming others by their actions. This is made clear at several points in the text. As Mill puts it in his final chapter:

the individual is not accountable to society for his actions in so far as these concern the interests of no person but himself. Advice, instruction, persuasion, and avoidance by other people, if thought necessary by them for their own good, are the only measures by which society can justifiably express its dislike or disapprobation of his conduct.

(Mill 1985 edn, p. 163)

This principle relies on there being some actions which affect only the individual concerned, or, rather, affect only the individual *adversely* (since the Harm Principle is concerned expressly with *harm*, not with all the ways in which one person is capable of affecting another). Mill assumes that we can make a distinction between actions which affect other people and those which affect only the individual. Some people have challenged this assumption, even going so far as to say that absolutely anything a person does, whether in public or in private, has the potential to affect and possibly harm other people. James Fitzjames Stephen, Mill's contemporary, took this position. He pointed out the way in which Mill's principle about purely self-regarding actions appears misguided in that it takes for granted that there are some such actions: 'It assumes that some acts regard the agent only, and that some regard other people. In fact, by far the most important part of our conduct regards both ourselves and others' (Fitzjames Stephen 1967 edn, p. 66).

Fitzjames Stephen points out that the fundamental and unstated assumption of Mill's argument is that there are important actions which affect only the person performing them. This fact needs to be established, since it is both important to Mill's Principle and at the same time controversial. Mill can't simply *assume* it. Fitzjames Stephen says that 'by far the most important part of our conduct regards both ourselves and others', and this is a view shared by many of Mill's critics.

If Fitzjames Stephen's challenge is well-founded, then the area of freedom protected by the Harm Principle will be very small. If almost every important action has the potential to harm other people, then very few actions can be protected against state interference by the Harm Principle. Of course many actions won't in fact harm other people, they may even benefit them, and so won't be subject to coercion.

What emerges from this discussion is the degree of Mill's individualistic assumptions. He believes that individuals are capable of many actions which do not seriously affect others and are not the concern of anyone else. His opponents such as Fitzjames Stephens and, more recently, Lord Devlin (as we will see in Chapter 5), make the assumption that just about every action an individual performs can potentially affect other members of that society adversely.

If I go out every night and stay out living wildly till three in the morning, this might on the face of it seem to be a purely self-regarding (and self-destructive) way of life. You might want to talk me out of a way of life that is gradually eroding my health; but according to Mill's Harm Principle you aren't justified in forcing me to stay in. Nor is it any of the state's business how I choose to spend my nights, provided that I'm not causing damage to anyone else. However, if I'm married or living with someone, it might reasonably be argued that my way of life seriously harms my partner's potential for a happy home life (assuming my partner wants to spend time with me). If I have people who are financially dependent on me and I end up spending all my money on expensive meals, drinks and night clubs, then surely in a sense my dependants are harmed by my actions. What seemed to be harmful only to myself might turn out to be harmful to other people too. Similarly, when the artist Paul Gauguin decided to sail away to Tahiti to spend the rest of his life painting his sensual pictures of islanders, exotic flowers and so on, this might have looked like a purely self-regarding action. In fact, though, he left dependants who suffered financially as a result of his choice.

But you don't need to have dependants for your apparently self-regarding actions to have harmful repercussions for other people. If you smoke heavily on your own in the privacy of your room (avoiding the problem that you might be harming involuntary passive smokers, and assuming that you are not pregnant), this might seem to be a paradigm case of a life choice which only has the potential to harm yourself. Yet, in a country such as Britain which operates a National Health system, your increased risk of serious disease potentially puts a strain on a provision that is operating with limited resources. It could be argued that you, and others like you, by smoking in private cumulatively harm others by your actions since you will quite likely make disproportionately large claims on a public health resource in later life. This will reduce the resources available for other people with serious illnesses.

Again, a politician whose private life is dissected in public by journalists, might try to argue that it is nobody else's business whether or not, for instance, he is a hypocrite; perhaps in Parliament being aggressively opposed to the lowering of the age of sexual consent for male homosexuals, while in private having a series of homosexual relationships with partners below the current age of consent. But it could be argued that his private actions, because they are potentially accessible to public scrutiny, can contribute to the undermining of public trust in the sincerity of politicians' public pronouncements. Perhaps the whole institution of representative democracy is damaged by such cases. Or it could be argued that the hypocrisy of people in high places in public life is harmful because they are, whether they like it or not, role models for those who eventually want to take their place.

What these sorts of cases show is that actions which at first glance may seem to be self-regarding can in fact harm other people. They also show the difficulty in drawing a line between what affects only yourself and what has the potential to affect others. Mill was well aware that apparently self-regarding actions can in some cases harm others; however, some of his critics feel that he did not give this consideration sufficient weight. The difficulties are exacerbated by the fact that Mill is so imprecise about what 'harm' means, so this kind of criticism is related to the first one discussed above. Nevertheless, it is implausible to conclude from this that *every* action which individuals perform and which is important to them can have significant harmful effects on others. Far more plausible is the view that what independent individuals, or consenting adults, do in private doesn't on the whole have the potential to harm other people significantly. We'll be considering this question in more detail in Chapter 5.

Let's now turn to the third major criticism of *On Liberty*, the suggestion that, despite Mill's claim to the contrary, its conclusions are not utilitarian ones.

CRITICISM 3: LIBERTY AND UTILITARIANISM

Although he professes to hold to the tenets of utilitarianism, and indeed was working on his book *Utilitarianism* at the same time as writing *On Liberty*, Mill ends up defending values other than happiness in the latter work. Or at least that is what many commentators have claimed. In other words, although he says that the various negative freedoms he defends are defensible on utilitarian grounds, he seems to end up valuing such things as diversity, truth and freedom to choose how you live your life as worth protecting because they are good in themselves rather than for any tendency they might have to maximize happiness. This is a charge of inconsistency.

As a professed utilitarian, Mill must believe that the ultimate value of the range of negative liberties he champions is that they will contribute to aggregate happiness. He states very clearly near the beginning of the work that utility is 'the ultimate appeal on all ethical questions' (Mill 1987 edn, p. 70). Yet Fitzjames Stephen pointed out that, for many people, providing a range of negative freedoms will have anything but beneficial consequences, and that coercion would be a better method in such cases for maximizing utility:

> Men are so constructed that whatever theory as to goodness and badness we choose to adopt, there are and always will be in the world an enormous mass of bad and indifferent people – people who deliberately do all sorts of things which they ought not to do, and leave undone all sorts of things which they ought to do. Estimate the proportion of men and women who are selfish, sensual, frivolous, idle, absolutely commonplace and wrapped up in the smallest of petty routines, and consider how far the freest of free discussion is likely to improve them. The only way by which it is practically possible to act upon them at all is by compulsion or restraint. Whether it is worth while to apply to them both or either I do not now inquire; I confine myself to saying that the utmost conceivable liberty which could be bestowed upon them would not in the least degree tend to improve them. It would be as wise to say to the water of a stagnant marsh, 'Why in the world do not you run into the sea? you are perfectly free. There is not a single hydraulic work within a mile of you. There are no pumps to suck you up, no defined channel down which you are compelled to run, no harsh banks and mounds to confine you to any particular course, no dams and no flood-gates; and yet there you lie, putrefying and breeding fever, frogs, and gnats, just as if you were a mere slave!' The water might probably answer, if it knew how, 'If you want me to turn mills and carry boats, you must dig proper channels and provide proper water-works for me.'
> (Fitzjames Stephen 1967 edn, pp. 72–3)

Fitzjames Stephen's view, which is pessimistic about the likely effects on the general population of increasing negative liberty, was not merely speculative; it was based on his breadth of experience as lawyer working in England and India. His work put him in touch with a far wider range of people than did Mill's. (Though, of course, wide experience in no way guarantees that your views about human nature are true. For some people, for example, travel narrows the mind.) If Fitzjames Stephen's view proved true, then to be consistent Mill would have to retreat from his advocacy of a wide range of negative freedoms for everyone, to the position that to provide such liberty was beneficial only for some people and detrimental for many others. A consistent utilitarian would at this point have to bite the bullet (i.e. accept the unpalatable consequences of strict application of the theory) and embrace the fact that the best way of maximizing happiness might be to coerce some weaker-willed people (probably the greater part of humanity) and guarantee extensive negative freedom only for those who were capable of making good use of it. Yet there is not the slightest hint in *On Liberty* that Mill would be prepared to jettison liberty for coercion in the light of such evidence.

It is an empirical question whether or not increasing negative liberties for everyone will maximize happiness. Mill doesn't provide sufficient empirical evidence to back up the claim that increased negative liberty for everyone is the most effective way of increasing overall happiness.

The French sociologist Emile Durkheim (1858–1917), unlike Mill, did carry out extensive empirical investigation into one particular aspect of society, namely the sorts of conditions which most frequently lead to suicide. His conclusion was that the removal of a wide range of social constraints on behaviour (i.e. an increase of negative freedom of the sort that Mill recommends) can bring about a condition which he labelled 'anomie'. This sense of loss of traditional values and limits on behaviour can be bewildering, and in extreme cases lead to suicide. Durkheim's empirical research seems to undermine Mill's fundamental belief that the removal of all sorts of constraints, both social and legal, on what an individual can do will tend to maximize utility. It is true that Mill's definition of 'happiness' is not simply of a blissful mental state but rather a condition 'grounded on the permanent interests of man as a progressive being' (Mill 1985 edn, p. 70). But this does not avoid the point that, if Durkheim was correct to link increases in negative freedom with an increase in a sense of anomie and an increase in the number of suicides, then the empirical evidence suggests that, in at least some circumstances, it would be wrong on utilitarian grounds to remove some constraints on behaviour. This would be so even though such people harm themselves rather than harm each other. In other words, a consistent utilitarian should, on the basis of this empirical evidence, propose a far narrower range of negative freedom than is indicated by Mill's Harm Principle. This is the contemporary philosopher Robert Paul Wolff's[1] assessment of Durkheim's research and its implications for Mill's Harm Principle:

> Durkheim marshals statistics to show that where the intensity of the collective life of a community diminishes – as their 'freedom', in Mill's sense, increases, therefore – the rate of suicide rises. Thus Protestant communities exhibit higher rates than Catholic communities, which in turn surpass the inward-turning Jewish communities. So too, education is 'positively' correlated with suicide, for although knowledge in itself is not harmful to the human personality, the independence of group norms and isolation which higher education carries with it quite definitely is inimical. One might almost see in the varying suicide rates a warning which society issues to those of its number who foolishly venture through the walls of the town into the limitless and lonely wastes beyond.
>
> It seems, if Durkheim is correct, that the very liberty and individuality which Mill celebrates are deadly threats to the integrity and health of the personality. So far from being superfluous constraints which thwart the free development of the self, social norms protect us from the dangers of anomie; and that invasive intimacy of each with each which Mill felt as suffocating is actually our principal protection against the soul-destroying evil of isolation.
>
> (Wolff, in Wolff *et al.* 1969, p. 41)

Perhaps, then, Mill's hypothesis that increases in negative freedom will have beneficial effects is just not borne out by the facts. That was Fitzjames Stephen's view, and seems also to follow from Durkheim's study of suicide (assuming, of course, that we can take suicide as an indicator of unhappiness). But the criticism of *On Liberty* that we are considering here is not simply that Mill got his facts wrong about the consequences of increasing negative freedom, but rather that, despite his claims to be grounding his theory on a utilitarian foundation, he was, rather, making an impassioned plea for increasing negative freedom as something good in itself, not simply for the consequences that it supposedly brings with it.

If Durkheim was correct about the impact of removing social and legal constraints on behaviour, then a consistent utilitarian would have to acknowledge that Mill's assumption that increased negative liberty results in increased aggregate happiness was simply mistaken. The utilitarian defence of negative liberty would crumble. However, many readers of *On Liberty* have been left with the strong suspicion that Mill's defence of liberty is not a utilitarian one at all. Rather, he seems to be defending the values of choosing for oneself and diversity within society as good independently of what effect they might have on aggregate happiness. Isaiah Berlin in his essay 'John Stuart Mill and the Ends of Life' puts this view forcefully, identifying what he takes to be the features of human existence which Mill *really* admires and champions as ends in themselves (despite his 'official' utilitarian view). This can be read as a gloss on what Mill meant by 'utility in the largest sense, grounded in the permanent interests of man as a progressive being' (Mill 1985 edn, p. 70):

> At the centre of Mill's thought and feeling lies, not his utilitarianism, nor the concern about enlightenment, nor about dividing the private from the public domain – for he himself at times concedes that the State may invade the private domain, in order to promote education, hygiene, or social security or justice – but his passionate belief that men are made human by their capacity for choice – choice of evil and good equally. Fallibility, the right to err, as a corollary of the capacity for self-improvement; distrust of symmetry and finality as enemies of freedom – these are the principles which Mill never abandons.
>
> (Berlin 1969, p. 192)

Again we need to ask how serious a criticism of Mill's whole position this is. At first glance it might seem to leave his project in tatters. However, against this view, it is worth noting that he barely mentions utilitarianism in the book, and that what he gives us is a powerful expression of the value of negative freedom based not on utilitarianism but on a view of what human beings are, namely, beings who achieve their humanity most fully by being given space to make fundamental decisions about their own lives. We don't want our lives to be lived for us; we want to be in the driving seat, even if the result is that we sometimes make decisions which make our lives go badly. This is certainly Berlin's view of the continuing value of Mill's book:

> From the days of James Stephen,[2] whose powerful attack on Mill's position appeared in the year of Mill's death, to the conservatives and socialists and authoritarian and totalitarians of our day, the critics of Mill have, on the whole, exceeded the number of his defenders.

Nevertheless, the inner citadel – the central thesis – has stood the test. It may need elaboration or qualification but it is still the clearest, most candid, persuasive, and moving exposition of the point of view of those who desire an open and tolerant society. The reason for this is not merely the honesty of Mill's mind, or the moral and intellectual charm of his prose, but the fact that he is saying something true and important about some of the most fundamental characteristics and aspirations of human beings.

(Berlin 1969, p. 201)

CONCLUSION

Despite the fact that Mill's approach in *On Liberty* is in some ways flawed, and vulnerable to all three types of criticism outlined above, it still provides an important defence of negative liberty. This becomes most apparent when we look at his more detailed analyses of the value of negative freedom in particular contexts, notably in the realm of expression of views and of choice of lifestyles. These are the subjects of the next two chapters.

CHAPTER SUMMARY

Mill's Harm Principle is the view that the only justification for exercising power over an adult is to prevent harm to others. The Harm Principle provides a necessary but not a sufficient condition for intervention. Mill defends it on utilitarian grounds. His approach is vulnerable to three major criticisms: that his notion of harm is imprecise; that it assumes some of our actions are purely self-regarding; and that it is not consistent with his utilitarianism. Nevertheless *On Liberty* provides a powerful statement and defence of a broad range of negative liberties.

READING

OVERVIEW

In the following passage Mill outlines the kinds of negative liberty he is going to defend in the rest of the book: principally freedom of conscience, freedom of speech and freedom of lifestyle. Read through the passage to get an overview of the topics we'll be discussing in the following sections.

This, then, is the appropriate region of human liberty. It comprises first, the inward domain of consciousness, demanding liberty of conscience in the most comprehensive sense, liberty of thought and feeling, absolute freedom of opinion and sentiment on all subjects, practical or speculative, scientific, moral, or theological. The liberty of expressing and publishing opinions may seem to fall under a different principle, since it belongs to that part of the conduct of an individual which concerns other people, but, being almost of as much importance as the liberty of thought itself and resting in great part on the same reasons, is practically inseparable from it. Secondly, the principle requires liberty of tastes and pursuits, of framing the plan of our life to suit our own character, of doing as we like, subject to such consequences as may follow, without impediment from our fellow creatures, so long as what we do does not harm them, even though they should think our conduct foolish, perverse, or wrong. Thirdly, from this liberty of each individual follows the liberty, within the same limits, of combination among individuals; freedom to unite for any purpose not involving harm to others: the persons combining being supposed to be of full age and not forced or deceived.

No society in which these liberties are not, on the whole, respected is free, whatever may be its form of government; and none is completely free in which they do not exist absolute and unqualified. The only freedom which deserves the name is that of pursuing our own good in our own way, so long as we do not attempt to deprive others of theirs or impede their efforts to obtain it. Each is the proper guardian of his own health, whether bodily *or* mental and spiritual. Mankind are greater gainers by suffering each other to live as seems good to themselves than by compelling each to live as seems good to the rest.

(Mill 1985 edn, pp. 71–2)

Now read 'The Place of Liberty' (Reading 3). This is an extract from Jonathan Wolff's *An Introduction to Political Philosophy*. It provides a useful overview of Mill's arguments and conclusions. In this case Wolff also provides a critical assessment of Mill's position. Reading this piece in advance of the extracts from Mill's book which we'll be looking at in the next two chapters should help you find your way through Mill's writing.

Reading
p. 149

FURTHER READING

The complete text of Mill's *On Liberty* is readily available in many different editions. However, I recommend that you finish the next two chapters before attempting to read the whole book from cover to cover. Mill's book *Utilitarianism* is also well worth reading, as is his *Autobiography*.

Roger Crisp's *Mill on Utilitarianism* (Routledge, Guidebook series, 1997) provides a clear and reliable introduction to Mill's moral philosophy including *On Liberty*.

Isaiah Berlin's essay 'John Stuart Mill and the Ends of Life' is in his book *Four Essays on Liberty* (Oxford University Press, 1969).

Jonathan Glover (ed.) *Utilitarianism and its Critics* (Macmillan, 1990) provides an excellent selection of writing on utilitarianism and its present-day descendants. The brief introductions written by Glover are particularly useful.

NOTES

1   Not to be confused with the philosopher Jonathan Wolff, whose account of Mill's *On Liberty* is included as Reading 3.
2   James Fitzjames Stephen, who is quoted above. His middle name 'Fitzjames' is usually included to distinguish him from several other members of his family who were also called James Stephen.

4 Freedom of speech

INTRODUCTION

Should members of a civilized society tolerate unlimited freedom of expression? Should everybody be allowed to say, print, publish, broadcast or communicate electronically any view whatsoever, no matter how sexist, racist, revolutionary, offensive or pornographic? Very few people believe that there should be no limits at all on the views people can express. Mill's Harm Principle provides a way of discriminating between those views which should be tolerated and those which should not. According to this principle, any view which does not harm others should be tolerated; only views which cause harm to others may be suppressed. Mill is explicit, as we have seen, in saying that mere offence to others doesn't amount to harm: someone applying Mill's Harm Principle in this area would not have suppressed the publication of Salman Rushdie's *The Satanic Verses*. The fact that it caused great offence to many Muslims would not alone amount to a sufficient reason for banning it. The Harm Principle requires a more tangible harm than mere offence in order to justify suppressing an individual's freedom to express his or her opinions. In contrast a speech which incited racial violence would be the sort of expression of opinion which a follower of Mill might be prepared to ban. The direct causal link with harm could be warrant enough to suppress such a speech. As Mill puts it:

> even opinions lose their immunity [i.e. from suppression] when the circumstances in which they are expressed are such as to constitute their expression a positive instigation to some mischievous act. An opinion that corn dealers are starvers of the poor, or that private property is robbery, ought to be unmolested when simply circulated through the press, but may justly incur punishment when delivered orally to an excited mob assembled before the house of a corn dealer, or when handed about among the same mob in the form of a placard. Acts, of whatever kind, which without justifiable cause do harm to others may be, and in the more important cases absolutely require to be, controlled by the unfavourable sentiments, and, when needful, by the active interference of mankind.
>
> (Mill 1985 edn, p. 119)

It is not simply what is said, but also the context in which it is said, which determines whether or not an opinion is harmful to others. The same words in one context can be spoken or published without censorship, but when spoken or published in another context may amount to incitement to violence, and so can justifiably be silenced by force.

In *On Liberty* Mill provides a sustained defence of the view that individuals should be free from restraints on their expressing or publishing their views, regardless of whether or not these views go against the orthodox opinions of the age, or, indeed, regardless of whether they are true or not. The chapter of *On Liberty* entitled 'Of the liberty of thought and discussion' provides a detailed case study of one kind of negative freedom that he believes it important to establish and preserve, a freedom which is justified by application of the Harm Principle, which as we have seen, is itself supposed to be justified on utilitarian grounds. In other words, Mill's official belief was that guaranteeing this kind of freedom would maximize happiness, and so was the morally right thing to do (though, as we saw in the previous chapter, there are grounds for believing that Mill wasn't a consistent utilitarian in *On Liberty*, and that he sometimes set the value of freedom higher than strictly utilitarian concerns would warrant).

For Mill, freedom of speech is a mark of a civilized society, and provides a valuable safeguard against stagnation and decay. Furthermore, it aids us in the pursuit of truth. The consequences of suppressing speech are, on the whole, bad. Utility will be maximized by preserving freedom of expression, even if in some particular cases it may at first glance seem to serve no useful purpose.

As Mill puts it:

> If all mankind minus one were of one opinion, mankind would be no more justified in silencing that one person than he, if he had the power, would be justified in silencing mankind. Were an opinion a personal possession of no value except to the owner, if to be obstructed in the enjoyment of it were simply a private injury, it would make some difference whether the injury was inflicted only on a few persons or on many. But the peculiar evil of silencing the expression of an opinion is that it is robbing the human race, posterity as

well as the existing generation – those who dissent from the opinion, still more than those who hold it. If the opinion is right, they are deprived of the opportunity of exchanging error for truth; if wrong, they lose, what is almost as great a benefit, the clearer perception and livelier impression of truth produced by its collision with error.

(Mill 1985 edn, p. 76)

We will return to the claims that Mill makes in this passage and assess them critically later in this chapter. However, for the moment what is important is identifying Mill's main arguments for preserving freedom of expression. He conveniently summarizes his four principal arguments at the end of the chapter:

First, if any opinion is compelled to silence, that opinion may, for aught we can certainly know, be true. To deny this is to assume our own infallibility.

Secondly, though the silenced opinion be an error, it may, and very commonly does, contain a portion of truth; and since the general or prevailing opinion on any subject is rarely or never the whole truth, it is only by the collision of adverse opinions that the remainder of the truth has any chance of being supplied.

Thirdly, even if the received opinion be not only true, but the whole truth; unless it is suffered to be, and actually is, vigorously and earnestly contested, it will, by most of those who receive it, be held in the manner of a prejudice, with little comprehension or feeling of its rational grounds. And not only this, but, fourthly, the meaning of the doctrine itself will be in danger of being lost or enfeebled, and deprived of its vital effect on the character and conduct: the dogma becoming a mere formal profession, inefficacious for good, but cumbering the ground and preventing the growth of any real and heartfelt conviction from reason or personal experience.

(Mill 1985 edn, pp. 115–16)

EXERCISE 4.1

MILL'S FOUR ARGUMENTS

Re-read the above passage. Summarize Mill's four arguments in your own words before reading on.

DISCUSSION

Mill's four main arguments are:

1   If we suppress a view, it might possibly turn out that the view we suppressed was true. If we assume that it isn't, this is equivalent to assuming that we can never make a mistake about such matters.

2   Even if the view we suppress is false, it can easily still contain an element of truth. Since widely held opinions are rarely if ever completely true, the only way that we can have any hope of discovering the missing true element is to allow largely false opinions to be heard, and a fuller truth to emerge thereby.

3   Even if the established opinion is the whole truth on the matter in question, if we don't allow it to be challenged and criticized, people will believe it without appreciating the reasons why they believe it. It will be a prejudice rather than a belief held on rational grounds.

4   There is also the risk that the established opinion won't continue to stir anyone to action unless it is challenged. People will say that they believe the established opinion, but they won't have any deep convictions about it as it won't mean anything in terms of their personal experience. Allowing the established opinion to be challenged will prevent this opinion's link with action from being severed.

We'll examine each of these arguments as Mill sets them out in his chapter. First, let's consider the Infallibility Argument, the claim that anyone who suppresses a view must assume that they can never be mistaken about where the truth lies.

THE INFALLIBILITY ARGUMENT

If you assume that you are infallible, you assume that you never make a mistake. Mill maintains that anyone who suppresses a view assumes that their own views on the subject cannot be mistaken. Mill's response is that human beings are fallible creatures, and that history has shown that many people who felt certain that they could not be wrong, were in fact wrong. So, it is absurd to assume infallibility on any issue, and therefore absurd to suppress any view on the grounds that the view is obviously false. Since the view suppressed may conceivably turn out to be true, those who suppress the view deprive humanity of the opportunity of jettisoning their false opinions and replacing them with true beliefs.

This argument, like most, is probably easier to follow if you consider a specific example. It is well known that in early seventeenth-century Europe anyone who suggested that the earth revolved around the sun (Copernicus's theory), rather than vice versa, risked censorship and at worst imprisonment or even death. The established and widely held opinion was that the reason that the sun rises in the morning and sinks below the horizon at dusk is that the sun is moving around the earth which is fixed. Those who held this view certainly had reasons for their belief. The Roman Catholic Church saw those, such as Galileo Galilei, who endorsed the Copernican theory, as dangerous because they were spreading false views about the nature of the universe. The General Congregation of the Index, effectively the voice of censorship for the Catholic Church, declared on 5 March 1616:

in order that this opinion may not insinuate itself any further to the prejudice of Catholic truth, the Holy Congregation has decreed that the said Nicolaus Copernicus' *De revolutionibus orbium* and Diego de Zuniga's *On Job* be suspended until they be corrected ...

(quoted in Koestler 1959, p. 456)

Galileo was eventually prosecuted for endorsing the Copernican view of the universe both in print and in his teaching. He was forced to recant these views, which he did by reading out a statement saying that he 'abjured, cursed and detested' his past errors (though there is no evidence whatsoever that his recantation was sincere). A comment in a contemporary letter about Galileo's recantation is revealing:

> The disputes of Signor Galileo have dissolved into alchemical smoke, since the Holy Office has declared that to maintain this opinion is to dissent manifestly from the infallible dogmas of the Church. So here we are at last, safely back on a solid Earth, and we do not have to fly with it as so many ants crawling around a balloon ...
>
> (Querengo, quoted in Koestler 1959, p. 461)

Notice the phrase here 'infallible dogmas of the Church'. There was, then, from the Church's point of view, no chance whatsoever of being wrong on the question of whether the sun travels round the earth or vice versa. The teachings of the Church were believed to be infallible. Mill's response to this would be that no such claim to empirical knowledge can be infallible; the best that human beings can hope for is a state of certainty which arises from a careful assessment of the available evidence on the matter.

Certainty is a psychological state; it is a sense that we have that our beliefs are true. But my certainty in no way guarantees that my beliefs *are* true. I might feel certain that I left my car keys on the mantelpiece; but the fact of the matter could still be that I left them in my coat pocket. When I reach into my coat pocket and discover them there I realize that I was completely mistaken about where I had left them. My feeling of certainty didn't guarantee that my belief about where I'd left the keys was true; empirical evidence shows that I misremembered.

In retrospect, astronomers such as Galileo have been vindicated. Scientific evidence, based on much more extensive empirical data than those available in the seventeenth century, has undermined the hypothesis that the sun revolves around the earth. The suppression of opposing views in the seventeenth century now seems particularly pernicious as the view suppressed turns out to be a more or less true one. Mill's point is simply that the certainty of the people who prevented the Copernican theory from being widely voiced did not guarantee that they were right. By the same sort of reasoning, we may feel certain about all kinds of beliefs that are now widely held, but that doesn't provide a good enough reason for suppressing opposing views. The views that we might suppress could turn out to be true. It may be highly unlikely that we are mistaken; but history shows that we could be. For this reason we should tolerate those people who continue to believe that the earth is flat or that the sun revolves around the earth. We should tolerate them, but, unless they can provide overwhelming evidence for their views, we shouldn't give their views any credence.

READING

Read the following passage from Mill's chapter 'Of the liberty of thought and discussion'. Don't worry if you have to re-read it several times to make sense of it. Some of the difficulty may simply be a result of the long, quite complex sentences that Mill uses, and have nothing to do with the intrinsic difficulty of the ideas he is setting forward.

First: the opinion which it is attempted to suppress by authority may possibly be true. Those who desire to suppress it, of course, deny its truth; but they are not infallible. They have no authority to decide the question for all mankind and exclude every other person from the means of judging. To refuse a hearing to an opinion, because they are sure that it is false, is to assume that *their* certainty is the same thing as *absolute* certainty. All silencing of discussion is an assumption of infallibility. Its condemnation may be allowed to rest on this common argument, not the worse for being common.

Unfortunately for the good sense of mankind, the fact of their fallibility is far from carrying the weight in their practical judgement, which is always allowed to it in theory; for while everyone well knows himself to be fallible, few think it necessary to take any precautions against their own fallibility, or admit the supposition that any opinion, of which they feel very certain, may be one of the examples of the error to which they acknowledge themselves to be liable. Absolute princes, or others who are accustomed to unlimited deference, usually feel this complete confidence in their own opinions on nearly all subjects. People more happily situated, who sometimes hear their opinions disputed and are not wholly unused to be set right when they are wrong, place the same unbounded reliance only on such of their opinions as are shared by all who surround them, or to whom they habitually defer; for in proportion to a man's want of confidence in his own solitary judgement does he usually repose, with implicit trust, on the infallibility of 'the world' in general. And the world, to each individual, means the part of it with which he comes in contact: his party, his sect, his church, his class of society; the man may be called, by comparison, almost liberal and large-minded to whom it means anything so comprehensive as his own country or his own age. Nor is his own faith in this collective authority at all shaken by his being aware that other ages, countries, sects, churches, classes, and parties have thought, and even now think, the exact reverse. He devolves upon his own world the responsibility of being in the right against the dissentient worlds of other people; and it never troubles him that mere accident has decided which of these numerous worlds is the object of his reliance, and that the same causes which make him a churchman in London would have made him a Buddhist or a Confucian in Peking. Yet it is as evident in itself, as any amount of argument can make it, that ages are no more infallible than individuals – every age having held many opinions which subsequent ages have deemed not only false but absurd; and it is as certain that many opinions, now general, will be rejected by future ages, as it is that many, once general, are rejected by the present.

(Mill 1985 edn, pp. 77–8)

The gist of this passage is that people frequently pay lip service to the fact that human beings are fallible. However, as regards their own behaviour, they typically act as if they were infallible, despite the fact that history has shown that many of the views held with certainty in one age, are likely to be found absurd and obviously false by subsequent generations.

At this point, Mill anticipates a possible objection. He plays devil's advocate against his own argument, putting forward the strongest objection he can imagine, only to demonstrate that he can meet the objection.

EXERCISE 4.2

PLAYING DEVIL'S ADVOCATE

Which of the following is the best definition of 'playing devil's advocate'?

1   Being argumentative for the sake of it.
2   Being a hypocrite.
3   Running rings around your opponent in argument.
4   Putting the strongest case against a position in order to test whether that opinion is true.
5   Using clever-sounding arguments to win a debate even though you don't have any faith in the arguments you are using.

Check your answer against the one at the back of the book before reading on.

READING

Here is the counter-argument to his own position that Mill provides. Read through it carefully, and try to anticipate the sort of response that Mill is going to make to it.

> The objection likely to be made to this argument would probably take some such form as the following. There is no greater assumption of infallibility in forbidding the propagation of error than in any other thing which is done by public authority on its own judgement and responsibility. Judgement is given to men that they may use it. Because it may be used erroneously, are men to be told that they ought not to use it at all? To prohibit what they think pernicious is not claiming exemption from error, but fulfilling the duty incumbent on them, although fallible, of acting on their conscientious conviction. If we were never to act on our opinions, because those opinions may be wrong, we should leave all our interests uncared for, and all our duties unperformed. An objection which applies to all conduct can be no valid objection to any conduct in particular. It is the duty of governments, and of individuals, to form the truest opinions they can; to form them carefully, and never impose them upon others unless they are quite sure of being right. But when they are sure (such reasoners may say), it is not conscientiousness but cowardice to shrink

from acting on their opinions and allow doctrines which they honestly think dangerous to the welfare of mankind, either in this life or in another, to be scattered abroad without restraint, because other people, in less enlightened times, have persecuted opinions now believed to be true. Let us take care, it may be said, not to make the same mistake; but governments and nations have made mistakes in other things which are not denied to be fit subjects for the exercise of authority: they have laid on bad taxes, made unjust wars. Ought we therefore to lay on no taxes and, under whatever provocation, make no wars? Men and governments must act to the best of their ability. There is no such thing as absolute certainty, but there is assurance sufficient for the purposes of human life. We may, and must, assume our opinion to be true for the guidance of our own conduct; and it is assuming no more when we forbid bad men to pervert society by the propagation of opinions which we regard as false and pernicious.

(Mill 1985 edn, pp. 78–9)

The key sentence in this passage, which sums up the whole object is, 'There is no such thing as absolute certainty, but there is assurance sufficient for the purposes of human life.' In other words, Mill is suggesting that perhaps we don't need to be infallible in order to have good reasons for suppressing some views. The objection is that the fact that we might turn out to be wrong in suppressing a view doesn't provide a good enough reason for us refraining from suppressing it. Governments have to act on the best available evidence. Not to act simply because there is a chance that you are wrong, is simply cowardice: 'Men and governments must act to the best of their ability.' If there is good evidence that a view is wrong, then surely there can be justification for suppressing it.

Mill, as we shall see, doesn't think this a devastating objection to his thesis. He is simply entertaining this idea in order to bring out what he takes to be the truth of the matter. In a sense here, in the way he sets out this chapter, he is demonstrating one of his views about the importance of allowing false views to be circulated. By entertaining this objection to his own opinion, he is showing us that the collision between true and false opinions can allow those holding basically true opinions to refine their views in the light of objections and to hold them with greater conviction as a result. Mill has anticipated the strongest argument that an opponent might put forward; he then proceeds to respond to it, thus pre-empting what might otherwise be taken to be a devastating criticism. This is a characteristic approach taken by philosophers: they very often anticipate and answer possible (and of course actual) objections to their positions. For this reason you should always be aware when reading a piece of philosophy that the idea being set out may not be one to which the author subscribes. In many cases philosophers present an idea in a plausible form in order to refute it. This is certainly the case with the passage from Mill quoted above. This isn't simply a clever debating strategy, but rather an important method for getting to the truth of the matter in question.

READING

Read the passage below. This is Mill's response to the objection that he has just anticipated, the notion that authorities don't need to assume their own infallibility in order to justify suppressing opinions which they believe to be false or pernicious.

There is the greatest difference between presuming an opinion to be true because, with every opportunity for contesting it, it has not been refuted, and assuming its truth for the purpose of not permitting its refutation. Complete liberty of contradicting and disproving our opinion is the very condition which justifies us in assuming its truth for purposes of action; and on no other terms can a being with human faculties have any rational assurance of being right.

When we consider either the history of opinion or the ordinary conduct of human life, to what is it to be ascribed that the one and the other are no worse than they are? Not certainly to the inherent force of the human understanding, for on any matter not self-evident there are ninety-nine persons totally incapable of judging of it for one who is capable; and the capacity of the hundredth person is only comparative, for the majority of the eminent men of every past generation held many opinions now known to be erroneous, and did or approved numerous things which no one will now justify. Why is it, then, that there is on the whole a preponderance among mankind of rational opinions and rational conduct? If there really is this preponderance – which there must be unless human affairs are, and have always been, in an almost desperate state – it is owing to a quality of the human mind, the source of everything respectable in man either as an intellectual or as a moral being, namely, that his errors are corrigible. He is capable of rectifying his mistakes by discussion and experience. Not by experience alone. There must be discussion to show how experience is to be interpreted. Wrong opinions and practices gradually yield to fact and argument; but facts and arguments, to produce any effect on the mind, must be brought before it. Very few facts are able to tell their own story, without comments to bring out their meaning. The whole strength and value, then, of human judgement depending on the one property, that it can be set right when it is wrong, reliance can be placed on it only when the means of setting it right are kept constantly at hand. In the case of any person whose judgement is really deserving of confidence, how has it become so? Because he has kept his mind open to criticism of his opinions and conduct. Because it has been his practice to listen to all that could be said against him; to profit by as much of it as was just, and to expound to himself, and upon occasion to others, the fallacy of what was fallacious. Because he has felt that the only way in which a human being can make some approach to knowing the whole of a subject is by hearing what can be said about it by persons of every variety of opinion, and studying all modes in which it can be looked at by every character of mind. No wise man ever acquired his wisdom in any mode but this; nor is it in the nature of human intellect to become wise

> in any other manner. The steady habit of correcting and completing his own opinion by collating it with those of others, so far from causing doubt and hesitation in carrying it into practice, is the only stable foundation for a just reliance on it; for, being cognizant of all that can, at least obviously, be said against him, and having taken up his position against all gainsayers – knowing that he has sought for objections and difficulties instead of avoiding them, and has shut out no light which can be thrown upon the subject from any quarter – he has a right to think his judgement better than that of any person, or any multitude, who have not gone through a similar process.
>
> (Mill 1985 edn, pp. 79–80)

The essence of Mill's response is contained in the first paragraph of this quotation. The second, much longer, paragraph elaborates the general points made in the first one. His central point is that we can have reason to believe that our opinions are right only if there have been opportunities for people to put the opposing case. If there is no freedom for other people to contradict our opinions, then we are not justified in feeling certain that our own views are correct.

He puts great stress on the fact that, throughout history, human beings have shown that their errors are corrigible. We can correct our mistakes, once either experience or discussion has demonstrated to us that they really are mistakes. Wrong opinions, he says, gradually yield to the onslaught of facts and arguments which undermine them. However, for this vitally important process to take place, the arguments need to be expressed. If you don't hear the counter-arguments to your position, you are unlikely to become aware of mistakes you have made in clinging to it. Mill stresses that to justify having confidence in our own beliefs, we need to know what can be said against them; only then can we rightly think our judgement superior to those who have not been through the same process. This won't make us infallible, but it will make our judgements more reliable. We need to hear both sides:

> To call any proposition certain, while there is no one who would deny its certainty if permitted, but who is not permitted, is to assume that we ourselves, and those who agree with us, are the judges of certainty, and judges without hearing the other side.
>
> (Mill 1985 edn, p. 81)

The effects of the assumption of infallibility involved in the suppression of ideas can be devastating:

> Who can compute what the world loses in the multitude of promising intellects combined with timid characters, who dare not follow out any bold, vigorous, independent train of thought, lest it should land them in something which would admit of being considered irreligious or immoral?
>
> (Mill 1985 edn, p. 95)

But it is not just that the world misses out on the possible contributions of potential great thinkers. Average human beings require freedom of expression in order to develop intellectually: 'There have been, and may again be, great individual thinkers in a general atmosphere of mental slavery. But there never has been, nor ever will be, in that atmosphere an intellectually active people' (Mill 1985 edn, p. 95). Mill would have found the impossibility of an intellectually active people a particularly undesirable state of affairs given his view that the highest and most important pleasures available to humanity are intellectual ones.

The main claim of the Infallibility Argument is that if you suppress another person's opinion, this implies that you are claiming infallibility for yourself. Mill's view here could be challenged however. Does it really follow? A possible objection to Mill at this point is that you can suppress views without assuming that your own *must* be right. You might have evidence which suggests that your own view is very probably correct, and that the view that you are suppressing is very probably false. So your assumption is not that you are infallible, only that your own view is very probably true. Presumably Mill would respond to this line of criticism by pointing to the number of times in history that this sort of reasoning has led to the suppression of views which turned out to be true. Even if you don't assume your own infallibility, the objection that history brims with examples of suppressed views which turned out to be true presents a strong case against the suppression of free speech.

You should remember that Mill, although he was against the suppression of views in general, could consistently advocate the suppression of any views which were likely to bring about harm (not offence). Thus his Harm Principle might tolerate racism which did not incite violence, but not racism that did. Toleration does not imply that you find the views that you tolerate congenial; you may well despise them. You are entitled to try to dissuade a racist from publishing his or her views. As a publisher you would have no responsibility to air such views. But there should be no law which prevents them from being published on grounds of their offensiveness. The Harm Principle would only justify a ban on publishing them if they were likely to incite violence or cause some other harm in Mill's sense of the term.

So far we've been considering the suppression of views which might conceivably turn out to be true. Now let's consider the second type of argument that Mill offers in favour of freedom of expression: the claim that even if the view in question is false, if expressed, it saves the received opinion from becoming dead dogma.

In the summary of his own arguments that we examined above, Mill gave this as the third type of argument he used. In the main body of the text, however, it crops up second. To avoid confusion we'll follow the order in which he discusses the ideas. This should make it easier to follow Mill's exposition if you decide to read the full text of his book.

THE DEAD DOGMA ARGUMENT

The main thrust of this argument is given in the following statement:

> However unwillingly a person who has a strong opinion may admit the possibility that his opinion may be false, he ought to be moved by the consideration that, however true it may be, if it is not fully, frequently, and fearlessly discussed, it will be held as a dead dogma, not a living truth.
>
> (Mill 1985 edn, pp. 96–7)

Ideas stay alive when they are challenged; become fossilized when left unquestioned and unexamined. Here one of Mill's main targets is the notion of 'truth by authority': the belief that simply because an authority, someone who is held in high prestige, asserts something, it must for that reason be true. If you believe in truth by authority, then in order to prove that an opinion is true you don't have to provide any reasons or evidence for believing it beyond demonstrating that it is a view that was held by a particular authority. So, for example, for a large part of the medieval period, showing that Aristotle held a view was considered a proof that the view was true. Any further argument was superfluous.

Mill, like any philosopher worthy of the name, was fundamentally opposed to the idea that the views held by authorities should not be challenged. Beliefs held independently of an examination of the reasons supporting them, and the possible objections, were prejudices – the equivalent of superstitions. Even if the views were true, they were held for the wrong reason: 'this is not the way in which truth ought to be held by a rational being.'

READING

Read the following passage on the topic of learning the grounds for your beliefs. For Mill, and for most philosophers, reasons supporting conclusions are all-important. Here he defends the idea that we should be able to defend our most important beliefs by giving reasons for them. Read through the passage several times, then answer the questions below.

If the cultivation of the understanding consists in one thing more than in another, it is surely in learning the grounds of one's own opinions. Whatever people believe, on subjects on which it is of the first importance to believe rightly, they ought to be able to defend against at least the common objections. But, someone may say, 'Let them be *taught* the grounds of their opinions. It does not follow that opinions must be merely parroted because they are never heard controverted. Persons who learn geometry do not simply commit the theorems to memory, but understand and learn likewise the demonstrations; and it would be absurd to say that they remain ignorant of the grounds of geometrical truths because they never hear anyone deny and attempt to disprove them.' Undoubtedly: and such teaching suffices on a subject like mathematics, where there is nothing at all to be said on the wrong side of the question. The peculiarity of the evidence of mathematical truths is that all the argument is on one side. There are no objections, and no answers to objections. But on every subject on which difference of opinion is possible, the truth depends on a balance to be struck between two sets of conflicting reasons. Even in natural philosophy, there is always some other explanation possible of the same facts; some geocentric theory instead of heliocentric, some phlogiston instead of oxygen; and it has to be shown why that other theory cannot be the true one; and until this is shown, and until we know how it is shown, we do not understand the grounds of our opinion. But when we turn to subjects infinitely more complicated, to morals, religion, politics, social relations, and the business of life, three-fourths of the arguments for every disputed opinion consist in dispelling the appearances which favour some opinion different from it. The greatest orator, save one, of antiquity, has left it on record that he always studied his adversary's case with as great, if not still greater, intensity than even his own. What Cicero practised as the means of forensic success requires to be imitated by all who study any subject in order to arrive at the truth. He who knows only his own side of the case knows little of that. His reasons may be good, and no one may have been able to refute them. But if he is equally unable to refute the reasons on the opposite side if he does not so much as know what they are, he has no ground for preferring either opinion. The rational position for him would be suspension of judgement, and unless he contents himself with that, he is either led by authority or adopts, like the generality of the world, the side to which he feels most inclination. Nor is it enough that he should hear the arguments of adversaries from his own teachers, presented as they state them, and accompanied by what they offer as reputations. That is not the way to do justice to the arguments or bring them into real contact with his own mind. He must be able to hear them from persons who actually believe them, who defend them in earnest and do their very utmost for them. He must know them in their most plausible and persuasive form; he must feel the whole force of the difficulty which the true view of the subject has to encounter and dispose of, else he will never really possess himself of the portion of truth which meets and removes that difficulty. Ninety-nine in a hundred of what are called educated men are in this condition, even of those who can argue fluently for their opinions. Their conclusion may be true, but it might be false for anything they know; they have never thrown themselves into the mental position of those who think differently from them, and considered what such persons may have to say; and, consequently, they do not, in any proper sense of the word, know the doctrine which they themselves profess. They do not know those parts of it which explain and justify the remainder – the considerations which show that a fact which seemingly conflicts with another is reconcilable with it, or that, of two apparently strong reasons, one and not the other ought to be preferred. All that part of the truth which turns the scale and decides the judgement of a completely informed mind, they are stranger to; nor is it ever really known but to those who have attended equally and impartially to both sides and endeavoured to see the reasons of both in the strongest light. So essential is this discipline to a real understanding of moral and human subjects that, if opponents of all-important truths do not exist, it is indispensable to imagine them and supply them with the strongest arguments which the most skilful devil's advocate can conjure up.

To abate the force of these considerations, an enemy of free discussion may be supposed to say that there is no necessity for mankind in general to know and understand all that can be said against or for their opinions by philosophers and theologians. That it is not needful for common men to be able to expose all the mis-statements or fallacies of an ingenious opponent. That it is enough if there is always somebody capable of answering them, so that nothing likely to mislead uninstructed persons remains unrefuted. That simple minds, having been taught the obvious grounds of the truths inculcated in them, may trust to authority for the rest and, being aware that they have neither knowledge nor talent to resolve every difficulty which can be raised, may repose in the assurance that all those which have been raised have been or can be answered by those who are specially trained to the task.

Conceding to this view of the subject the utmost that can be claimed for it by those most easily satisfied with the amount of understanding of truth which ought to accompany the belief of it, even so, the argument for free discussion is noway weakened. For even this doctrine acknowledges that mankind ought to have a rational assurance that all objections have been satisfactorily answered; and how are they to be answered if that which requires to be answered is not spoken? Or how can the answer be known to be satisfactory if the objectors have no opportunity of showing that it is unsatisfactory? If not the public, at least the philosophers and theologians who are to resolve the difficulties must make themselves familiar with those difficulties in their most puzzling form; and this cannot be accomplished unless they are freely stated and placed in the most advantageous light which they admit of.

(Mill 1985 edn, pp. 97–100)

EXERCISE 4.3

COMPREHENSION

1   Why does Mill believe that it is not sufficient simply to be *taught* the grounds of your opinions in the areas of morals, religion, politics, social relations, and the business of life? Why not learn them parrot fashion?

2   Why does Mill think it important not just to know the possible counter-arguments to your opinion, but also to hear them from people who actually believe them?

3   What is the point of playing devil's advocate and in what circumstances is it necessary?

4   Identify the point in this passage where Mill is himself playing devil's advocate.

5   What is Mill's response to the objection he puts forward as devil's advocate?

DISCUSSION

1   If you just learn the reasons for your opinions by heart then you won't fully appreciate the arguments on the other side. If you can't refute the possible counter-arguments to your position, then you should withhold judgement.

2   Real, imaginative understanding of the counter-arguments requires hearing them in their most plausible, persuasive form. Mill seems to be suggesting that only someone who sincerely believes in a counter-argument will be capable of putting it in this form. It is only by hearing the counter-arguments in their strongest form that the defender of a view will come to appreciate the full force of the objections. Appreciating the force of counter-arguments and being able to meet these objections leads to the kind of knowledge which Mill values so highly and away from the parroting of dead dogma.

3   The point of playing devil's advocate is to present the strongest possible counter-arguments to your position in order to show that it is unassailable. Mill describes this technique of argument as 'indispensable' when opponents of centrally important truths don't happen to exist.

4   Mill plays devil's advocate when he spells out a possible objection to his own thesis; that is, when he suggests that an enemy of free discussion might argue that the common people need not be able to defend their opinions; they can rely on a specially-trained minority examining the arguments and counter-arguments.

5   Even if it were true that the common people don't need to be able to defend their most important beliefs against possible objections (a view which Mill is only conceding for the sake of argument – there is no indication that he believed this), then it would still follow that the negative freedom of expression should be preserved. This is because at least a sub-section of society would need to be able to examine objections in order to come to conclusions on these matters.

A consequence of Mill's view that opinions need to be challenged to keep them alive is that apparently negative and highly critical ways of thinking have their part to play in preventing rigor mortis of thought:

> It is the fashion of the present time to disparage negative logic – that which points out weaknesses in theory or errors in practice without establishing positive truths. Such negative criticism would indeed be poor enough as an ultimate result, but as a means to attaining any positive knowledge or conviction worthy the name it cannot be valued too highly …
>
> (Mill 1985 edn, p. 107)

He exempts mathematics from the need for constant challenge. But, as far as other subjects are concerned, it is only through defending them against the challenges of dissenting opinion that we keep them alive. If there is no one

challenging your ideas as you set them forth, it is your intellectual duty to anticipate what a critic might say; hence the value of learning to think critically, and in
a sense negatively.

Philosophers are sometimes despised by those trained in other disciplines for
their constant readiness to take issue with and criticize other people's views.
Superficially it can seem a very negative subject: although philosophers do in
many cases put forward important positive views, they seem to spend a great deal
of their time tearing other people's ideas apart. Some seem intent even on
ripping their own ideas into ribbons. Mill's comments about the skills of criti-
cizing arguments are pertinent here; the point of such apparently negative
thought is to get at the truth, and to make sure that you are not holding any views
simply as prejudices. To keep your thought alive, you need to be able to defend it
against the strongest possible criticisms which could be made of it. If you can't do
that, you may well not be justified in holding the views that you do, even if, by
good fortune they turn out to be true. When studying philosophy it is important
to remember that if we subject a philosopher's opinions to close scrutiny this is
not mere nit-picking. We are interested in discovering the truth, and believe that
the best way to do so is by employing our powers of reason. If there are weaknesses in someone else's argument, then we should point these out. If pointing
out the apparent flaws in someone's argument leads them to reformulate it in a
clearer or better-argued form, so much the better.

The Dead Dogma Argument is summed up in Mill's aphoristic comment,
'Both teachers and learners go to sleep at their post as soon as there is no enemy
in the field' (Mill 1985 edn, p. 105). James Fitzjames Stephen had a clever
response to Mill's Dead Dogma Argument. He pointed out that, far from leading
to the conclusion that we should tolerate freedom of speech, Mill's beliefs should
have led him to advocate vigorous persecution:

> The facts that whilst a doctrine is struggling for ascendancy it is full of meaning, and that
> when it has become a received opinion its living power begins to decline, surely prove that
> coercion and not liberty is favourable to its appreciation. A 'struggle for ascendancy' does
> not mean mere argument. It means reiterated and varied assertion persisted in, in the face
> of the wheel, the stake, and the gallows, as well as in the face of contradiction. If the
> Protestants and Catholics or the Christians and the Pagans had confined themselves to
> argument, they might have argued for ever, and the world at large would not have cared. It
> was when it came to preaching and fighting, to 'Believe, and be saved,' 'Disbelieve, and be
> damned,' 'Be silent, or be burned alive,' 'I would rather be burned than be silent,' that the
> world at large listened, sympathized, and took one side or the other. The discussion became
> free just in proportion as the subjects discussed lost their interest.
>
> (Fitzjames Stephen 1967 edn, pp. 107–8)

Here Fitzjames Stephen is arguing that Mill drew the wrong conclusion from the
observation that unchallenged opinions atrophy into dead dogma. Citing a religious precedent, he suggests that it is coercion and persecution which keep the
meaning of a doctrine alive: when people might have to die for their beliefs, these
beliefs have a living power which they lose when the threat recedes. Fitzjames
Stephen is not saying that we ought to persecute any views; he is indicating the

consequences of Mill's Dead Dogma Argument, and providing some empirical evidence from history to illustrate his claim. That is, he is suggesting that absurd consequences follow from Mill's belief that unchallenged views end up as dead dogma.

Another way of attacking Mill's Dead Dogma Arguments is by pointing to what it might mean in practice. In recent years, some overtly anti-Semitic organizations have been publishing and circulating pamphlets in which they claim that the Holocaust never happened. They have been putting forward their completely implausible views in the teeth of detailed and overwhelming evidence ranging from eyewitness testimony of survivors, and even of the perpetrators of horrendous crimes, through bureaucratic documents written by Nazi administrators, film and photographic records, right down to physical remains of the mechanisms of death, and of the bodies and possessions of those who died. To deny that millions of Jews, gypsies and homosexuals were systematically executed or left to die, often after having been subjected to gruesome torture, such as being forced to participate in Nazi medical experiments or to work as slaves in labour camps, is a bizarre stance to take. It is like denying that Adolf Hitler ever existed, or that there ever was such a thing as the Nazi party. It is scarcely credible that the views expressed in these pamphlets are intended as serious factual hypotheses. A far more likely explanation is that they are simply intended to anger and hurt members of the Jewish community. However, if we are to take Mill's Infallibility Argument seriously, we will have to concede the value of allowing dissenting opinion even on areas about which there can be no serious doubt. This is made clear in the following quotation:

> Strange it is that men should admit the validity of the arguments for free discussion, but object to their being 'pushed to an extreme', not seeing that unless the reasons are good for an extreme case, they are not good for any case. Strange that they should imagine that they are not assuming infallibility when they acknowledge that there should be free discussion on all subjects which can possibly be *doubtful*, but think that some particular principle or doctrine should be forbidden to be questioned because it is so *certain*, that is, because *they are certain* that it is certain. To call any proposition certain, while there is anyone who would deny its certainty if permitted, but who is not permitted, is to assume that we ourselves, and those who agree with us, are the judges of certainty, and judges without hearing the other side.
>
> (Mill 1985 edn, p. 81)

EXERCISE 4.4

APPLYING MILL'S ARGUMENTS

What would Mill's (1) Harm Principle, (2) Infallibility Argument and (3) Dead Dogma Argument each imply about the circulation of the views expressed by those who deny that the Holocaust took place? Write a short answer to this three-part question before reading my longer response below.

DISCUSSION

1   The Harm Principle

An important point to establish is whether anyone would be put at serious risk of harm by the circulation of such views. If these pamphlets aren't likely to stir up actual violence against Jews or anyone else, then, according to Mill's account of 'harm', the fact that large numbers of people would be deeply disturbed and angered by their circulation would not be sufficient grounds for forcibly censoring them.

However, Mill's Principle would allow coercive intervention if the Holocaust-deniers circulated their pamphlets to an angry mob of neo-Nazis outside a synagogue, i.e. if they were using them to stir up an anti-Semitic resentment that would very likely lead to violence. This would be analogous to Mill's case of declaring that corn-dealers are starvers of the poor to the angry mob outside a corn-dealer's house – a situation in which speech could justifiably be censored because of a serious risk of its leading to physical harm.

It could be countered, in response to this argument for the freedom to express offensive and obviously false views about so serious an event in world history, that the deep offence caused to those who lived through the Holocaust or whose relatives and friends were tortured and killed by the Nazis should be treated as a genuine harm, a psychological rather than a physical harm. Mill argued that taking offence should never be considered a harm. However, his account of what constitutes harm could be extended, particularly in the light of our greater knowledge about psychology, so that some cases of people being psychologically damaged could be considered cases of harming them, and so coercive preventative measures would in those cases be justified. The trouble with this approach, however, is that, as Mill realized, there is a very wide range of views to which people take great offence.

2   The Infallibility Argument

To suppress such views implies infallibility: you can't be absolutely certain that what you believe is true until you've heard what people who think it is false actually believe. Those countries which have chosen to make Holocaust denial against the law have, on this view, overstepped the mark. They do greater damage by silencing an obviously false view that has the potential to keep knowledge of recent history a living truth, than they would have done by allowing such views to be freely circulated. Censorship of such views would prevent 'the clearer perception and livelier impression of truth produced by its collision with error' (Mill 1985 edn, p. 76).

3   The Dead Dogma Argument

Mill's line would have to be that, obviously false as the views expressed are, they serve a useful function in forcing historians to be careful about how they document the evidence about the Holocaust, and in keeping awareness of what actually happened a living belief, rather than a dead dogma parroted by people who aren't really aware of the evidence which supports their beliefs.

The Infallibility Argument rests on the possibility that the view to be suppressed might conceivably turn out to be true; the Dead Dogma Argument provides reasons for allowing even false opinions to be expressed and circulated. The next argument we'll be looking at, the Partly True Argument, relies on the possibility that views which are largely false may contain an element of truth that might never surface if these views are suppressed.

THE PARTLY TRUE ARGUMENT

Mill points out that received opinion is rarely the whole truth on any matter, and that views which are, when taken as a whole, false, may contain important elements which are true. To illustrate this point Mill cites the example of Jean-Jacques Rousseau's protestations about the corruption brought about by civilization. In the mid-eighteenth century Rousseau's celebration of the 'noble savage' and of a simple rural existence ran counter to popular opinion:

> in the eighteenth century, when nearly all the instructed, and all those of the uninstructed who were led by them, were lost in admiration of what is called civilization, and of the marvels of modern science, literature, and philosophy, and while greatly overrating the amount of unlikeness between the men of modern and those of ancient times, indulged the belief that the whole of the difference was in their own favour; with what a salutary shock did the paradoxes of Rousseau explode like bombshells in the midst, dislocating the compact mass of one-sided opinion and forcing its elements to recombine in a better form and with additional ingredients. Not that the current opinions were on the whole farther from the truth than Rousseau's were; on the contrary, they were nearer to it; they contained more of positive truth, and very much less of error. Nevertheless there lay in Rousseau's doctrine, and has floated down the stream of opinion along with it, a considerable amount of exactly those truths which the popular opinion wanted [i.e. lacked]; and these are the deposit which was left behind them when the flood subsided. The superior worth of simplicity of life, the enervating and demoralizing effect of the trammels and hypocrisies of artificial society are ideas which have never been entirely absent from cultivated minds since Rousseau wrote …

> (Mill 1985 edn, pp. 109–10)

The choice of Rousseau as an example is particularly pertinent as several of his books were suppressed in France. Mill's point is that Rousseau's attack on the alleged fruits of civilization is, for the most part, misguided:[1] there is more truth in the view that he attacked, namely that society was progressing and benefiting greatly from advances in science and the arts. However, there were important elements of truth in what Rousseau had to say, and had his views been completely suppressed these elements of truth might not have emerged and become incorporated in the views of 'cultivated minds', as Mill suggests they have done. Even though much of what Rousseau had to say was false, this did not give sufficient grounds for state censorship. The cost of such censorship would have been the loss of important elements of the truth.

THE LINK WITH ACTION ARGUMENT

Mill's fourth argument for freedom of thought and expression, the claim that unchallenged views lose their power to stir people to action, is closely linked with his Dead Dogma Argument. When a belief isn't challenged it ends up being held as simply a verbal formula incapable of stirring anyone to action. Mill cites the example of the majority of Christians in his day. These, he says, in principle believe a number of ethical maxims, principles which should guide their behaviour; however, because their Christianity has become a dead dogma held simply as a prejudice, these maxims have lost their power to influence how they live:

> All Christians believe that the blessed are the poor and humble, and those who are ill-used by the world; that it is easier for a camel to pass through the eye of a needle than for a rich man to enter the kingdom of heaven; that they should judge not, lest they be judged; that they should swear not at all; that they should love their neighbour as themselves; that if one take their cloak, they should give him their coat also; that they should take no thought for the morrow; that if they would be perfect they should sell that they have and give it to the poor. They are not insincere when they say that they believe these things. They do believe them, as people believe what they have always heard lauded and never discussed. But in the sense of that living belief which regulates conduct, they believe these doctrines just up to the point to which it is usual to act upon them. The doctrines in their integrity are serviceable to pelt adversaries with; and it is understood that they are to be put forward (when possible) as the reasons for whatever people do that they think laudable. But anyone who reminded them that the maxims require an infinity of things which they never even think of doing would gain nothing but to be classed among those very unpopular characters who affect to be better than other people.
>
> (Mill 1985 edn, pp. 103–4)

Here Mill is not just accusing the majority of Christians of his day of being hypocrites – not practising what they preach – but also explaining what he takes to be the source of their hypocrisy. Because they hold their views as dead dogma, the living link with action has been severed. His suggestion is that if they had to defend their views against opposing arguments it would stimulate their minds in such a way that there would be an intimate link between what they believe and how they live their lives. In the absence of serious debate of their principles, their religious and ethical opinions harden into husks and shells. Their beliefs just become formulae to be trotted out when appropriate, but which, nevertheless, have no influence on how they live. So the negative effect of dead dogma is not just that the meaning of a belief can be lost, but also that all connection between the belief and action can wither away.

Is this argument a good one? Mill's evidence in support of his notion that unchallenged dogmas lose their power to stimulate action is anecdotal and limited. There may well have been many other reasons why so many Victorian Christians had lapsed into hypocrisy. To attribute the decline to the absence of challenge to orthodox teaching alone (in itself a controversial view of nineteenth-century history) is simplistic. The fact that members of some fundamentalist religions living in countries where all challenge to orthodoxy is forbidden by law have been amongst the most ready to realize the aims of their religion through action provides empirical evidence that lack of challenge to orthodox dogma need not sever the link with action.

Nevertheless it is certainly true that some opinions are kept alive by being challenged.

MILL AND MILTON

The great English poet John Milton (1608–74) published a pamphlet in 1644 entitled *Areopagitica* (its subtitle was 'A Speech of Mr John Milton for the Liberty of Unlicensed Printing to the Parliament of England'). This was a reaction to Parliament's decision to introduce censorship by requiring every printing press to be licensed. Censors could refuse to license a press which published any unorthodox or subversive material: the Order of 1643, mentions the printing of many 'false, forged, scandalous, seditious, libellous and unlicensed papers, pamphlets and books, to the great defamation of religion and government' (Milton 1993 edn, p. 619).

Milton was passionately opposed to this censorship of views before they had been heard in public. His *Areopagitica* presents numerous arguments and uses many persuasive techniques intended to convince Parliament that it should reinstate freedom of expression for writers. Some of these, such as his linking of censorship with the Catholic Church, are largely rhetorical. However, there are a number of points at which Milton's arguments in support of this particular freedom of expression come very close to Mill's. It is even possible that Mill was influenced by Milton's pamphlet.

EXERCISE 4.5

MILL AND MILTON

Read the following quotations from Milton's *Areopagitica*. Put the central point of each quotation in your own words. Do you see any parallel with Mill's arguments? Is Milton's point in each case compatible with Mill's approach? Bear in mind that, unlike Mill, Milton was concerned not just with the censorship of views that were thought to be false, but also with those that were thought to be evil. Don't be put off by the archaic language. If you find you can't make much sense out of these passages, then you can use the answers at the back of the book to help you to understand them.

1   'Since therefore the knowledge and survey of vice is in this world so necessary to the constituting of human virtue, and the scanning of error to the confirmation of truth, how can we more safely, and with less danger, scout into the regions of sin and falsity than by reading all manner of tractates and hearing all manner of reason? And this is the benefit which may be had of books promiscuously read' (Milton 1993 edn, p. 590).

2   'Besides another inconvenience ... how shall the licensers [censors] themselves be confided in [trusted], unless we can confer upon them, or they
assume to themselves above all others in the land, the grace of infallibility
and uncorruptedness?' (p. 593).

3   'Well knows he who uses to consider, that our faith and knowledge thrives by
exercise, as well as our limbs and complexion. Truth is compared in Scripture
to a streaming fountain; if her waters flow not in a perpetual progression,
they sicken into a muddy pool of conformity and tradition. A man may be a
heretic in the truth; and if he believe things only because his pastor says so ...
without knowing other reason, though his belief be true, yet the very truth he
holds becomes his heresy' (p. 604).

4   'When a man hath been labouring the hardest labour in the deep mines of
knowledge, hath furnished out his findings in all their equipage, drawn forth
his reasons as it were a battle [army] ranged, scattered and defeated all
objections in his way, calls out his adversary into the plain, offers him the
advantage of wind and sun, if he please, only that he may try the matter by
dint of argument: for his opponents then to skulk, to lay ambushments, to
keep a narrow bridge of licensing where the challenger should pass, though it
be valour enough in soldiership, is but weakness and cowardice in the wars of
Truth' (p. 614)

5   '[...]if it come to prohibiting, there is not aught more likely to be prohibited
than truth itself; whose first appearance to our eyes, bleared and dimmed
with prejudice and custom, is more unsightly and unplausible than many
errors ... ' (p. 615).

Compare your answers with the ones at the back of the book before reading on.

EXERCISE 4.6

APPLYING MILL'S PRINCIPLES

Before reading the next section, think what Mill might have said about the issue of
whether pornography should be banned. If you think his principles would lead him
to say that it should be banned under some circumstances, what would those
circumstances be? Jot down some notes, then read on.

PORNOGRAPHY: A CASE FOR RESTRICTING FREEDOM OF EXPRESSION?

Mill did not discuss the issue of whether or not his Harm Principle would justify
state censorship of pornography. However, this is one of the commonest areas in
which principles of freedom of speech and expression have been challenged in
recent years. A number of people have argued that there are good grounds for
restricting individuals' negative freedom to create, purchase and consume various

kinds of pornography, and that a civilized society should censor a wide range of pornographic publications. Despite the fact that Mill did not himself address this question directly, *On Liberty* is frequently cited in the pornography debate, both by those who want to preserve freedom from state intervention in this area *and* by those who want to set some quite stringent limits on what kinds of pornography should be available to adults. The authors of *The Williams Report on Obscenity and Film Censorship* (1979), for example, mention that several of those who presented submissions to the committee cited Mill's book in their support; the authors of the report, despite the uneven quality of Mill's arguments, did not consider this out of place: 'Some of Mill's reasons [for defending freedom of expression] we believe to be still very relevant today. Some of his arguments, however, were always flimsy and are yet more so in modern conditions' (Williams 1979, pp. 53–4).

The pornography debate, then, provides a case study of an attempt to restrict negative liberty; it also provides an illustration of how Mill's arguments can be applied to developments that he did not foresee.

A conspicuous limitation of Mill's chapter 'Of the Liberty of Thought and Expression' is its focus on truth. All four of the arguments he uses to defend freedom from interference in the publication and dissemination of ideas are underpinned by his notion that truth is beneficial to society and that the best way of discovering, keeping alive, and acting on the basis of truth is to guarantee freedom of expression right up to the point at which others are put at serious risk of physical harm.

However, many of the publications that those who are opposed to pornography object to don't put forward theses which could be considered either true or false. It is hard to see how a pin-sharp pornographic photograph of a sexual act could be considered to put forward an opinion: the sorts of truth which it might contribute to certain branches of medical science are extremely limited, and that is certainly not the point of such a photograph. Pornographic photographs are meant to arouse viewers sexually. Indirectly, such photographs could, and have been thought to, express a view about human sexuality, or about women, or, indeed, about men. But this is very much an indirect, and usually an unintended consequence of their publication. The Supreme Court of the United States (controversially) seems to have accepted this line of argument. It has endorsed the censorship of some hardcore pornography despite the First Amendment of the Constitution which declares that Congress shall not make any laws which abridge freedom of speech. Presumably the reasoning behind this exemption is that pornography doesn't typically put forward opinions, and so need not be protected in the way that other sorts of publication should.

Mill's discussion of freedom of thought and expression is focused exclusively on issues of truth and falsity, and thus is more limited in scope than it might first appear. Nevertheless, we can attempt to apply Mill's Harm Principle in this area and see what conclusions it will support.

PORNOGRAPHY AND THE HARM PRINCIPLE

The usual reason given for banning some kinds of pornography is that it is harmful in some sense. Yet there are many different kinds of harm, only some of which Mill would admit as warranting restrictions on individual liberty. In particular, you will remember, Mill stipulated that taking of offence should not be considered a genuine harm.

Those who want to restrict individuals' negative freedom of publishing and consuming pornography have identified several different kinds of harm which they believe result from toleration of pornography.

These are the main candidates:

1   Physical harm in the production of pornography. This may take the form of injury (as in certain kinds of non-consensual sadomasochism), or, perhaps, risk of various sexually transmitted diseases.
2   Physical harm perpetrated as a direct result of the use of pornography. Many people believe that some rapes and other forms of sexual violence are caused by pornography.
3   General harm to women. Women are often stereotyped as passive and subservient 'victims' in pornography. The claim is that those who use pornography carry this attitude over to the way they treat real women, thus harming them by encouraging sexual inequality.

HARM TO PARTICIPANTS

Mill's Harm Principle would certainly justify a legal prohibition on the production of any pornography which physically harmed those involved in making it. However, he does endorse the principle that if you give free and informed consent to someone to cause you physical damage, you are not then harmed by their actions. Without this principle a whole range of activities such as tattooing, physical contact sports, surgery and so on could justifiably be prohibited. Those most likely to be harmed in producing pornography are children (who cannot give free and informed consent), and those involved against their will in making some kinds of sadistic videos or photographs. The genre of the so-called 'snuff movie', in which an unsuspecting victim is mutilated and killed in front of the camera, provides the extreme example of such harm (fortunately, most alleged snuff movies turn out to be simulations rather than records of actual crimes). In such cases, issues about freedom of expression are irrelevant since the Harm Principle gives a clear-cut assessment as to why these practices should not be tolerated, namely because they harm participants in a very obvious way.

HARM PERPETRATED BY USERS

Many opponents of access to pornography have claimed that it can cause people to commit various acts of sexual violence. Access to pornography allegedly increases the likelihood of women (or in some cases men) being raped or assaulted. This is an empirical claim. If it were shown to be true, then, provided that the increased risk of sexually motivated violence were sufficiently high, the Harm Principle would indicate that access to such pornography could justifiably be restricted, or perhaps even prohibited altogether. The problem is that it is extremely difficult to demonstrate beyond reasonable doubt that there is such a causal connection. When the Williams Committee submitted its report in 1979, after considering all the available empirical evidence on this alleged causal connection, they did not rule out the possibility of such a connection. However, the Committee concluded:

> It is not possible, in our view, to reach well-based conclusions about what in this country has been the influence of pornography on sexual crime. But we unhesitatingly reject the suggestion that the available statistical information for England and Wales lends any support at all to the argument that pornography acts as a stimulus to the commission of sexual violence.
>
> (Williams 1979, p. 80)

If, however, such conclusive evidence were to emerge, then the Harm Principle would support a restriction or (where that proves unfeasible) a ban on at least some types of pornography. But it would only advocate such a ban provided that driving pornography underground would not be likely to result in a more ready supply of this kind of pornography and so an increased risk of pornography-related crimes.

GENERAL HARM TO WOMEN

A common claim is that much pornography is inherently degrading to women and so fosters sexist attitudes which have repercussions throughout women's lives. The women allegedly harmed by the toleration of pornography aren't just those who are involved in the sex industry that produces it, but also all those women who interact with men who use pornography. The claim is that male users of pornography tend to treat women as passive, sexual objects, and that this leads to unfair treatment both in the workplace and in domestic life. This attack can only consistently be applied to pornography that does actually have this effect (assuming there is some pornography that does) and so does not provide any argument against, for example, male homosexual pornography being freely available to adults. It also usually ignores the fact that some women use pornography and that it is plausible that if some pornography is degrading to women, some is also degrading to men.

Applying Mill's Harm Principle here is difficult. It is clear that if the alleged degrading aspect of pornography is simply a matter of it being found peculiarly offensive by women, then Mill would argue that this does not amount to sufficient grounds for restricting adult access to it. But if there were genuinely some well-established and significant harm done to women in society, such as that the existence of pornography made it impossible for women to reach top jobs, or to get equal pay with men, then perhaps Mill's principle could be invoked to justify either a total ban on pornography, or else a ban on the sorts of pornography which tended to produce this effect. However, as with the alleged link between pornography and actual sexual violence, it is extremely difficult to produce conclusive evidence about such a causal connection. The risk of genuine harm has to be shown to be severe, and the harm great, otherwise the Harm Principle could, for example, be used to justify banning all car driving on the grounds that there is an undeniable causal link between people driving cars and a large number of people getting injured in road accidents (an uncontroversial example of people being harmed). The harm done must outweigh any counterbalancing good brought about by a general freedom to publish. Evidence has yet to be produced that there is a high risk of severe harm. However, as with the supposed link between pornography and sexual crimes, it is possible that such empirical evidence might one day emerge. In the absence of such evidence, however, many people believe that there should be a presumption in favour of freedom of expression and freedom about what sorts of pictures we can look at, and they frequently mention Mill's arguments about the value of free speech in this connection.

However, it could be argued that, as Mill's arguments in favour of free speech are almost entirely concerned with opinions which can be true or false (or, perhaps, partly true), they are completely unilluminating about this aspect of the pornography debate.

This could be countered by bringing out the implications of banning pornography on the grounds that it is degrading to women. A great deal of advertising and other representations of women in magazines and on television is sexist. In fact, such representations of women, being so widespread and generally thought acceptable, are likely to have a far more pernicious effect on the treatment of women than are representations of women in pornography. If this is accepted, then consistency seems to demand that those who call for a ban on pornography on the grounds that it degrades women should also be calling (and perhaps more strongly) for a general ban on sexist media representations of women. This argument is of the same form as the one that Locke used against Christian persecutors of heretics: he pointed out that consistent application of their expressed principles would seem to demand that they persecute the far more widespread 'evils' of, for example, prostitution and adultery, rather than concentrate all their energy on religious dissenters (see Chapter 2). A possible retort to this is that pornography in fact has a more severe effect than the milder sexism found in representations of women in advertisements. However, such a statement would only have force if it were backed up with reliable empirical evidence.

THE HARM PRINCIPLE AND PORNOGRAPHY

The pornography debate points up some difficulties of applying Mill's principles about freedom of expression in the present-day context. Mill's specific arguments about this topic are far more pertinent when what is at issue is the fate of opinions which can be true, false or partly true. He simply did not address the issue of the possible benefits to humanity of the toleration of access to pornographic representations. What is clear, however, is that merely finding such representations offensive would not, on his principles, give good grounds for state interference with their production and publication. Some harm, beyond a feeling of disgust or revulsion, would have to result from the availability of such representations to justify a restriction on negative liberty in this area.

Reading
p. 167

First read the extract from the *Williams Report* (Reading 4) which makes explicit the relevance of Mill's Harm Principle to debates about censorship. Then

Reading p. 179

read Ronald Dworkin's essay 'Liberty and Pornography' (Reading 5) in which he links Isaiah Berlin's essay on the two concepts of liberty with recent attempts to restrict access to a wide range of allegedly pornographic material.

CONCLUSION

This chapter has focused on Mill's defence of freedom of speech and on its relevance for present-day arguments about censorship. In the next chapter we will be looking at another application of the Harm Principle, this time in the area of what Mill called 'experiments of living'.

CHAPTER SUMMARY

Mill presents four main arguments in favour of free speech. The Infallibility Argument is that those who censor assume that they never make mistakes. The Dead Dogma Argument involves the claim that unless views are challenged we will lose our capacity to provide good reasons in their defence and they will be held dogmatically. The Partly True Argument is that even views which are for the most part false can contain elements of truth that may be lost if these views are suppressed. The Link with Action Argument is that unchallenged views, even if true, lose their power to stir people to action. The present-day debates about the censorship of pornography bring out some of the difficulties of applying Mill's Harm Principle.

FURTHER READING

The complete text of Milton's *Areopagitica* is certainly worth reading, though the language in which it is expressed can be quite difficult to follow at first. It is available in various editions.

An abridged version of the *Williams Report* is available as a book, *Obscenity and Film Censorship*, edited by Bernard Williams (Cambridge University Press, 1981).

Ronald Dworkin gives a fuller discussion of his position on pornography in 'Do We Have a Right to Pornography?', in Ronald Dworkin, *A Matter of Principle* (Harvard University Press, 1985), Chapter 17.

Alan Haworth's *Free Speech* (Routledge, 1998) provides an interesting account of the philosophical problem of free speech. It includes discussion of Mill, Locke and Milton.

NOTE

1   See, for instance, his 'Discourse on the Science and the Arts' (1750) where this is the main theme of the piece. Scepticism about the value of progress in science and art is to be found throughout Rousseau's work.

5 'Experiments of living'

The four principal arguments that Mill used to defend the negative freedom of expression also apply to the choice of how we live our lives. If, to use Berlin's terminology, you believe in a 'final solution', a single way of life which all human beings should adopt, then you will probably have fewer qualms about imposing this pattern on everyone than if you aren't certain that you have all the answers. Mill suggests that to impose a particular way of life on others reveals your assumption of infallibility on the matter of how life should be lived, just as in the realm of expression of ideas suppressing a view because you 'know' it is false reveals your assumption of infallibility about what is true. Some fundamentally misguided ways of living are likely to contain parts of the truth about what will make people's lives go well; diversity of ways of life contributes to society by challenging people to think through how they live, rather than living according to some pre-arranged system that may have lost all vitality. In both these respects there are obvious parallels with the arguments Mill uses to defend freedom of thought and expression. This is how Mill makes the link between arguments for freedom of thought and expression and arguments for freedom of action or way of life:

That mankind are not infallible; that their truths, for the most part, are only half-truths; that

> unity of opinion, unless resulting from the fullest and freest comparison of opposite opin-
> ions, is not desirable, and diversity not an evil, but a good, until mankind are much more
> capable than at present of recognizing all sides of the truth, are principles applicable to
> men's modes of action not less than to their opinions.
>
> (Mill 1985 edn, p. 120)

Here he is outlining the benefits which he thinks result from toleration of diversity within a society. The only limit he wants to set on how people choose to live
is that they shouldn't be permitted to harm other people. You should be
permitted to offend others, and to lead a bizarre and eccentric existence, if that is
what you want to do, and there are likely to be tangible benefits to society if
many different approaches to life are tolerated. However, at the point at which
your way of living causes or is likely to cause harm to other people, your activities can justifiably be curtailed. What Mill calls 'experiments of living' are
beneficial to society in the way that divergent opinions are beneficial:

> As it is useful that while mankind are imperfect there should be different opinions, so it is
> that there should be different experiments of living; that free scope should be given to vari-
> eties of character, short of injury to others; and that the worth of different modes of life
> should be proved practically, when anyone thinks fit to try them. It is desirable, in short, that
> in things which do not primarily concern others, individuality should assert itself. Where not
> the person's own character but the traditions or customs of other people are the rule of
> conduct, there is wanting one of the principal ingredients of human happiness, and quite the
> chief ingredient of individual and social progress.
>
> (Mill 1985 edn, p. 120)

The gist of this passage is that if you get your way of life 'off the peg', simply
accepting the traditions and customs of the society in which you happen to find
yourself, you miss out on the possibility of an important kind of fulfilment. This is
the fulfilment that comes from designing your own life for yourself, rather than
having a pattern imposed on you (this is a point which Berlin wholeheartedly
endorses in his essay 'Two Concepts of Liberty'). A flourishing society depends
on the negative freedom of its members to invent and put into practice their own
experiments of living. Only when there is a risk of injuring other people in the
process should the state or anyone else intervene and forcibly restrain you from
expressing your individuality through the choices that you make for yourself.

Here Mill is explicitly supporting his views with utilitarian arguments: aggregate happiness will be maximized in a society which does not prevent individuals
from putting into practice their ideas about how best to live, even if in some cases
the individuals concerned do not themselves end up particularly content with
their lives.

Mill is not advocating complete licence about experiments of living: he
doesn't believe it acceptable for you to do absolutely anything that takes your
fancy. In particular, he does not want to grant extensive negative liberty to those
who aren't yet fully responsible for their choices. He believes that paternalism is
entirely appropriate towards those not yet at an age at which they can make
responsible decisions. Part of the point of education is to teach us which ways of

living are most likely to prove beneficial to us, based on the accumulated experience of how people have in the past chosen to live. Education can also instil, by force if necessary, good habits, which will serve us throughout our lives. However, once we reach an age at which we can be considered adults, then there is no longer any justification for coercing us into a particular way of life, apart from risk of harm to other people. But this proviso, provided by the Harm Principle, *does* rule out many ways of life: you wouldn't, in Mill's ideal world, be free to take up a career as a torturer, a mugger or a serial killer. These sorts of experiments of living are non-starters on account of the harm they cause to other people. Provided, however, that you stay within the bounds set by the Harm Principle, you should be free to live as you please. As long as you are capable of making informed choices for yourself about your life, then it is up to you how and whether you choose to benefit from what you have learnt of other people's choices:

> it is the privilege and proper condition of a human being, arrived at the maturity of his faculties, to use and interpret experience in his own way. It is for him to find out what part of recorded experience is properly applicable to his own circumstances and character.
>
> (Mill 1985 edn, p. 122)

EXERCISE 5.1

COMPREHENSION

Read the following passage carefully. Note down in your own words three reasons Mill gives against simply adopting customs and traditions as a guide as to how to live.

> The traditions and customs of other people are, to a certain extent, evidence of what their experience has taught *them* – presumptive evidence, and as such, have a claim to his [i.e. to the adult deciding how to live his life] deference: but, in the first place, their experience may be too narrow, or they may have not interpreted it rightly. Secondly, their interpretation of experience may be correct, but unsuitable to him. Customs are made for customary circumstances and customary characters; and his circumstances or his character may be uncustomary. Thirdly, though the customs be both good as customs and suitable to him, yet to conform to custom merely *as custom* does not educate or develop in him any of the qualities which are the distinctive endowment of a human being.
>
> (Mill 1985 edn, p. 122)

Compare your answer with the one at the back of the book before reading on.

Underlying the last of the three points that Mill makes is a view about what human beings are. Where Darwin, in his *The Origin of Species* (published in 1859, the same year as *On Liberty*), emphasized the continuity, at least in evolutionary terms, between apes and human beings, Mill emphasized the value of choice for human beings. Our capacity for making choices about how we live is an all-important one:

> He who lets the world, or his own portion of it, choose his plan of life for him has no need of any other faculty than the ape-like one of imitation. He who chooses his plan for himself employs all his faculties. He must use observation to see, reasoning and judgement to foresee, activity to gather materials for decision, discrimination to decide, and when he has decided, firmness and self-control to hold to his deliberate decision ... It is possible that he might be guided in some good path, and kept out of harm's way, without any of these things. But what will be his comparative worth as a human being? It really is of importance, not only what men do, but also what manner of men they are that do it ... Human nature is not a machine to be built after a model, and set to do exactly the work prescribed for it, but a tree, which requires to grow and develop itself on all sides, according to the tendency of the inward forces which make it a living thing.
>
> (Mill 1985 edn, p. 123)

In this passage Mill seems to have moved from defending the consequential value of not interfering with how other people live, to making a plea for a particular kind of self-mastery or self-realization through choosing for oneself. In other words, this passage seems to be presenting a positive rather than a negative idea of freedom. Though he doesn't go quite this far, he could almost have written 'True freedom is making your own choices for yourself rather than having them imposed on you by others'; this contrasts with the negative freedom, which he certainly defends, the notion that freedom consists in the absence of constraints on how you might possibly live. Nevertheless, these two aspects of his philosophy are not in conflict: they are complementary.

GENIUSES

One reason that Mill gives for permitting individuals to organize their own lives as they see fit is that without this sort of freedom those highly original individuals we label 'geniuses' would not be likely to develop. The great originality of geniuses prevents society sliding into complacent dogmatism:

> without them, human life would become a stagnant pool. Not only is it they who introduce good things which did not before exist; it is they who keep the life in those which already exist. If there were nothing new to be done, would human intellect cease to be necessary? Would it be a reason why those who do the old things should forget why they are done, and do them like cattle, not like human beings? There is only too great a tendency in the best beliefs and practices to degenerate into the mechanical; and unless there were a succession of persons whose ever-recurring originality prevents the grounds of those beliefs and practices from becoming merely traditional, such dead matter would not resist the smallest shock from anything really alive, and there would be no reason why civilization should not die out ...
>
> (Mill 1985 edn, p. 129)

This passage echoes the Dead Dogma Argument that Mill used in defence of freedom of expression. Geniuses, by their originality (even, presumably, when their views are misguided), keep a society's central beliefs alive by challenging them. They stimulate defenders of the traditionally accepted views to give the grounds of their beliefs, rather than simply to hold these beliefs because everyone else has always held them. Geniuses, then, even though they are always a small minority of any population, help a society and its members to flourish: 'but in order to have them, it is necessary to preserve the soil in which they grow. Genius can only breathe freely in an *atmosphere* of freedom' (Mill 1985 edn, p.129).

His reason for believing that genius requires an atmosphere of freedom is that geniuses are by definition more individual than other people. They are, he says,

> less capable, consequently, of fitting themselves, without hurtful compression, into any of the small number of moulds which society provides in order to save its members the trouble of forming their own character. If from timidity they consent to be forced into one of these moulds, and to let all that part of themselves which cannot expand under the pressure remain unexpanded, society will be little the better for their genius.
>
> (Mill 1985 edn, pp. 129–30)

Geniuses, then, by their nature, won't fit comfortably into 'off-the-peg' ways of living: they need to tailor their own lives to the measure of their individuality. If society squashes them into unsuitable moulds, moulds that are completely satisfactory for the mediocre majority, then we won't receive the possible benefits of their genius. Mill's point is that a society which preserves negative freedom about how individuals live allows geniuses 'to breathe freely'. He doesn't rule out the possibility of geniuses emerging in more repressive societies, but clearly believes that the best way of cultivating them is to give them room to develop in their chosen ways, just so long as no one is harmed by the way they choose to live. Mill's argument about genius can be stated as follows:

Premise 1	Only in an atmosphere of freedom can genius breathe freely.
Premise 2	Societies which restrict negative freedom don't provide an atmosphere of freedom.
Conclusion	So such societies won't permit genius to breathe freely.

The message seems to be that if you want genius to breathe freely, then you ought to arrange society so that this is possible, i.e. provide an atmosphere of freedom. A great deal turns on what Mill means by 'breathe freely' here. Presumably his view is that in a society in which a range of negative freedoms are protected there is a better chance of geniuses emerging and developing than in a more oppressive society in which individuals' behaviour is restricted either by law or social pressures to conform. Such societies, he hints, are only likely to breed mediocrity, to the detriment of the societies and indeed to humanity in general.

Mill's argument in part rests on the assumption that more oppressive societies do not provide sufficient room for geniuses to develop and realize their potential. Yet, even though this view has some initial plausibility, it seems, as a generalization, to be contradicted by historical evidence. The character Harry Lime, in Graham Greene's screenplay for the film *The Third Man*, makes this point forcefully to his friend Holly:

> In Italy for thirty years under the Borgias they had warfare, terror, murder, bloodshed – they produced Michelangelo, Leonardo da Vinci and the Renaissance. In Switzerland they had brotherly love, 500 years of democracy and peace, and what did that produce … ? The cuckoo clock.
>
> (Quoted in Sherry 1994, p. 254)

Some of the most original geniuses have managed to produce their greatest works under conditions of censorship and oppression. We have already seen in Chapter 4 how, for instance, Galileo lived in a society which, at times, certainly did not provide an atmosphere in which he could breathe freely; yet he still managed to make significant original contributions to science. Some societies have preserved a wide range of negative liberties without being blessed with many geniuses as a result. It is not, then, obviously true that genius requires a range of negative liberties; some people even argue that censoring views is the surest way of giving them life. In the stifling atmosphere of an oppressive regime, those who hold dissenting views typically hold them with a passion that stirs them to action. Providing a range of negative freedoms in no way guarantees that genius will flourish as a result.

Although there is an initial plausibility in Mill's idea that, because geniuses are by definition more individual than the great mass of humanity, and will not be able to develop and bloom in an atmosphere that cramps all kinds of originality, this idea could be overturned by empirical evidence. Harry Lime's point about the surprising conditions under which past geniuses have flourished is a reminder that the ideal conditions for the cultivation of geniuses cannot be determined simply by imagining which conditions might suit them best. In the end it is only by looking at the actual conditions under which geniuses have emerged and have made their contributions to humanity that we can decide this issue.

HUMAN DIVERSITY AS AN ARGUMENT FOR LIBERTY

One of Mill's strongest arguments in defence of preserving an area of freedom for each individual is that we differ considerably in what we desire and in what will make us happy. A mode of life which would suit one person would utterly crush and constrain another:

> Human beings are not like sheep; and even sheep are not undistinguishably alike. A man cannot get a coat or pair of boots to fit him unless they are either made to his measure or he has a whole warehouseful to choose from; and is it easier to fit him with a life than with a coat, or are human beings more like one another in their whole physical and spiritual conformation than in the shape of their feet? If it were only that people have diversities of taste, that is reason enough for not attempting to shape them all after one model. But different persons also require different conditions for their spiritual development; and can no more exist healthily in the same moral, than all the variety of plants can in the same physical,

atmosphere and climate. The same things which are helps to one person towards the cultivation of his higher nature are hindrances to another. The same mode of life is a healthy excitement to one, keeping all his faculties of action and enjoyment in their best order, while to another it is a distracting burden which suspends or crushes all internal life. Such are the differences among human beings in their sources of pleasure, their susceptibilities of pain, and the operation on them of different physical and moral agencies that, unless there is a corresponding diversity in their modes of life, they neither obtain their fair share of happiness, nor grow up to the mental, moral, and aesthetic stature of which their nature is capable.

(Mill 1985 edn, p. 133)

Imposing a single way of life on all members of a society would be like treating an orchid, a cactus, a lettuce and a sunflower all in the same way. The conditions in which orchids thrive would very soon kill most cacti, and most lettuces would turn limp and shrivel in the optimum conditions for a sunflower. Human beings differ too much for there to be any sense in attempting to make all members of a society conform to one model of the good life.

IMPLICATIONS FOR CHANGING CRIMINAL LAW

Mill was at least as concerned with the effects of social pressures as with legal ones. However, the influence of *On Liberty* is most apparent today in debates about changes to the criminal law. The publication of the Wolfenden Report in 1957, which recommended decriminalizing male homosexual activity in England and Wales (provided that it occurred in private between consenting adults) ignited a public exchange of views about the philosophical justification for the criminal law. The main participants in the debate were Lord Devlin (a judge) and H.L.A. Hart (Professor of Jurisprudence at Oxford). Devlin opposed the principle on which the Wolfenden Report was based, that there should be a realm of private morality (and immorality) which is none of the law's business. Hart, on the other hand, defended the Wolfenden Report, using adaptations of Mill's arguments from *On Liberty*. More recently, in 1990 in England in the so-called 'Spanner Trial', fifteen men were prosecuted for participating in consensual sadomasochistic sexual activity. This again raised the question of whether there is any justification for curtailing negative freedom concerning choices about how to live which apparently affect only consenting participants.

In this section we'll look at the challenge to Mill's arguments about experiments of living provided by Devlin's reaction to the Wolfenden Report. In the next, we'll consider the implications of the Spanner Case in the light of Mill's ideas.

THE WOLFENDEN REPORT

The underlying principle of the Wolfenden Report differs very little from Mill's Harm Principle:

In this field [laws on prostitution and on male homosexuality], its [the criminal law's] function, as we see it, is to preserve public order and decency, to protect the citizen from what is offensive or injurious, and to provide sufficient safeguards against exploitation and corruption of others, particularly those who are specially vulnerable because they are young, weak in body or mind, inexperienced, or in a state of special physical, official or economic dependence.

It is not, in our view, the function of the law to intervene in the private lives of citizens, or to seek to enforce any particular pattern of behaviour, further than is necessary to carry out the purposes we have outlined.

(Wolfenden, quoted in Wasserstrom 1971, pp. 25–6)

EXERCISE 5.2

THE HARM PRINCIPLE AND THE WOLFENDEN REPORT

In which respects do the principles of the Wolfenden Report resemble those embodied in Mill's Harm Principle? What are the main differences?

Write down a brief answer to this question before reading on.

DISCUSSION

The principles of the Wolfenden Report are very similar to those of Mill's Harm Principle as elaborated in *On Liberty*. Both see the prime function of restrictions on liberty as being to prevent harm to others. Both agree that the law should not concern itself with matters of private morality, and certainly should not enforce a particular way of life on anyone unless this is the only way of avoiding significant risk of harm to others.

The authors of the Wolfenden Report appear to differ from Mill slightly in their view as to what counts as harming someone. They suggest that part of the law's purpose is to preserve decency and to protect the citizen from anything that is offensive. It is not clear what 'decency' amounts to here, but presumably, in view of the later remarks about private and public morality, it must refer only to whatever is done in public.

However, Mill himself notes that some sorts of action, even though they only directly harm the person performing them, if performed in public, can be forcibly prevented not on the grounds that they are condemnable actions themselves, but that when performed in public they amount to offences against decency. So perhaps there is no real difference here between the views (whether Mill's statement on this point is consistent with the rest of his views, is another question). However, Mill *is* clear that finding an expressed opinion offensive doesn't in itself provide a sufficient ground for outlawing it. If the word 'offensive' is meant to cover the expression of opinions as well as indecent public actions, then it is clear that the authors of the Wolfenden Report and Mill differ on this point.

Implicit in the quotation from the Wolfenden Report and explicit in Mill's *On Liberty* is the view that individuals' freedom to engage in experiments of living should not be curbed simply to enforce a particular code of morality.

DEVLIN'S ATTACK

Devlin's attack on the principles of the Wolfenden Report might just as well have been focused directly on Mill's Harm Principle. It is an attack on the assumption that toleration has beneficial effects on society; it is also an attack on the view that private morality is none of the law's business. His fundamental belief is that any society, if it is to survive, requires a single public morality. Devlin makes this point by drawing an analogy between the law which prevents treason and laws which the state might impose to enforce morality:

> The law of treason is directed against aiding the king's enemies and against sedition from within. The justification for this is that established government is necessary for the existence of society and therefore its safety against violent overthrow must be secured. But an established morality is as necessary as good government to the welfare of society. Societies disintegrate from within more frequently than they are broken up by external pressures. There is disintegration when no common morality is observed and history shows that the loosening of moral bonds is often the first stage of disintegration, so that society is justified in taking the same steps to preserve its moral code as it does to preserve its government and other essential institutions.
>
> (Devlin, in Dworkin 1977, pp. 76–7)

EXERCISE 5.3

DEVLIN'S ANALOGY

What exactly is the analogy that Devlin is drawing in this passage? Is the analogy a good one?

    Write down an answer to this question before reading on. You should be clear which two things are being compared, how similar they actually are, and whether Devlin is justified in drawing the conclusion that he does on the basis of this analogy.

DISCUSSION

The two things being compared in this passage are the law of treason and laws which serve to enforce morality. The law of treason protects the government. Government is necessary for society. So the law of treason indirectly protects society by protecting what is necessary for it. Similarly, according to Devlin, a common morality, like government, is necessary for society. Remove common morality and you risk the disintegration of society. So, Devlin concludes, the argument from analogy shows that we are as justified in imposing laws which enforce morality as we are in enforcing laws which forbid treason. The consequences of relaxing laws in both areas can be disastrous for the cohesion of society.

    Arguments from analogy rely on the two things being compared being relevantly similar. The alleged similarity on which the argument turns, between treason and immorality (and the laws which prohibit them), is that if left unchecked both sorts of activity are likely to contribute to the disintegration of society from within. However, the analogy between treason and immorality is not as straightforward as Devlin takes it to be.

The belief that allegedly immoral acts performed in private are likely to undermine society is not obviously true. It is hard to see how, for instance, a sexual liaison of a supposedly immoral kind performed in private between two consenting adults could shake the stability of a society in the way that an act of treason could. If the idea is simply false, then the whole analogy between treason and immorality is just misleading: they aren't relevantly similar, and so a conclusion based on a comparison of their similarities is unwarranted. The analogy is, then, only very weak. And a weak analogy can provide only weak support for any conclusion drawn on the basis of it.

Devlin has a response to this sort of criticism of his analogy. The criticism rests on the point that it is difficult to see how an action which seems to affect only two consenting adults can be compared to an act of treason which may affect a whole state. But Devlin rejects the idea that what you do in private affects only you and whoever you do it with. He points out both that whatever you do has an effect on your character, which may have repercussions in your future interactions with other people, and that if one person quietly performs an act of vice in private this may not be significant in itself, but if large numbers of people are doing likewise then this can have a wider effect on society. Like James Fitzjames Stephen before him, then, he seriously questions whether there is such a thing as a private sphere of purely self-affecting actions. Like treason, apparently self-affecting vice can contribute to the downfall of a whole society, and so should be controlled by law:

> The suppression of vice is as much the law's business as the suppression of subversive activities; it is no more possible to define a sphere of private morality than it is to define one of private subversive activity. It is wrong to talk of private morality or of the law not being concerned with immorality as such or to try to set rigid bounds to the part which the law may play in the suppression of vice. There are no theoretical limits to the power of the State to legislate against treason and sedition, and likewise I think there can be no theoretical limits to legislation against immorality. You may argue that if a man's sins affect only himself it cannot be the concern of society. If he chooses to get drunk every night in the privacy of his own home, is anyone except himself the worse for it? But suppose a quarter or a half of the population got drunk every night, what sort of society would it be? You cannot set a theoretical limit to the number of people who can get drunk before society is entitled to legislate against drunkenness.
>
> (Devlin, in Dworkin 1977, pp. 77–8)

Mill's approach throughout *On Liberty* emphasizes the importance of being rational in human affairs. We should hold our views not as prejudices, but on the basis of reasons and evidence. We should be able to provide arguments in defence of what we believe. Toleration in most matters is the best policy, since we are fallible creatures, and can never achieve completely reliable knowledge on such issues as the question of how best to live. Devlin's approach contrasts sharply with this. As we have seen, he believes that immorality can pose a threat to the whole of a society, even if the alleged immorality is apparently victimless, and only carried out in private between consenting adults.

Devlin believes that public morality is relatively easy to discern: it is revealed by the strong emotions of members of the society. Public morality is revealed in the judgements of 'the reasonable man'. Public morality doesn't require complete agreement of all members of the society, nor is it simply what the majority believe:

> How is the law-maker to ascertain the moral judgments of society? It is surely not enough that they should be reached by the opinion of the majority; it would be too much to require the individual assent of every citizen. English law has evolved and regularly uses a standard which does not depend on the counting of heads. It is that of the reasonable man. He is not to be confused with the rational man. He is not expected to reason about anything and his judgment may be largely a matter of feeling. It is the viewpoint of the man in the street – or to use an archaism familiar to all lawyers – the man in the Clapham omnibus.
>
> (Devlin, in Dworkin 1977, p. 78)

Where Mill emphasized the importance of being able to give reasons for your opinions, Devlin's reasonable man may simply have strong views about right and wrong. But for Devlin not every action which the 'reasonable man' considers immoral need be prohibited by law. There are different intensities of feeling that the 'reasonable man' may feel towards different actions. When the feelings reach a threshold level of a combination of intolerance, indignation and disgust, society is justified in imposing a legal ban on the activity in question, since these feelings reveal it as a threat to society.

Let's look at the structure of Devlin's main argument.

Summary of Devlin's main argument

Premise 1	Any activity which seriously contravenes public morality threatens society's existence.
Premise 2	The strong feelings of a 'reasonable person' reveal the content of public morality (presumably by 'reasonable man' Devlin means 'reasonable person', whether man or woman).
Intermediate conclusion and Premise 3	So any activity which the reasonable person strongly feels to be immoral threatens society's existence.
Premise 4	Society is justified in imposing laws for the purpose of safe-guarding its existence.
Main conclusion	Therefore society is justified in making laws to enforce the strong moral feelings of a reasonable person.

In the above summary of Devlin's main argument, the intermediate conclusion follows from the combination of Premises 1 and 2. This intermediate conclusion then acts as a premise (Premise 3) in the second part of the argument; combined with Premise 4 it leads to the main conclusion of the whole argument.

EXERCISE 5.4

DEVLIN'S PREMISES

As you will probably have realized, Devlin's argument is an extremely controversial one. Critics of it have challenged several of its premises. Look back over my summary of the structure of the argument. Which, if any, of the premises do you think controversial? Why?

DISCUSSION

Premise 2 is particularly controversial. It relies on the rather vague concept of the 'reasonable person'. As anyone who uses public transport knows, there is unlikely to be a moral consensus on many issues, even amongst people travelling in one bus in Clapham. Even if there were such a consensus, the idea that we could simply determine what public morality was by asking this supposed 'reasonable man' which activities he finds morally repugnant, amounts to relying on gut reactions and prejudices for determining what the law should or shouldn't proscribe. This is especially true in light of the fact that Devlin allows that the 'reasonable man' need not have any reasons for holding the moral views that he does.

If we were to take Devlin's suggestions seriously and apply them to what went on in Nazi Germany in the late 1930s, then it seems that, by asking the 'reasonable man' on the Berlin tram whether or not there should be laws forbidding Jews from marrying non-Jews, we would probably get the answer that his feelings of intolerance, indignation and disgust at this activity were justification enough for instituting a law prohibiting such marriages. Not to have such laws would have been considered a 'risk' to that society (itself a somewhat vague notion). If such obviously immoral laws can be seen to be justified by applying Devlin's argument to this sort of case, then there must be something seriously amiss with his argument. The most obvious flaw is his assumption that the moral prejudices of a 'reasonable man' are worth taking seriously when no reasons whatsoever are provided for them. He might respond to this that an anti-Semite on the Berlin tram wouldn't count as a 'reasonable man'. But in this case the rather vague notion of the 'reasonable man' seems to be smuggling in preconceptions about the nature of public morality.

There is also the suspicion that Devlin is using a circular definition of 'reasonable man' here. If what he means by a 'reasonable man' is simply 'someone who makes correct moral judgements', and if the only way we have of knowing which moral judgements are correct is to ask a 'reasonable man' what he thinks, then this part of Devlin's argument is viciously circular. He defines two key concepts (the 'reasonable man' and 'public morality') each in terms of the other without providing any independent way of understanding either of them. The emptiness of this strategy should be obvious. It's the equivalent of saying: 'If you want to know what "yes" means, it's the opposite of "no". And "no"? That's the opposite of "yes".'

Not all circularity in definitions is to be avoided; a good dictionary, for instance, will involve circular definitions in the sense that every word used in the definitions should also appear as an entry in the dictionary. However, when the circle of definition is as small as it seems to be with Devlin's definitions of 'a reasonable man' and 'public morality' then this is usually described as 'vicious' circularity. Vicious circularity is certainly to be avoided since it is spectacularly uninformative while often giving the superficial appearance of making a contribution to a discussion. It is important to realize that showing that someone is arguing in a vicious circle doesn't prove that their conclusion is false, only that the kind of argument they have used is entirely uninformative.

EXERCISE 5.5

VICIOUS CIRCULARITY

Which of the following are examples of vicious circularity?

1 I'm taller than my sister. She's taller than my brother. So I'm taller than my brother.

2 All real works of art produce an aesthetic emotion in a sensitive viewer. What do you mean by 'an aesthetic emotion'? Oh, it's the feeling that is characteristically experienced by sensitive people when they are in the presence of real works of art.

3 What does 'freedom' mean in the social context? It means not being prevented from acting in various ways by other people. What does 'slavery' mean, then? Having most of your freedoms taken away.

4 Every word in the Bible is true. How do you know? It's the word of God. But how do you know that it's the word of God? It says so in the Bible.

Check your answers against the ones at the back of the book before reading on.

READING

Reading
p. 189

Read the article by Hart, 'Immorality and Treason' (Reading 6). Then write down answers to the questions below.

1 What is the difference between Devlin's 'reasonable man' and a rational person?

2 Why, according to Hart, does Devlin believe that it would be inappropriate to have a law against fornication, but appropriate to have one against homosexuality, given that Devlin thinks both contravene public morality?

3 What are the two questions which Hart thinks we should ask ourselves in situations in which public opinion has reached a high level of intolerance, indignation and disgust? Put the questions in your own words.

4 Why does Hart believe 'private subversive activity' to be a contradiction in

terms? What implications does this point have for Devlin's analogy between treason and private immorality?

5   What is the 'wider, perhaps deeper' criticism that Hart thinks Devlin's analogy is open to?

6   What does Hart suggest should replace Devlin's 'man in the Clapham omnibus' test?

DISCUSSION

1   Despite the connotations of the word 'reasonable', Devlin doesn't mean that such a person needs to have reasons for their moral beliefs, nor to be capable of justifying the beliefs. Devlin's 'reasonable man' has strong, reliable feelings about what is and is not morally acceptable. In contrast, a rational person has good reasons for his or her beliefs.

2   Public feeling against fornication is not now at the high level of intolerance, indignation and disgust that indicates that a legal ban is justified. The balance between protecting society and protecting individual liberty is swayed in favour of individual liberty in this case. However, according to Devlin, the public feeling against homosexuality may have reached such an intensity that 'reasonable' people may believe that its existence is dangerous to society; on these grounds, Devlin seems to be saying, a legal ban on homosexual activity is appropriate.

3   (a) Is the activity harmful in itself? (b) Will the activity in question *really* endanger society as a whole if there is no law made against it?

4   Hart's point is that subversive activity, by its very nature, involves attempting to undermine a government, which is a public entity. So there can be no such thing as acting in a subversive way which puts no one else at risk of harm. In contrast, the allegedly immoral private sexual behaviour of adults does not necessarily affect anyone else; so the analogy seems to break down. If Devlin replies that such immoral behaviour, left unchecked, has a tendency to undermine public morality and thus endanger the fabric of society, then the onus is on him to demonstrate that this is true. As Hart points out,

> we have ample evidence for believing that people will not abandon morality, will not think any better of murder, cruelty, and dishonesty, merely because some private sexual practice which they abominate is not punished by the law.
>
> (Hart, in Dworkin 1977, p. 86)

This leads to Hart's conclusion that Devlin's analogy between subversive activity and treason is simply absurd.

5   By relying on feelings of intolerance rather than rational argument, Devlin's approach to morality seems to have the consequence that if there is a widespread feeling of intolerance, indignation and disgust felt by 'reasonable people' towards, for example, marriage between people of different ethnic backgrounds, then it is perfectly appropriate that a law should be brought in to maintain such a public morality (as, for example, under apartheid in South

Africa). The feelings are sufficient to justify the law, regardless of rational considerations. Hart clearly (and surely rightly) finds this an unpalatable and unacceptable conclusion following from Devlin's stance.

6   Hart suggests that the appropriate question is not about what happens to make the 'reasonable man' feel sick. Rather we should subject general moral feelings to critical scrutiny, investigate whether they are based on superstition, ignorance or misunderstanding. We should also be aware of the possibly destructive consequences of bringing in laws against allegedly immoral behaviour. Reason, sympathetic understanding and critical intelligence should all be applied; Devlin, in contrast, is content to seek the views of someone whose judgements may be based on none of these.

THE 'SPANNER' CASE

The 1990 'Spanner' trial of fifteen men for engaging in consensual sadomasochistic activity resurrected many of the debates about the acceptable limits on individual freedom in a civilized state that had been the focus of the Hart/Devlin controversy. These men were prosecuted for voluntarily inflicting on each other, in private and by mutual agreement, less serious injuries than are often sustained in a rugby match, though, it must be said, in more sensitive parts of the body.[1]

EXERCISE 5.6

APPLYING THE HARM PRINCIPLE

Consider how Mill might have viewed the Spanner Case. Write down some notes on how you think he might have applied his Harm Principle in such a case. What would Lord Devlin have had to say on the matter?

DISCUSSION

At first glance you might suppose that sado-masochistic sex carried out in private which results in injury could be ruled out by Mill's Harm Principle on the grounds that physical injuries are a clear case of harms. However, Mill is explicit that not only self-inflicted 'harms' are immune from this principle:

> there is a sphere of action in which society, as distinguished from the individual, has, if any, only an indirect interest: comprehending all that portion of a person's life and conduct which affects only himself, *or, if it also affects others, only with their free, voluntary, and undeceived consent and participation*.
>
> (Mill 1985 edn, p. 71; my italics)

In other words, if you give your consent to be injured, and this consent is given freely (i.e. you are not forced to give it), and you are not deceived about what it is you are consenting to (no one has tricked you into agreeing to more than you intended), then even if you sustain physical injuries, these don't count as 'harms' from the point of view of Mill's Harm Principle. Mill doesn't directly address the issue of consenting to the infliction of bodily injury, but this seems a plausible interpretation of his comments, and consistent with his view that, 'Neither one person, nor any number of persons, is warranted in saying to another human creature of ripe years that he shall not do with his life for his own benefit what he chooses to do with it' (Mill 1985 edn, p. 142).

Certainly some present-day liberal philosophers, whose views are heavily influenced by Mill's Harm Principle, have argued that the principle enshrined in Roman Law known as *volenti non fit injuria* ('to one who consents, no injury is done') is a reasonable one. In the Spanner Case there was never any doubt that the defendants had given their informed consent to be injured. They had not misled each other about the nature of the injuries they would inflict. And none of them was under age (i.e. not old enough to give consent). So, on this interpretation of Mill's Harm Principle, the defendants in the Spanner Case should not have been punished by the law for their private consensual activities.

Lord Devlin would probably have argued that there were excellent grounds for using the law to curb such activities. Setting aside the fact that the activity in question was homosexual, no doubt Devlin would have considered it immoral to get sexual gratification from inflicting injury on someone else, or on having it inflicted on yourself. If after consulting the man on the Clapham omnibus he concluded that there was, among 'reasonable' people, a sufficiently strong feeling of intolerance, indignation and disgust, then he would have argued that this was indication enough that such activities should be outlawed, that his conception of public morality should be enforced.

Reading
p. 195

Now read the article entitled 'Consent and the Harm Principle' (Reading 7). This is an extract from the Law Commission Consultation Paper *Consent in the Criminal Law*. It sets out the position of philosophical liberalism (a position substantially influenced by Mill's arguments in *On Liberty*) on the issue of consent.

THE ATTEMPT TO BAN BOXING

EXERCISE 5.7

APPLYING THE HARM PRINCIPLE

Do you think from your understanding of *On Liberty* that Mill would have been sympathetic to recent attempts to ban boxing on the grounds that it is dangerous to participants? Give reasons for your answer.

DISCUSSION

It is clear from *On Liberty* that if, as some medical experts have claimed, boxing carries with it a severe risk of cumulative brain damage (i.e. real irreversible physical harm), then Mill would have thought a ban on children boxing entirely appropriate.[2] Children are not mature enough to make informed decisions about putting themselves in positions of extreme risk, and so a degree of paternalism is needed. Here, protecting them from risk of brain damage by preventing them from boxing at school, for instance, may be justified. However, it has to be pointed out that many activities in which young people often participate such as playing rugby, and even soccer, carry with them reasonably high risks of injury, the risks varying according to the quality of training and supervision provided. Even cycling to school (or catching the bus) carries some risk. Mill's Harm Principle does not give us any way of drawing the line between acceptable and unacceptable levels of risk. However, it is clear that children need to be protected against participation in particularly risky activities, and that the Harm Principle does not rule out intervention to prevent harm to them, even when they apparently give consent; the point is that the 'consent' children give cannot be considered genuine consent.

When it comes to adults' choices about how they live their lives and the risks they take, Mill's principle is easier to apply. In the case of boxing, provided that adult participants give their free and informed consent, then even if you find the sport offensive (in which case you are likely to put the word 'sport' in inverted commas), the most that you would be justified in doing would be to attempt to educate would-be boxers about the risks of participating in the activity. Your finding boxing offensive doesn't constitute a harm in Mill's sense of the term, even if you are one of those people who feel that they are psychologically harmed by the knowledge that our society tolerates boxing. Adults are in a better position than younger people to know what is likely to make their lives go well, and even if they make mistakes about this, the mistakes they make are theirs and not the result of coercion. Provided no one is harmed in the process (and those who have given free and informed consent can't be harmed by what they have consented to), Mill thinks such a situation more conducive to maximizing happiness than one in which individuals' choices about the risks they take are severely constrained for their own sake. Such paternalism is appropriate only towards children. We should recognize and respect adults' autonomy, their power to give direction to their own lives.

This interpretation of Mill is relatively uncontroversial so far as it concerns the apparent harm that boxers inflict on each other in private. However, many boxing matches take place in public. Joyce Carol Oates, in her classic examination of the sport, *On Boxing*, compares the public spectacle of boxing to pornography in some respects:

> The spectacle of human beings fighting each other for whatever reason, including, at certain well-publicized times, staggering sums of money, is enormously disturbing because

it violates a taboo of our civilization. Many men and women, however they steel themselves, cannot watch a boxing match because they cannot allow themselves to see what it is they are seeing. One thinks helplessly, this can't be happening, even as, and usually quite routinely, it *is* happening. In this way boxing as a public spectacle is akin to pornography: in each case the spectator is made a voyeur, distanced, yet presumably involved, in an event that is not supposed to be happening as it is happening.

(Oates 1994, pp. 105–6)

In one passage in *On Liberty*, Mill seems to be saying that, whether or not they harm anyone, some acts should not be permitted in public:

there are many acts which being directly injurious only to the agents themselves, ought not to be legally interdicted, but which, if done publicly, are a violation of good manners and, coming thus within the category of offences against others, may rightly be prohibited.

(Mill 1985 edn, p. 168)

Here Mill is clearly thinking of sexual acts which, if carried out in the privacy of one's home, are entirely innocuous, but which if practised, for example, on the Clapham omnibus, would amount to acts of indecency, and would no doubt shock and offend some of one's fellow travellers. On the grounds that such public acts are offensive, he appears to be saying, a ban is justified. However, it is difficult to reconcile this with the rest of *On Liberty* where he is adamant that being offended doesn't count as a harm from the point of view of his theory. The fact that the man on the Clapham omnibus is offended by what the couple in front of him are doing is on that principle irrelevant to the question of whether the activity should be banned. The fact is that most of *On Liberty* is concerned with how people choose to behave in private and does not provide much in the way of elucidation about how we are to cope with public actions. The most plausible explanation of Mill's example is that he was presenting it as an exception to his general principles (otherwise it would seem to contradict the idea that the Harm Principle provides a necessary condition for any justified intervention or coercion). If we take Mill at his word, however, then it seems that those who are deeply offended by boxing taking place in public might have a case for banning it as a spectator sport. Defenders of boxing in public might point out in response to this that there is an important disanalogy between the two sorts of activity. Those who watch boxing choose to do so, and have a good idea what to expect. Someone going home on a bus presumably hasn't chosen to watch an indecent act. So perhaps Mill could consistently prevent the indecent act and yet tolerate the boxing match on the grounds that there are significant differences between the two public activities.

If there were reliable empirical evidence which demonstrated beyond reasonable doubt that boxing was a catalyst to actual violence in society (i.e. people harming each other without consent), then Mill's Harm Principle could provide grounds for banning the sport. However, until such evidence emerges there can be no serious justification for banning the sport on the grounds that it harms society, at least not any that derives from Mill's arguments in *On Liberty*.

CONCLUSION

Mill's arguments in *On Liberty* provide a framework within which to discuss the question of how free we should be to live as we please. They are the starting point for many contemporary debates on the issue. However, Mill's arguments are largely in favour of a concept of negative freedom, freedom from interference; in the next chapter we'll be considering the strongest arguments that can be put in favour of a concept of positive freedom.

CHAPTER SUMMARY

Mill's arguments about the value of experiments of living derive from his view of the human situation as one of choice-making. Only when we are given sufficient freedom to choose how we live our lives are we likely to realize our humanity to the fullest extent and thus maximize happiness. Geniuses benefit society, yet they require an atmosphere of freedom to flourish. Diversity of lifestyle within a society is also of benefit since it allows very different individuals to find fulfilling ways of living. The Wolfenden Report used principles very similar to Mill's. Devlin's attack on it was based on his belief that society needs a single public morality, and that this morality should be enforced on all, for the good of all. Devlin believed that public morality should take as its standard the convictions of a reasonable person. Hart provided a range of arguments against Devlin's position, arguing for the need for reason in assessing moral convictions and rejecting Devlin's analogy between immorality and treason. The case studies (the 'Spanner' Case and the question of whether boxing should be banned) demonstrate the continuing relevance of Mill's ideas.

FURTHER READING

Devlin and Hart provide more detailed defences of their respective positions on morality and the law in P. Devlin, *The Enforcement of Morals* (Oxford University Press, 1963/1983) and H.L.A. Hart, *Law, Liberty and Morality* (Oxford University Press, 1963).

Richard A. Wasserstrom (ed.) *Morality and the Law* (Wadsworth, 1971) is an interesting collection of articles on philosophical justifications for the criminalization of various activities.

Nigel Warburton, 'Freedom to Box' (*Journal of Medical Ethics*, 1998, vol. 24, pp. 56–60) is a critical examination of the logic of those who argue that boxing should be banned. It is reprinted in Nigel Warburton (ed.) *Philosophy: Basic Readings* (Routledge, 1999).

NOTE

1   The Spanner defendants were convicted of assaults occasioning actual bodily harm contrary to Section 47 of the Offences Against the Person Act of 1861, and of wounding contrary to section 20.

6 Positive freedom

INTRODUCTION

Negative freedom is freedom from constraints – a matter of how many doors lie unlocked for you, and of what lies behind those doors. Positive freedom, you should remember from Chapter 1, is a question of what you are actually free to do – which doors you can actually go through, and whether these are the doors you genuinely want to go through.

Defenders of positive freedom argue that just because no one is preventing you from doing something it doesn't follow that you are free; you may, for example, have inner psychological obstacles to doing what you *really* want to do, and these can prevent you just as effectively as chains or prison bars. If you have a genuine writer's block then you can no more write than someone who is in a coma. Or else society might be arranged in such a way that you can't come to realize that, although in principle a particular course of action lies open to you, you really could choose to follow it through.

Isaiah Berlin argued that historically the concept of positive freedom has been most open to abuse. It is this concept which has been perverted by various totalitarian regimes which have oppressed their subjects in the name of freedom. Some readers of his essay 'Two Concepts of Liberty' have come away with the impression that he was arguing that theories based on a concept of negative freedom are the only sort worth defending; that theories which draw on a positive concept are obviously flawed. However, as we saw in Chapter 1, this is a misreading of his views, one which he has been at pains to correct. Indeed, he has even gone so far as to say that some form of positive freedom is necessary for a decent existence. In this chapter we'll be looking at one of the most famous accounts of society based on a concept of positive freedom, Jean-Jacques Rousseau's. We'll also be examining Charles Taylor's arguments to the effect that opponents of positive freedom have tended to focus on extreme examples of the application of this notion, and that, in any case, the extreme concept of negative freedom, which identifies lack of freedom simply with external obstacles to the fulfilment of my desires, collapses into a positive concept.

ROUSSEAU'S *THE SOCIAL CONTRACT*

In his most important work of political philosophy, *The Social Contract* (1762), Rousseau set out his view of an ideal society. Central to his approach is his distinctive attitude to freedom. For Rousseau, freedom is definitely not just a matter of having a range of opportunities available to you; it isn't a matter of no one preventing you from doing what you might want to do. Rousseau's theory is not based on a concept of negative freedom but on a concept of positive freedom. Famously he came to the conclusion that, under some circumstances it would be right to force citizens to be free.

For anyone who holds a concept of negative freedom, the notion of forcing someone to be free is a self-contradictory one; if someone is *forced* to do something, then in that respect they are not free. You might have overriding reasons for forcing someone to do or refrain from some action, such as that otherwise they run the risk of harming someone else; but these are cases of justified restrictions on liberty, they don't make anyone free. It just can't be true both that you were forced and yet free. Negative freedom is a matter of the absence of coercion, never of its presence. How, then did Rousseau arrive at the conclusion that it could be right to force people to be free?

The Social Contract opens with one of the best-known philosophical quotations: 'Man was born free, and everywhere he is in chains' (World Classics edn, p. 45). The task Rousseau sets himself is to outline a society in which it is possible to preserve our freedom, and thus our essential humanity, while at the same time reap the benefits of life in a society in terms of mutual protection and co-operation. At first glance this seems an impossible goal to achieve. For most political theorists, life in society requires that individuals give up a whole range of freedoms in order to gain the greater prizes that come from co-operation. You have to curb your desires and actions in numerous ways if you are to live with other people, but this is a price worth paying. This was the sort of argument that Thomas Hobbes used in his *Leviathan* (1651), where he suggested that to avoid a miserable existence outside of society, condemned to a life which would be 'solitary, poor, nasty, brutish and short', individuals group together and agree to give up certain freedoms in return for protection. The agreement that individuals make to form a body politic is known as a *social contract*. For Hobbes it was obvious that agreeing to be a member of society necessarily meant that you were in many respects less free than you would have been outside it. What's distinctive about Rousseau's approach, in contrast, is his desire to have his cake and eat it: he wants to show how a particular arrangement of society can leave its members as free as they would have been outside of society. The freedom that we would have outside of a society he calls 'natural' freedom; that within a society 'civil' freedom. To understand how he reaches his conclusion that such a state of affairs is possible (although not yet achieved) we need to consider his notion of the 'general will'.

THE GENERAL WILL

The phrase 'the general will' is, for Rousseau, a technical term. At first hearing it might sound like the sort of thing that could be determined by taking a vote and abiding by majority decisions. On that understanding the general will would be the equivalent of general consensus, or what you get when you add together what everybody in the society happens to want. But that is not what Rousseau means by it at all. The general will is not to be confused with the will of all. The will of all *is* the summation of what everybody happens to want. But you don't arrive at the general will by asking everybody what they want. The general will is the common interest.

EXERCISE 6.1

ROUSSEAU'S GENERAL WILL

Read the short extract below from Jonathan Wolff's *An Introduction to Political Philosophy*, then answer the questions that follow.

So what is the general will? A helpful illustration is this: suppose a company has 1000 employees, and a fixed sum of £1 million available for wage increases. It is in each individual's interests to get as much of this money as possible, so, at the limit, we could say the particular will of each individual is to try to gain an extra £1 million. Adding these particular wills together we get the will of all: a demand for £1000 million, which, of course, was not on offer. But suppose the employees are represented by a trade union, which acts equally in the interests of all its members. The union can do nothing but put in a claim for the £1 million, and then share it out equally between all of its members, giving them £1000 each. This result represents the general will: the policy equally in the interests of all the members. This is not in anyone's special interests, although it is in the common interest. Hence we see an illustration of the difference between the particular wills of all the citizens, and the

> general will. The general will demands the policy which is equally in everyone's inter-
> ests.
>
> (Wolff 1996, p. 87)

Which of the following statements are true and which are false?

1   If you add together everyone's particular will you get the general will.
2   What the union does in the above example is consistent with the will of all.
3   In the above example, giving everyone £1000 is the policy demanded by the general will.
4   The will of all gives the best solution in the above example.
5   The general will is just another way of saying the will of all.

Check your answers at the back of the book before reading on.

In Rousseau's ideal society the citizens, by entering into a social contract, become a new entity, a special kind of composite person. Each individual citizen is transformed and takes on a new role in this composite person, the state:

> Immediately, this act of association produces, in place of the individual persons of every contracting party, a moral and collective body, which is composed of as many members as there are votes in the assembly, and which, by the same act, is endowed with its unity, its common self, its life, and its will.
>
> (Rousseau 1994 edn, p. 56)

The citizens will of course have desires about what is best for them as individuals; but these can always be overridden by what is in the common interest. As citizens they should always vote for and implement whatever is consistent with the general will. For example, you may personally despise all sports and healthy pastimes. Nevertheless, this personal view of their relevance to you shouldn't cloud your judgement about the importance for society of providing good sporting facilities and the opportunity to engage in healthy leisure activities. If you have to vote on whether such facilities should be provided you should not allow your individual feelings on the matter to sway you; you should vote for what is in the common interest.

Here we see the split that any citizen in Rousseau's ideal state might experience between individual personal desires and the general will. The general will is what the individual in society should rationally choose, since it is in the common interest. If as a citizen you choose according to the general will, then you are truly free. If you allow your individual desires to hold sway then you threaten the whole principle of association underlying society. These are the circumstances when, Rousseau asserts, the state is justified in forcing you to be free, which means forcing you to comply with the general will.

> For each individual can have, as a man, a personal will that is contrary or dissimilar to the

general will that he has as a citizen. His personal interest can speak to him quite differently from the common interest: his mode of existence, absolute and independent, can make him regard what he owes to the common cause as a gratuitous contribution, the loss of which will be less onerous to others than its payment is for him; and envisaging the artificial person, in which the state consists, as an abstract being, on the grounds that it is not a man, he would thus enjoy the rights of a citizen while declining to fulfil the duties of a subject, an example of injustice which, if it were to spread, would bring the ruin of the body politic.

In order therefore that the social pact should not be an empty formula, it contains an implicit obligation which alone can give force to the others, that if anyone refuses to obey the general will he will be compelled to do so by the whole body; which means nothing else than that *he will be forced to be free* …

(Rousseau 1994 edn, p. 58; my italics)

In this passage Rousseau reveals himself as a defender of a concept of positive freedom. The individual citizen has two aspects, two selves you might even say. First, he (we'll assume he's male) is an individual with his personal will (desires for what he happens to want or need for himself). But, more importantly for Rousseau, as a citizen joined with others by the social contract (or 'social pact' as he sometimes calls it), he is part of the body politic, the state. As such, he should always subdue his personal will in favour of the general will, the common interest. Subduing the personal will to the general will is the very condition of true freedom. And when a citizen allows the personal will to predominate, the other citizens should force him to be free. What this means is they should force him to act according to the general will. That is just the cost of living in society. The cost is usually far outweighed by the benefit of protection of life and property that society can provide.

The individual concerned may in this situation feel coerced. According to the concept of negative freedom, he would be having his freedom curbed since some of his possible choices would be impeded by other people's actions. However, according to Rousseau's concept of positive freedom, by being forced to comply with the general will, to act according to his better self, the one which he has by being part of a state, he actually increases his freedom when acting under this compulsion. For Rousseau, then, there is no paradox involved in forcing someone to be free. The state remains in control of its destiny by bringing its parts (individual citizens) into line where necessary.

For anyone sympathetic to the sort of theory of negative freedom that Mill argues for in *On Liberty*, the idea that we should force individuals to be free is not only self-contradictory, but also frightening. It is frightening because it is a small step from allowing that individuals can be forced to be free to rationalizing oppression in the name of freedom. As Mill would presumably have pointed out, those who force individuals to act according to what they take to be the common interest, the general will, assume the state's own infallibility on the matter. Mill, as we have seen, like Rousseau, believes that there is a right answer to the question, 'What is in the common interest?' The answer, Mill thinks, is whatever will maximize aggregate happiness. We may not be able to arrive at the right answer, because of the limited information we have at our disposal, and the difficulties inherent in calculating the consequences of actions, but, at least in principle, for Mill such a question has a right answer.

Berlin is more pessimistic; human goals are so diverse, that there might not be one single answer to the question. For him, those who have believed there to be some single 'final' solution and have imposed this on everyone else because it was, in their view, in the common interest (or, in Rousseau's terminology, in accordance with the general will), have destroyed the lives of numerous individuals. Recall the passage from Berlin's essay quoted in Chapter 1:

> One belief, more than any other, is responsible for the slaughter of individuals on the altars of the great historical ideals – justice or progress or the happiness of future generations, or the sacred mission or emancipation of a nation or race or class, or even liberty itself, which demands the sacrifice of individuals for the freedom of society. This is the belief that somewhere, in the past or in the future, in divine revelation or in the mind of an individual thinker, in the pronouncements of history or science, or in the simple heart of an uncorrupted good man, there is a final solution.
>
> (Berlin 1969, p. 167)

Rousseau's belief that it can sometimes be right to force citizens to be free presupposes such a 'final solution' and that it can be known. It relies on the conviction that other people might know better than you what you as a rational being truly want, and what will make you free. Rousseau's arguments could be used (or 'misused' according to his defenders) to pave the way to a totalitarian regime in which anyone whose views do not conform with that society's picture of what is in the common interest can be compelled to conform, on the grounds that this is the way to make them free.

Some theorists, particularly in the economic sphere, have argued that the best overall situation for everyone will be achieved by letting individuals act according to their personal interests. In other words, the aims of the general will are most likely to be met by giving free rein to everyone's personal will. On this sort of view, there is a 'hidden hand' that operates, a sort of natural selection of, for example, prices, businesses, and techniques of buying and selling, which operates to preserve the ways of doing business most suited to the environment and context in question. Theorizing about what might be the common interest, on this view, is no substitute for letting economic processes run their course. So, if this theory is true, then there need be no conflict between personal wills and the general will: do what you as an individual want to do and the likely effect is that everyone will be better off. Mill seems to be saying that a similar principle operates in the area of choices about how we are to live. Society is better served by allowing individuals to run their own experiments of living than by imposing a single pattern on human life from above: a kind of natural selection of lifestyles will operate, tending to produce a greater aggregate happiness than any other policy would.

Rousseau's concept of positive freedom provides the core of his political philosophy. It is a view that is open to abuse. His is the sort of theory that is most often called upon in discussions of positive liberty, partly because, with its notion of the legitimacy of forcing citizens to be free, it so clearly reveals the inherent dangers in basing political theories on the view that individuals' own feelings about their freedom may not be the best guide as to whether they are genuinely free. Rousseau was writing in the eighteenth century, but in case you are tempted to believe that defences of forcing people to be free are merely of historical interest, I want to examine a more recent example of this type of argument.

MARCUSE'S ARGUMENTS FOR INTOLERANCE

Herbert Marcuse (1898–1979) has some sympathy for Rousseau's idea that in certain circumstances it is appropriate to force people to be free. In his book *One-Dimensional Man* (first published in 1964) he argues that modern industrial society has indoctrinated the general population to such an extent that they are no longer aware of their 'real' needs and desires. By means of advertising and an obsession with comfort and affluence, modern society has suffocated and obscured individuals' real desires, making it impossible for them to achieve genuine freedom. In these circumstances, the apparent freedoms achieved in Western societies, such as freedom of the press, are obstacles to true freedom:

> In the last analysis, the question of what are true and false needs must be answered by the individuals themselves, but only in the last analysis; that is, if and when they are free to give their own answer. As long as they are kept incapable of being autonomous, as long as they are indoctrinated and manipulated (down to their very instincts), their answer to this question cannot be taken as their own …
>
> The distinguishing feature of advanced industrial society is its effective suffocation of those needs which demand liberation – liberation also from that which is tolerable and rewarding and comfortable – while it sustains and absolves the destructive power and repressive function of the affluent society. Here, the social controls exact the overwhelming need for the production and consumption of waste; the need for stupefying work where it is no longer a real necessity; the need for modes of relaxation which soothe and prolong this stupefaction; the need for maintaining such deceptive liberties as free competition at administered prices, a free press which censors itself, free choice between brands and gadgets.
>
> Under the rule of a repressive whole, liberty can be made into a powerful instrument of domination. The range of choice open to the individual is not the decisive factor in determining the degree of human freedom, but *what can* be chosen and what *is* chosen by the individual … Free choice among a wide variety of goods and services does not signify freedom if these goods and services sustain social controls over a life of toil and fear …
>
> (Marcuse 1991, pp. 6–8)

Here Marcuse is challenging the assumptions of those who believe that an increase in possible choices is an increase in liberty, namely those who adopt the concept of negative liberty in its simplest form. An increase in the range of products available to the consumer would on that view be an increase in the consumer's freedom. Every new brand of instant coffee or new flavour of yoghurt increases this sort of freedom. Marcuse suggests that such an increase in 'liberty' actually undermines genuine liberty because it presents the consumer with a range of meaningless choices, while at the same time obscuring the fact that presenting a range of attractive goods simply seduces consumers into a life of alienating toil in order to be able to purchase those goods. Greater apparent freedom is, then, the cause of less *real* freedom.

Being free to choose between ten different brands of washing powder instead of two is not a significant gain in freedom; but it is the type of choice that, according to Marcuse, serves to blind us to the real choices that we might make for ourselves. Like most of those who espouse a concept of positive freedom, Marcuse suggests that in our present benighted state we might not even be able to recognize our genuine needs and desires. According to Marcuse, free speech of the kind defended by Mill can itself be an obstacle to genuine freedom. In his essay 'Repressive Tolerance' (1965) (note the deliberately paradoxical title), he claimed that: 'what is proclaimed and practised as tolerance today, is in many of its most effective manifestations serving the cause of oppression' (Marcuse, in Wolff *et al*. 1969, p. 95).

Marcuse clearly believes that most people living in affluent societies cannot benefit from negative freedoms, the kinds advocated by those who see the merits of universal toleration: 'Universal toleration becomes questionable when … tolerance is administered to manipulated and indoctrinated individuals who parrot, as their own, the opinion of their masters' (Marcuse, in Wolff *et al*. 1969, p. 104). His solution is to repress the expression of some right-wing views in order that left-wing ones (the ones he believes to be true) can be heard and absorbed – a view he labels 'discriminating tolerance'.

Marcuse's argument relies on the dubious premise that most people in affluent societies have been conditioned in such a way that some of their true needs are obscured. Presumably recognizing the truth of what Marcuse says is not such a true need, otherwise most of its readers would have been incapable of doing this because of their repressive conditioning. A serious criticism of Marcuse's use of this premise as the foundation of his argument is that he provides virtually no evidence to support it. His comment about the evidence for his views is unintentionally revealing in this respect:

> Perhaps the most telling evidence can be obtained by simply looking at television or listening to the AM radio for one consecutive hour for a couple of days, not shutting off the commercials, and now and then switching the station.
>
> (Marcuse 1991, p. xliv)

Presumably, if you do this and fail to find what he thinks you will find you must already be too heavily indoctrinated by the media to appreciate what is really going on. But, on the other hand, if you try this experiment and *do* notice it, it suggests that radio and television have a less serious effect than he suggests. So either way the experiment fails to provide support for his view (unless for some reason the person carrying out the experiment is exempt from the sorts of effects that television and radio are supposed generally to have). Certainly, he presents insufficient empirical evidence to warrant the strong claim that he makes. This doesn't show that his conclusion is false – it might turn out to be true. However, the 'evidence' he cites does not prove it to be true.

Marcuse's notion of discriminating tolerance also involves precisely the sort of misuse of the concept of positive freedom that Isaiah Berlin attacks in 'Two Concepts of Liberty'. Norman Barry summarizes the main objections to Marcuse's strategy and shows how Berlin's essay has exposed it:

> Even if Marcuse's ideas are presented in the most favourable light they seriously distort the facts of the modern world and our notions of freedom and reason ... What is remarkable is his contempt for the majority of mankind; most people are incapable of resisting the pressures of modern civilization and must be liberated by an enlightened minority. While it is true that many of the consumption habits of individuals in liberal societies may not be desirable, this in itself illustrates an essential property of freedom; that is, freedom involves the making of choices, many of which may turn out to be mistaken. Marcuse merely equates freedom with pursuing activities which he regards as desirable. Furthermore, his intolerance of other philosophical and political ideas removes the essential element required for human progress – rational criticism. Equally sinister is his critique of the freedom of expression and opinion in Western liberal democracies as a system of 'repressive tolerance', since it removes the distinction between societies which have clear and genuine impediments to freedom for thought, discussion and communication, and those which do not. His identification of freedom and 'truth' prevents that competition between ideas which is the mark of a free society.
>
> Berlin easily exposes the trickery involved in the argument for positive liberty. It depends crucially on a special interpretation of the self; it assumes not just that there is a realm of activity towards which the individual ought to direct himself but that he is being liberated when he is directed towards it. The route to totalitarianism is plainly laid out when the higher purposes of the individual are made equivalent to those of collectivities such as classes, nations and races.
>
> (Barry 1989, p. 205)

Not all theories of freedom based on a concept of positive freedom are so obviously unattractive as Rousseau's and Marcuse's; nor so easily refuted. If we think of the concept of positive freedom as a concept of self-realization, then it is probably true that most of us see it, in some form, as a valuable goal, one which is worth struggling for. We saw in Chapter 1 that Isaiah Berlin thinks that the concepts of both negative and positive freedom have their parts to play in a civilized society. In order to endorse a concept of positive freedom it is not necessary to believe that it is sometimes acceptable to force people to be free, nor need you believe that suppressing some free speech actually increases the freedom of a society. What positive theories of freedom have in common is their focus on the question of who is in control. You are only truly free if you are in control of your life; or if you are in a just society which is collectively in control of its destiny. It is important to realize that even if the theories of Rousseau and Marcuse are ultimately unsatisfactory, it doesn't follow that every theory of positive freedom is worthless – far from it. At the individual level of being one's own master, and at the political level of being a member of a society which collectively is its own master, positive freedom remains an important and attractive concept. However, as Berlin so convincingly argues, when those with power convince themselves that there is only one way in which such self- or collective mastery can occur, one pattern for the whole of humanity, then totalitarianism raises its terrifying head. The dangers of negative freedom, on the other hand, are the dangers of giving free rein for the rich, powerful or fortunate to thrive at the expense of the poor, weak and unlucky.

TAYLOR: 'WHAT'S WRONG WITH NEGATIVE LIBERTY'

If, as Berlin thinks, both negative and positive liberty are necessary for a decent existence, the positive liberty needed surely can't be of the extreme 'forced to be free' type advocated by Rousseau and Marcuse. In his article 'What's wrong with negative liberty' (1979), Charles Taylor presents an argument to the effect that a simple theory of negative liberty as absence of external obstacles is untenable. Indeed, simple negative theories, when examined closely, will be seen to collapse into positive theories very quickly when implicit assumptions are made explicit. Instead, we need to develop a theory of freedom which embodies ideas about the importance of self-realization. This, he suggests, need not take the form of the totalitarian line justifying the use of force to make people free. By focusing on freedom as self-realization he presents a far more attractive view of positive freedom than you might have got from the discussion of Rousseau and Marcuse above.

The view that Taylor is attacking is one which is usually attributed to Hobbes, namely that you are free to the extent that you are not prevented from various courses of action by external obstacles. Taylor terms this sense of 'freedom' an 'opportunity concept' (i.e. freedom is determined by the opportunities you have rather than by what you actually do); in contrast, he labels the notion of 'freedom' supporting theories which emphasize actual self-realization an 'exercise concept'. Mill, as we have seen, at times apparently opts for a purely opportunity-based approach. However, Mill's theory is not purely a negative one but also includes some ideas about the nature and importance of achieving self-realization. As such it partly relies on an exercise concept of freedom. Hobbes's account of freedom, in contrast, sees it as purely an opportunity concept.

What are Taylor's arguments against the simple Hobbesian view of negative freedom, that it is just the absence of external obstacles? The first stage in his argument is to establish that even the simplest theory of negative freedom must discriminate between different sorts of obstacles to different sorts of activity. The idea of freedom only makes sense in relation to our understanding that some goals and activities are more significant to our lives than others. In Taylor's example, we would scarcely be likely to describe a new traffic light as curtailing our freedom, though in the Hobbesian sense it does provide an obstacle to our free movement. In contrast a law forbidding me from worshipping in the way I want to would be a serious infringement of my freedom. This is because, undeniably, some activities have a higher significance for us than do others. But what makes some freedoms more significant than others? Taylor argues that it is not simply the case that the freedoms we happen to want most strongly are the most significant for us. If you are an agnostic in a hurry waiting for the traffic lights to change you may at that moment have an overwhelming desire that your movement around the city wasn't so impeded by traffic control measures. You might experience this as a far stronger desire than that people should be allowed to worship freely. However, the desire that freedom of worship be preserved may still be more *significant* for you than that traffic control systems be removed. Taylor explains the source of significance as being our capacity for what he calls 'strong evaluation'. We don't just have desires (known as first-order desires), we also can have desires about our desires (known as second-order desires). For instance, in the above example, you might have a first-order desire that there weren't any obstacles to your travelling around the city in your car; but you might also have a second-order desire, a desire about your desire, to the effect that you wish you didn't get so worked up about what, in the scheme of things, is a relatively trivial desire.

EXERCISE 6.2

FIRST AND SECOND-ORDER DESIRES

Which of the following statements are first-order desires? Which are second-order desires?

1   I'd like to be able to fly.
2   I wish I didn't have this overwhelming desire to fly.
3   I'd rather I didn't desperately want to win at all costs. But I do.
4   I wish I could read faster. I'd make better use of my study time.
5   I wish I could play the violin.

Check your answers against those at the back of the book before reading on.

We are capable of experiencing and recognizing some of our desires as more significant than others, irrespective of whether we experience the first-order desires as strong desires. Our capacity for strong evaluation in this sense is what allows us to make judgements of the relative significance of our desires for various freedoms. And some of our first-order desires can overwhelm the ones that we nevertheless recognize as more significant. An irrational fear can stop me doing what I really want to do. Similarly, in another of Taylor's examples, my spiteful reactions which I can barely inhibit might undermine an important relationship for me.

In such cases, a strong desire impedes the satisfaction of a significant one, much as in the case of Boswell's night of whoring quoted in Chapter 1. In no case is there an external obstacle restricting negative freedom; yet, Taylor suggests, these are cases in which freedom is restricted due to internal obstacles, psychological rather than physical ones:

> they seem to be cases in which the obstacles to freedom are internal; and if this is so, then freedom can't simply be interpreted as the absence of *external* obstacles; and the fact that I'm doing what I want, in the sense of following my strongest desire, isn't sufficient to establish that I'm free. On the contrary, we have to make discriminations among

> motivations, and accept that acting out of some motivations, for example irrational fear or
> spite, or this too great need for comfort, is not freedom, is even a negation of freedom.
>
> (Taylor 1991, p. 154)

So, if you admit that some desires are more significant than others (which we surely must do), this seems to lead to the view that strong yet relatively insignificant desires can be obstacles to our freedom. Another way of putting this is that less significant desires may prevent us achieving what we *really* want to do. Furthermore, Taylor argues, we can make mistakes about what we *really* want. Other people can, conceivably, be in a better position than I am to judge which are my authentically significant desires. Taylor mentions the example of Charles Manson, who presumably would have considered his desire to send his followers out to commit murders as a significant desire. In this case Manson's belief that this was one of his fundamental purposes was, Taylor maintains (using an unfortunate turn of phrase), 'shot through with confusion and error'. In other words, Manson was mistaken to think that this desire of his was significant. If we follow Taylor this far through his argument, then we are left with the conclusion that the pure concept of negative freedom collapses into a positive form, since he has shown that any plausible use of the concept will involve judgements of the relative significance of various desires, and that other people may be in a better position than you to recognize which of your desires are most significant. Taylor's conclusion is that the pure opportunity concept of freedom is untenable: to be truly free you need to exercise self-understanding at a level that allows you to realize some of your significant desires: 'we are forced to abandon the pure opportunity-concept of freedom.'

> For freedom now involves my being able to recognize adequately my more important
> purposes, and my being able to overcome or at least neutralize my motivational fetters, as
> well as my way of being free of external obstacles. But clearly the first condition (and I
> would argue, also the second) require me to have become something, to have achieved a
> certain condition of self-clairvoyance and self-understanding. I must be actually exercising
> self-understanding in order to be truly or fully free. I can no longer understand freedom just
> as an opportunity concept.
>
> (Taylor 1991, p. 162)

To be free, then, is a matter not just of having opportunities available to you, but also of being sufficiently in control to take advantage of them.

Now read Charles Taylor's article 'What's wrong with negative liberty' (Reading 8).

CONCLUSION

If Taylor is right (and his arguments *are* plausible) we should not be prevented by Berlin's warnings about historical misuses of the concept of positive freedom from endorsing theories of freedom based on a positive concept. Such a view will have to take into account not only external obstacles to action, but internal psychological ones too. Berlin's comment that a decent existence requires both negative and positive freedoms is a wise one. It is worth bearing in mind, however, that freedom of one sort or another isn't the only goal worth pursuing. Equality or justice, for instance, can be just as important goals, and can potentially conflict with the aims of freedom. This may be a further consequence of the human situation as described by Berlin: we have to make choices between incompatible goals, and there is no 'final solution' which will reconcile once and for all the various conflicting aims that we have.

CHAPTER SUMMARY

Rousseau's theory of positive freedom involves his notion of the general will. This is not the same as the will of all (the sum of what everyone wants). Rather it is whatever is in the common interest. Those who follow their personal wills rather than acting in the common interest should be 'forced to be free'. More recently, Marcuse has argued that people living in advanced industrial societies are suffocated by having a range of insignificant choices. Free speech can be an obstacle to their gaining genuine freedom. Taylor argues that a pure-opportunity concept of freedom is untenable. Freedom must be an exercise concept, that is, it must be a form of positive freedom.

FURTHER READING

You might like to read the complete text of Jean-Jacques Rousseau's *The Social Contract*. There are several translations readily available.

N.J. Dent, *A Rousseau Dictionary*, Blackwell, 1992 is a useful reference book.

Herbert Marcuse, *One-Dimensional Man*, 2nd edn, Routledge, 1991 is not an easy read. If you want to learn more about Marcuse, Alasdair MacIntyre's short and highly critical introduction *Marcuse*, Fontana Modern Masters, 1970 is recommended.

David Miller (ed.) *Liberty*, Oxford University Press, Oxford Readings in Politics and Government, 1991. This is a very good collection of essays with a useful introduction by the editor.

Jonathan Wolff, *Political Philosophy: An Introduction*, Oxford University Press, 1996 provides a clear and interesting introduction to political philosophy. A substantial part of one chapter, 'The Place of Liberty', is included in the Readings. If you want to learn more about political philosophy this book would be a very good place to begin.

Readings

1 'Two Concepts of Liberty'

Isaiah Berlin

Isaiah Berlin's essay 'Two Concepts of Liberty' is one of the most important pieces of post-war political philosophy. It was originally given as a lecture in Oxford in 1958 and has been much discussed since then (this version comes from Isaiah Berlin, *The Proper Study of Mankind*, Pimlico, 1998, pp. 191–206). In this extract from the lecture Berlin identifies the two different concepts of freedom – negative and positive – which provide the framework for his wide-ranging discussion. Negative freedom is, roughly, a matter of which doors lie open to you, it is concerned exclusively with opportunities. Positive freedom is a question of whether or not you can go through the doors, whether you are master of your life. Berlin points out that, historically, the concept of positive freedom has been used to control and repress individuals in the name of liberty.

I

To coerce a man is to deprive him of freedom – freedom from what? Almost every moralist in human history has praised freedom. Like happiness and goodness, like nature and reality, it is a term whose meaning is so porous that there is little interpretation that it seems able to resist. I do not propose to discuss either the history of this protean word or the more than two hundred senses of it recorded by historians of ideas. I propose to examine no more than two of these senses – but they are central ones, with a great deal of human history behind them, and, I dare say, still to come. The first of these political senses of freedom or liberty (I shall use both words to mean the same), which (following much precedent) I shall call the 'negative' sense, is involved in the answer to the question 'What is the area within which the subject – a person or group of persons – is or should be left to do or be what he is able to do or be, without interference by other persons?' The second, which I shall call the 'positive' sense, is involved in the answer to the question 'What, or who, is the source of control or interfer-ence that can determine someone to do, or be, this rather than that?' The two questions are clearly different, even though the answers to them may overlap.

THE NOTION OF NEGATIVE FREEDOM

I am normally said to be free to the degree to which no man or body of men interferes with my activity. Political liberty in this sense is simply the area within which a man can act unobstructed by others. If I am prevented by others from doing what I could otherwise do, I am to that degree unfree; and if this area is contracted by other men beyond a certain minimum, I can be described as being coerced, or, it may be, enslaved. Coercion is not, however, a term that covers every form of inability. If I say that I am unable to jump more than ten feet in the air, or cannot read because I am blind, or cannot understand the darker pages of Hegel, it would be eccentric to say that I am to that degree enslaved or coerced. Coercion implies the deliberate interference of other human beings within the area in which I could otherwise act. You lack political liberty or freedom only if you are prevented from attaining a goal by human beings.[1] Mere incapacity to attain a goal is not lack of political freedom.[2] This is brought out by the use of such modern expressions as 'economic freedom' and its counterpart, 'economic slavery'. It is argued, very plausibly, that if a man is too poor to afford something on which there is no legal ban – a loaf of bread, a journey round the world, recourse to the law courts – he is as little free to have it as he would be if it were forbidden him by law. If my poverty were a kind of disease which prevented me from buying bread, or paying for the journey round the world or getting my case heard, as lameness prevents me from running, this inability would not naturally be described as a lack of freedom, least of all political freedom. It is only because I believe that my inability to get a given thing is due to the fact that other human beings have made arrangements whereby I am, whereas others are not, prevented from having enough money with which to pay for it, that I think myself a victim of coercion or slavery. In other words, this use of the term depends on a partic-ular social and economic theory about the causes of my poverty or weakness. If my lack of material means is due to my lack of mental or physical capacity, then I begin to speak of being deprived of freedom (and not simply about poverty) only if I accept the theory.[3] If, in addition, I believe that I am being kept in want by a specific arrangement which I consider unjust or unfair, I speak of economic slavery or oppression. The nature of things does not madden us, only ill will does, said Rousseau.[4] The criterion of oppression is the part that I believe to be played by other human beings, directly or indirectly, with or without the intention of doing so, in frustrating my wishes. By being free in this sense I mean not being interfered with by others. The wider the area of non-interference the wider my freedom.

This is what the classical English political philosophers meant when they used this word.[5] They disagreed about how wide the area could or should be. They supposed that it could not, as things were, be unlimited, because if it were, it would entail a state in which all men could boundlessly interfere with all other men; and this kind of 'natural' freedom would lead to social chaos in which men's minimum needs would not be satisfied; or else the liberties of the weak would be suppressed by the strong. Because they perceived that human purposes and activities do not automatically harmonise with one another, and because (whatever their official doctrines) they put high value on other goals, such as justice, or happiness, or culture, or security, or varying degrees of equality, they were prepared to curtail freedom in the interests of other values and, indeed, of freedom itself. For, without this, it was impossible to create the kind of association that they thought desirable. Consequently, it is assumed by these thinkers that the area of men's free action must be limited by law. But equally it is assumed, especially by such libertarians as Locke and Mill in England, and Constant and Tocqueville in France, that there ought to exist a certain minimum area of personal freedom which must on no account be violated; for if it is overstepped, the individual will find himself in an area too narrow for even that minimum development of his natural faculties which alone makes it possible to pursue, and even to conceive, the various ends which men hold good or right or sacred. It follows that a frontier must be drawn between the area of private life and that of public authority. Where it is to be drawn is a matter of argument, indeed of haggling. Men are largely interdependent, and no man's activity is so completely private as never to obstruct the lives of others in any way. 'Freedom for the pike is death for the minnows';[6] the liberty of some must depend on the restraint of others. Freedom for an Oxford don, others have been known to add, is a very different thing from freedom for an Egyptian peasant.

This proposition derives its force from something that is both true and important, but the phrase itself remains a piece of political claptrap. It is true that to offer political rights, or safeguards against intervention by the State, to men who are half-naked, illiterate, underfed and diseased is to mock their condition; they need medical help or education before they can understand, or make use of, an increase in their freedom. What is freedom to those who cannot make use of it? Without adequate conditions for the use of freedom, what is the value of freedom? First things come first: there are situations in which – to use a saying satirically attributed to the nihilists by Dostoevsky – boots are superior to Pushkin; individual freedom is not everyone's primary need. For freedom is not the mere absence of frustration of whatever kind; this would inflate the meaning of the word until it meant too much or too little. The Egyptian peasant needs clothes or medicine before, and more than, personal liberty, but the minimum freedom that he needs today, and the greater degree of freedom that he may need tomorrow, is not some species of freedom peculiar to him, but identical with that of professors, artists and millionaires.

What troubles the consciences of Western liberals is, I think, the belief, not that the freedom that men seek differs according to their social or economic conditions, but that the minority who possess it have gained it by exploiting, or, at least, averting their gaze from, the vast majority who do not. They believe, with good reason, that if individual liberty is an ultimate end for human beings, none should be deprived of it by others; least of all that some should enjoy it at the expense of others. Equality of liberty; not to treat others as I should not wish them to treat me; repayment of my debt to those who alone have made possible my liberty or prosperity or enlightenment; justice, in its simplest and most universal sense – these are the foundations of liberal morality. Liberty is not the only goal of men. I can, like the Russian critic Belinsky, say that if others are to be deprived of it – if my brothers are to remain in poverty, squalor and chains – then I do not want it for myself, I reject it with both hands and infinitely prefer to share their fate. But nothing is gained by a confusion of terms. To avoid glaring inequality or widespread misery I am ready to sacrifice some, or all, of my freedom: I may do so willingly and freely; but it is freedom that I am giving up for the sake of justice or equality or the love of my fellow men. I should be guilt-stricken, and rightly so, if I were not, in some circumstances, ready to make this sacrifice. But a sacrifice is not an increase in what is being sacrificed, namely freedom, however great the moral need or the compensation for it. Everything is what it is: liberty is liberty, not equality or fairness or justice or culture, or human happiness or a quiet conscience. If the liberty of myself or my class or nation depends on the misery of a number of other human beings, the system which promotes this is unjust and immoral. But if I curtail or lose my freedom in order to lessen the shame of such inequality, and do not thereby materially increase the individual liberty of others, an absolute loss of liberty occurs. This may be compensated for by a gain in justice or in happiness or in peace, but the loss remains, and it is a confusion of values to say that although my 'liberal', individual freedom may go by the board, some other kind of freedom – 'social' or 'economic' – is increased. Yet it remains true that the freedom of some must at times be curtailed to secure the freedom of others. Upon what principle should this be done? If freedom is sacred, untouchable value, there can be no such principle. One or other of these conflicting rules or principles must, at any rate in practice, yield: not always for reasons which can be clearly stated, let along generalised into rules or universal maxims. Still, a practical compromise has to be found.

Philosophers with an optimistic view of human nature and a belief in the possibility of harmonising human interest, such as Locke or Adam Smith or, in some moods, Mill, believed that social harmony and progress were compatible with reserving a large area for private life over which neither the State nor any other authority must be allowed to trespass. Hobbes, and those who agreed with him, especially conservative or reactionary thinkers, argued that if men were to be prevented from destroying one another and making social life a jungle or a wilderness, greater safeguards must be instituted to keep them in their places; he wished correspondingly to increase the area of centralised control and decrease that of the individual. But both sides agreed that some portion of human existence must remain independent of the sphere of social control. To invade that preserve, however small, would be despotism. The most eloquent of all defenders of freedom and privacy, Benjamin Constant, who had not forgotten the Jacobin dictatorship, declared that at the very least the liberty of religion, opinion, expression, property must be guaranteed against arbitrary invasion. Jefferson, Burke, Paine, Mill compiled different catalogues of individual liberties, but the argument for keeping authority at bay is always substantially the same. We must preserve a minimum area of personal freedom if we are not to 'degrade or deny our nature'.[7] We cannot remain absolutely free, and must give up some of our liberty to preserve the rest. But total self-surrender is self-defeating. What then must the minimum be? That which a man cannot give up without offending against the essence of his human nature. What is this essence? What are the standards which it entails? This has been, and perhaps always will be, a matter of infinite debate. But whatever the principle in terms of which the area of non-interference is to be drawn, whether it is that of natural law or natural rights, or of utility, or the pronouncements of a categorical imperative, or the sanctity of the social contract, or any other concept with which men have sought to clarify and justify their convictions, liberty in this sense means liberty *from*; absence of interference beyond the shifting, but always recognisable, frontier. 'The only freedom which deserves the name, is that of pursuing our own good in our own way', said the most celebrated of its champions.[8] If this is so, is compulsion ever justified? Mill had no doubt that it was. Since justice demands that all individuals be entitled to a minimum of freedom, all other individuals were of necessity to be restrained, if need be by force, from depriving anyone of it. Indeed, the whole function of law was the prevention of just such collisions: the State was reduced to what Lassalle contemptuously described as the functions of a night-watchman or traffic policeman.

What made the protection of individual liberty so sacred to Mill? In his famous essay he declares that, unless the individual is left to live as he wishes in 'the part [of his conduct] which merely concerns himself',[9] civilisation cannot advance; the truth will not, for lack of a free market in ideas, come to light; there will be no scope for spontaneity, originality, genius, for mental energy, for moral courage. Society will be crushed by the weight of 'collective mediocrity'.[10] Whatever is rich and diversified will be crushed by the weight of custom, by men's constant tendency to conformity, which breeds only 'withered' capacities, 'pinched and hidebound', 'cramped and dwarfed' human beings. 'Pagan self-assertion' is as worthy as 'Christian self-denial'.[11] 'All errors which [a man] is likely to commit against advice and warning, are far outweighed by the evil of allowing others to constrain him to what they deem his good.'[12] The defence of liberty consists in the 'negative' goal of warding off interference. To threaten a man with persecution unless he submits to a life in which he exercises no choices of his goals; to block before him every door but one, no matter how noble the prospect upon which it opens, or how benevolent the motives of those who arrange this, is to sin against the truth that he is a man, a being with a life of his own to live. This is liberty as it has been conceived by liberals in the modern world from the days of Erasmus (some would say of Occam) to our own. Every plea for civil liberties and individual rights, every protest against exploitation and humiliation, against the encroachment of public authority, or the mass hypnosis of custom or organised propaganda, springs from this individualistic, and much disputed, conception of man.

Three facts about this position may be noted. In the first place Mill confuses two distinct notions. One is that all coercion is, in so far as it frustrates human desires, bad as such, although it may have to be applied to prevent other, greater evils; while non-interference, which is the opposite of coercion, is good as such, although it is not the only good. This is the 'negative' conception of liberty in its classical form. The other is that men should seek to discover the truth, or to develop a certain type of character of which Mill approved – critical, original, imaginative, independent, non-conforming to the point of eccentricity, and so on – and that truth can be found, and such character can be bred, only in conditions of freedom. Both these are liberal views, but they are not identical, and the connection between them is, at best, empirical. No one would argue that truth or freedom of self-expression could flourish where dogma crushes all thought. But the evidence of history tends to show (as, indeed, was argued by James Stephen in his formidable attack on Mill in his *Liberty, Equality, Fraternity*) that integrity, love of truth and fiery individualism grow at least as often in severely disciplined communities, among, for example, the puritan Calvinists of Scotland or New England, or under military discipline, as in more tolerant or indifferent societies; and if this is so, Mill's argument for liberty as necessary condition for the growth of human genius falls to the ground. If his two goals proved incompatible, Mill would be faced with a cruel dilemma, quite apart from the further difficulties created by the inconsistency of his doctrines with strict utilitarianism, even in his own humane version of it.[13]

In the second place, the doctrine is comparatively modern. There seems to be scarcely any discussion of individual liberty as a conscious political ideal (as opposed to its actual existence) in the ancient world. Condorcet had already remarked that the notion of individual rights was absent from the legal conceptions of the Romans and Greeks; this seems to hold equally of the Jewish, Chinese and all other ancient civilisations that have since come to light.[14] The domination of this ideal has been the exception rather than the rule, even in the recent history of the West. Nor has liberty in this sense often formed a rallying cry for the great masses of mankind. The desire not to be impinged upon, to be left to oneself, has been a mark of high civilisation on the part of both individuals and communities. The sense of privacy itself, of the area of personal relationships as something sacred in its own right, derives from a conception of freedom which, for all its religious roots, is scarcely older, in its developed state, than the Renaissance or the Reformation.[15] Yet its decline would mark the death of a civilisation, of an entire moral outlook.

The third characteristic of this notion of liberty is of greater importance. It is that liberty in this sense is not incompatible with some kinds of autocracy, or at any rate with the absence of self-government. Liberty in this sense is principally concerned with the area of control, not with its source. Just as a democracy may, in fact, deprive the individual citizen of a great many liberties which he might have in some other form of society, so it is perfectly conceivable that a liberal-minded despot would allow his subjects a large measure of personal freedom. The despot who leaves his subjects a wide area of liberty may be unjust, or encourage the wildest inequalities, care little for order, or virtue, or knowledge; but provided he does not curb their liberty, or at least curbs it less than many other regimes, he meets with Mill's specification.[16]

Freedom in this sense is not, at any rate logically, connected with democracy or self-government. Self-government may, on the whole, provide a better guarantee of the preservation of civil liberties than other regimes, and has been defended as such by libertarians. But there is no necessary connection between individual liberty and democratic rule. The answer to the question 'Who governs me?' is logically distinct from the question 'How far does government interfere with me?' It is in this difference that the great contrast between the two concepts of negative and positive liberty, in the end, consists.[17] For the 'positive' sense of liberty comes to light if we try to answer the question, not 'What am I free to do or be?', but 'By whom am I ruled?' or 'Who is to say what I am, and what I am not, to be or do?' The connection between democracy and individual liberty is a good deal more tenuous than it seemed to many advocates of both. The desire to be governed by myself, or at any rate to participate in the process by which my life is to be controlled, may be as deep a wish as that for a free area for action, and perhaps historically older. But it is not a desire for the same thing. So different is it, indeed, as to have led in the end to the great clash of ideologies that dominates our world. For it is this, the 'positive' conception of liberty, not freedom from, but freedom to – to lead one prescribed form of life – which the adherents of the 'negative' notion represent as being, at times, no better than a specious disguise for brutal tyranny.

II

THE NOTION OF POSITIVE FREEDOM

The 'positive' sense of the word 'liberty' derives from the wish on the part of the individual to be his own master. I wish my life and decisions to depend on myself, not on external forces of whatever kind. I wish to be the instrument of my own, not of other men's, acts of will. I wish to be a subject, not an object; to be moved by reasons, by conscious purposes, which are my own, not by causes which affect me, as it were, from outside. I wish to be somebody, not nobody; a doer – deciding, not being decided for, self-directed and not acted upon by external nature or by other men as if I were a thing, or an animal, or a slave incapable of playing a human role, that is, of conceiving goals and policies of my own and realising them. This is at least part of what I mean when I say that I am rational, and that it is my reason that distinguishes me as a human being from the rest of the world. I wish, above all, to be conscious of myself as a thinking, willing, active being, bearing responsibility for my choices and able to explain them by reference to my own ideas and purposes. I feel free to the degree that I believe this to be true, and enslaved to the degree that I am made to realise that it is not.

The freedom which consists in being one's own master, and the freedom which consists in not being prevented from choosing as I do by other men, may, on the face of it, seem concepts at no great logical distance from each other – no more than negative and positive ways of saying much the same thing. Yet the 'positive' and 'negative' notions of freedom historically developed in divergent directions, not always by logically reputable steps, until, in the end, they came into direct conflict with each other.

One way of making this clear is in terms of the independent momentum which the, initially perhaps quite harmless, metaphor of self-mastery acquired. 'I am my own master'; 'I am slave to no man'; but may I not (as Platonists or Hegelians tend to say) be a slave to nature? Or to my own 'unbridled' passions? Are these not so many species of the identical genus 'slave' – some political or legal, others moral or spiritual? Have not men had the experience of liberating themselves from spiritual slavery, or slavery to nature, and do they not in the course of it become aware, on the one hand, of a self which dominates, and, on the other, of something in them which is brought to heel? This dominant self is then variously identified with reason, with my 'higher nature', with the self which calculates and aims at what will satisfy it in the long run, with my 'real', or 'ideal', or 'autonomous' self, or with my self 'at its best'; which is then contrasted with irrational impulse, uncontrolled desires, my 'lower' nature, the pursuit of immediate pleasures, my 'empirical' or 'heteronomous' self, swept by every gust of desire and passion, needing to be rigidly disciplined if it is ever to rise to the full height of its 'real' nature. Presently the two selves may be represented as divided by an even larger gap; the real self may be conceived as something wider than the individual (as the term is normally understood), as a social 'whole' of which the individual is an element or aspect: a tribe, a race, a Church, a State, the great society of the living and the dead and the yet unborn. This entity is then identified as being the 'true' self which, by imposing its collective, or 'organic', single will upon its recalcitrant 'members', achieves its own, and therefore their, 'higher' freedom. The perils of using organic metaphors to justify the coercion of some men by others in order to raise them to a 'higher' level of freedom have often been pointed out. But what gives such plausibility as it has to this kind of language is that we recognise that it is possible, and at times justifiable, to coerce men in the name of some goal (let us say, justice or public health) which they would, if they were more enlightened, themselves pursue, but do not, because they are blind or ignorant or corrupt. This renders it easy for me to conceive of myself as coercing others for their own sake, in their, not my, interest. I am then claiming that I know what they truly need better than they know it themselves. What, at most, this entails is that they would not resist me if they were rational and as wise as I and understood their interests as I do. But I may go on to claim a good deal more than this. I may declare that they are actually aiming at what in their benighted state they consciously resist, because there exists within them an occult entity – their latent rational will, or their 'true' purpose – and that this entity, although it is belied by all that they overtly feel and do and say, is their 'real' self, of which the poor empirical self in space and time may know nothing or little; and that this inner spirit is the only self that deserves to have its wishes taken into account.[18] Once I take this view, I am in a position to ignore the actual wishes of men or societies, to bully, oppress, torture them in the name, and on behalf, of their 'real' selves, in the secure knowledge that whatever is the true goal of man (happiness, performance of duty, wisdom, a just society, self-fulfilment) must be identical with his freedom – the free choice of his 'true', albeit often submerged and inarticulate, self.

This paradox has been often exposed. It is one thing to say that I know what is good for X, while he himself does not; and even to ignore his wishes for its – and his – sake; and a very different one to say that he has *eo ipso* chosen it, not indeed consciously, not as he seems in everyday life, but in his role as a rational self which his empirical self may now know – the 'real' self which discerns the good, and cannot help choosing it once it is revealed. This monstrous impersonation, which consists in equating what X would choose if he were something he is not, or at least not yet, with what X actually seeks and chooses, is at the heart of all political theories of self-realisation. It is one thing to say that I may be coerced for my own good, which I am too blind to see: this may, on occasion, be for my benefit; indeed it may enlarge the scope of my liberty. It is another to say that if it is my good, then I am not being coerced, for I have willed it, whether I know this or not, and am free (or 'truly' free) even while my poor earthly body and foolish mind bitterly reject it, and struggle with the greatest desperation against those who seek, however benevolently, to impose it.

This magical transformation, or sleight of hand (for which William James so justly mocked the Hegelians), can no doubt be perpetrated just as easily with the 'negative' concept of freedom, where the self that should not be interfered with is no longer the individual with his actual wishes and needs as they are normally conceived, but the 'real' man within, identified with the pursuit of some ideal purpose not dreamed of by his empirical self. And, as in the case of the 'positively' free self, this entity may be inflated into some super-personal entity – a State, a class, a nation, or the march of history itself, regarded as a more 'real' subject of attributes than the empirical self. But the 'positive' conception of freedom as self-mastery, with its suggestion of a man divided against himself, has in fact, and as a matter of history, of doctrine and of practice, lent itself more easily to this splitting of personality into two: the transcendent, dominant controller, and the empirical bundle of desires and passions to be disciplined and brought to heel. It is this historical fact that has been influential. This demonstrates (if demonstration of so obvious a truth is needed) that conceptions of freedom directly derive from views of what constitutes a self, a person, a man. Enough manipulation of the definition of man, and freedom can be made to mean whatever the manipulator wishes. Recent history has made it only too clear that the issue is not merely academic.

NOTES

1 I do not, of course, mean to imply the truth of the converse.
2 Helvétius made this point very clearly: 'The free man is the man who is not in irons, not imprisoned in a gaol, nor terrorised like a slave by the fear of punishment.' It is not lack of freedom not to fly like an eagle or swim like a whale. (*De l'esprit*, First Discourse, Chapter 4.)
3 The Marxist conception of social laws is, of course, the best-known version of this theory, but it forms a large element in some Christian and utilitarian, and all socialist, doctrines.
4 *Émile*, Book 2, p. 320 in *Oeuvres complètes*, ed. Bernard Gagnebin and others (Paris, 1959), vol. 4.
5 'A free man', said Hobbes, 'is he that ... is not hindered to do what he has a will to.' *Leviathan*, Chapter 21, p. 146 in Richard Tuck's edition (Cambridge, 1991). Law is always a fetter, even if it protects you from being bound in chains that are heavier than those of the law, say some more repressive law or custom, or arbitrary despotism or chaos. Bentham says much the same.
6 R. H. Tawney, *Equality* (1931), 3rd edn (London, 1938), Chapter 5, Section 2, 'Equality and Liberty', p. 208 (not in previous editions).
7 Constant, *Principes de politique*, Chapter 1, p. 275 in Benjamin Constant, *De la liberté chez les modernes: écrits politiques*, ed. Marcel Gauchet (Paris, 1980).
8 J.S. Mill, *On Liberty*, Chapter 1, p. 226 in *Collected Works of John Stuart Mill*, ed. J.M. Robson (Toronto/London, 1981), vol. 18.
9 Ibid., p. 224.
10 Ibid., Chapter 3, p. 268.
11 Ibid., pp. 265–6.
12 Ibid., Chapter 4, p. 277.
13 This is but another illustration of the natural tendency of all but a very few thinkers to believe that all the things they hold good must be intimately connected, or at least compatible, with one another. The history of thought, like the history of nations, is strewn with examples of

inconsistent, or at least disparate, elements artificially yoked together in a despotic system, or held together by the danger of some common enemy. In due course the danger passes, and conflicts between allies arise, which often disrupt the system, sometimes to the great benefit of mankind.

14   See the valuable discussion of this in Michel Villey, *Leçons d'histoire de la philosophie du droit* (Paris, 1957), which traces the embryo of the notion of subjective rights to Occam.

15   Christian (and Jewish or Muslim) belief in the absolute authority of divine or natural laws, or in the equality of all men in the sight of God, is very different from belief in freedom to live as one prefers.

16   Indeed, it is arguable that in the Prussia of Frederick the Great or in the Austria of Joseph II men of imagination, originality and creative genius, and, indeed, minorities of all kinds, were less persecuted and felt the pressure, both of institutions and custom, less heavy upon them than in many an earlier or later democracy.

17   'Negative liberty' is something the extent of which, in a given case, it is difficult to estimate. It might, prima facie, seem to depend simply on the power to choose between at any rate two alternatives. Nevertheless, not all choices are equally free, or free at all. If in a totalitarian State I betray my friend under threat of torture, perhaps even if I act from fear of losing my job, I can reasonably say that I did not act freely. Nevertheless, I did, of course, make a choice, and could, at any rate in theory, have chosen to be killed or tortured or imprisoned. The mere existence of alternatives is not, therefore, enough to make my action free (although it may be voluntary) in the normal sense of the word. The extent of my freedom seems to depend on (a) how many possibilities are open to me (although the method of counting these can never be more than impressionistic; possibilities of action are not discrete entities like apples, which can be exhaustively enumerated); (b) how easy or difficult each of these possibilities is to actualise; (c) how important in my plan of life, given my character and circumstances, these possibilities are when compared with each other; (d) how far they are closed and opened by deliberate human acts; (e) what value not merely the agent, but the general sentiment of the society in which he lives, puts on the various possibilities. All these magnitudes must be 'integrated', and a conclusion, necessarily never precise, or indisputable, drawn from this process. It may well be that there are many incommensurable kinds and degrees of freedom, and that they cannot be drawn up on any single scale of magnitude. Moreover, in the case of societies, we are faced by such (logically absurd) questions as 'Would arrangement X increase the liberty of Mr A more than it would that of Messrs B, C and D between them, added together?' The same difficulties arise in applying utilitarian criteria. Nevertheless, provided we do not demand precise measurement, we can give valid reasons for saying that the average subject of the King of Sweden is, on the whole, a good deal freer today [1958] than the average citizen of Spain or Albania. Total patterns of life must be compared directly as wholes, although the method by which we make the comparison, and the truth of the conclusions, are difficult or impossible to demonstrate. But the vagueness of the concepts, and the multiplicity of the criteria involved, are attributes of the subject-matter itself, not of our imperfect methods of measurement, or of incapacity for precise thought.

18   'The ideal of true freedom is the maximum of power for all members of human society alike to make the best of themselves', said T.H. Green in 1881. *Lecture on Liberal Legislation and Freedom of Contract*, p. 200 in T.H. Green, *Lectures on the Principles of Political Obligation and Other Writings*, ed. Paul Harris and John Morrow (Cambridge, 1986). Apart from the confusion of freedom with equality, this entails that if a man chose some immediate pleasure – which (in whose view?) would not enable him to make the best of himself (what self?) – what he was exercising was not 'true' freedom: and if deprived of it, he would not lose anything that mattered. Green was a genuine liberal: but many a tyrant could use this formula to justify his worst acts of oppression.

2 | 'Locke: toleration and the rationality of persecution'

Jeremy Waldron

The contemporary philosopher Jeremy Waldron concentrates on one argument from Locke's *A Letter Concerning Toleration* (abridged from Horton and Mendus 1991), namely the argument that it is irrational to attempt to force someone to adopt a religious belief since such beliefs cannot be adopted at will. This is the argument that I have referred to in Chapter 2 as the Irrationality Argument. Waldron is particularly concerned to examine the argument that Locke used rather than to dwell on historical circumstances and religious debates of the seventeenth century when the letter was written and published. His conclusion is that, despite an initial plausibility, Locke's Irrationality Argument fails because, even if it proves impossible to coerce religious belief by direct means, indirect coercion is still possible. This sort of objection was first raised by one of Locke's contemporaries, Jonas Proast, and, Waldron concludes, has never met with a satisfactory response. Locke's argument is, then, 'inadequate and unconvincing'.

I

This is a paper about John Locke's argument for toleration, or, more accurately, it is a paper about the main line of argument which appears in Locke's work *A Letter on Toleration*.[1] It is *not* intended – as so many papers on Locke's political philosophy are these days – as an historical analysis of his position. I am not going to say very much at all about the development (in some ways the quite remarkable development) of Locke's views on the subject, or about the contemporary debate on religious toleration in which Locke, first as an academic then as a political agitator, was involved, or about the historical circumstances of the *Letter*'s composition.[2] Rather, I want to consider the Lockean case as a political argument – that is, as a practical intellectual resource that can be abstracted from the antiquity of its context and deployed in the modern debate about liberal theories of justice and political morality.[3] To put it bluntly, I want to consider whether Locke's case is worth anything as an argument which might dissuade someone here and now from actions of intolerance and persecution.[4]

There is a further somewhat more abstract reason for examining the Lockean argument. In its content and structure the Lockean case is quite different from the more familiar and more commonly cited arguments of John Stuart Mill.[5] Even if, as I shall claim, it turns out to be an inadequate and unconvincing argument, one that in the last resort radically underestimates the complexity of the problem it addresses, still its distinctive structure and content tell us a lot about the possibilities and limits of liberal argumentation in this area. Those insights and the contrast with the more familiar arguments of Mill may well contribute considerably to our understanding of modern liberal theories of toleration and the 'neutral' state.[6]

II

I have said that I am going to concentrate on the main line of argument in the *Letter on Toleration*. But perhaps it is worth saying a word or two about one subordinate line of argument that I will largely overlook in the rest of my discussion.

At the beginning of the *Letter*, Locke takes some pains to emphasize the peculiarly Christian character of toleration. 'The toleration of those that differ from others in matters of religion', he maintains, is not only consistent with and 'agreeable to' the gospel of Jesus Christ (p. 65) but actually required by Christian teaching. Persecution, he points out, with the denial of love and charity which it involves, is repugnant to the Christian faith (pp. 59–65).

Historically, there is no doubting the importance of this aspect of Locke's case. As an *ad hominem* argument addressed to the Christian authorities, it is of course devastating for it exposes an evident and embarrassing inconsistency between the content of their theory and their practice in propagating it. It is significant that much of the immediate reaction to the publication of the *Letter* concerned this part of the Lockean case and that many of the issues taken up in Locke's boring and inordinately repetitive *Second*, *Third*, and (mercifully) uncompleted *Fourth Letter on Toleration* had to do with the argument from Christian premises.[7]

But, however effective and historically important this line of argument might have been, it is uninteresting from a philosophical point of view. We are interested in the question of whether the state *as such* is under a duty of toleration and we want an argument addressed to state officials in their capacity as wielders of the means of coercion, repression and persecution. An argument which addresses them instead in their capacity as members of a Christian congregation is insufficiently general to be philosophically interesting because it leaves us wondering what if anything we would have to say to someone who proposed persecution in the name of a more militant and less squeamish faith. Certainly, it would be an untidy and unsatisfactory state of affairs if we had to construct a fresh line of argument for toleration to match each different orthodoxy that was under consideration.

Locke, I think, recognizes this, and the bulk of the *Letter* is devoted to consid-

erations which proceed on a more general front and which purport to show the
irrationality of intolerance and not just its uncongeniality to a particular religious
point of view. It is this argument – the argument by which Locke attempts to
show that religious persecution is irrational – that I want to examine in my
paper.

III

An argument for toleration is an argument which gives a reason for not interfering with a person's beliefs or practice even when we have reason to hold that
those beliefs or practices are mistaken, heretical or depraved. (Questions of
toleration do not arise in relation to beliefs or practices which are regarded as
good or true.)[8] ...

IV

The crux of [Locke's] argument – the step which dominates it and on which
everything else depends – is the claim that religious belief cannot be secured by
the coercive means characteristic of state action. This is the essence of Locke's
challenge to the rationality of religious persecution: that what the persecutors
purport to be up to is something that, in the nature of the case, they cannot hope
to achieve.

To make this case, he needs to show that this is true *in principle*. It is not
enough to show that coercion is *inefficient* as a means of religious discipline or
that it is less efficient than the citizens' means of argument and persuasion. For
that would leave open the possibility of using coercion as a last resort, and it
would also make the case for toleration vulnerable to a reassessment of the relative values of the various effects of coercive action. Locke needs to show
impossibility here. He must show that there is a gap between political means and
religious ends which cannot in principle be bridged.

On Locke's account, that causal gap between political coercion and religious
belief is framed, as it were, by two important propositions: (1) that coercion
works by operating on a person's will, that is, by pressurizing his decision-making
with the threat of penalties; and (2) that belief and understanding are not subject
to the human will, and that one cannot acquire a belief simply by intending or
deciding to believe. If I do not believe in the truth of the Resurrection, for
example, there is nothing I can do, no act of will that I can perform, to *make*
myself believe it. (There is no way of holding my mouth or concentrating which
is going to get me into the state of having this belief.) Of course, I may change
my mind about the Resurrection, and people often do. But there is a sense in
which even if that happens it is not my doing: it happens rather as a result of the
work of what Locke calls 'light and evidence' on the understanding and not as the
upshot of *my* conscious decision-making.

The effect of these two claims then – that coercion works through the will and
that belief is not subject to the will – if they are true, is to render religious belief
or unbelief effectively immune from coercive manipulation. Laws, Locke says,
are of no force without penalties (p. 69), and the whole point of penalties is to

bring pressure to bear on people's decision-making by altering the pay-offs for various courses of action, so that willing one particular course of action (the act required or prohibited by law) becomes more or less attractive to the agent than it would otherwise be. But this sort of pressurizing is crazy in cases of actions which men are incapable of performing no matter how attractive the pay-off or unattractive the consequences. Sincerely believing a proposition that one takes to be false (like jumping 20 feet into the air) is an action in this category. As Locke puts it: 'What is gained in enjoining by law what a man cannot do, however much he may wish to do it? To believe this or that to be true is not within the scope of our will' (p. 121). The imposition of belief, then, by civil law has been shown to be an absurdity. Intolerance and persecution, at least for religious reasons, have been shown to be irrational.

This is the sort of conclusion that every moral philosopher dreams of when he starts out making an argument. To justify his belief that a certain practice is wrong, he does not want to have to appeal in a Humean fashion to contingent desires and attitudes: he can never be certain that his audience shares them, and even if they do this sort of argument often appears to establish nothing more than the undesirability of the practice. Rather he wants to be able to show (if he can) that the wrong practice is also an irrational practice – that it involves in itself the sort of inconsistency or rational absurdity which every philosopher wants to avoid in his life as well as in his arguments.[9] Everyone in his audience – or at least everyone in his philosophical audience – accepts standards of rationality; they are part of the tools of the trade, even for one who is, in other respects, the most rabid of moral sceptics ...

V

This is the crux of Locke's argument for toleration. Before going on to indicate some of the difficulties in the argument, I want to make two or three general observations.

The first point to notice is that this argument for toleration does not rest on any religious doubt, religious scepticism or epistemic misgivings in relation either to the orthodox position Locke is considering or to the beliefs and practices that are being tolerated. It is sometimes said that toleration is the child of doubt, and that there is a philosophical as well as a historical connection between the rise of secular liberalism and the decline of religious certainty. Similarly, it is often said that there is a philosophical as well as a historical connection between liberal doctrine and doubts about the objectivity of ethics.[10] I have to confess that these conceptual connections escape me; and that the view that moral non-cognitivism generates a principle of ethical *laissez-faire* seems to me simply incoherent.[11] Be that as it may, Locke (like most of the great thinkers in the early liberal tradition) has little truck with arguments of this sort. He is adamant that there is a God, that His existence can be established very readily,[12] that this God requires certain things of us in the way of ethical practice, belief and worship, and 'that man is obliged above all else to observe these things, and he must exercise his utmost care, application and diligence in seeking out and performing them' (pp. 123–5). We should, however, note that although Locke believed that there is 'only one way to heaven', he did suggest at one point that the case for toleration might be even stronger if there were more than one right answer to questions about religious practice: 'if there were several ways, not even a single pretext for compulsion could be found' (p. 91). But this is a mistake. The truth of something like religious pluralism ... would still leave open the question of what to do about those heretics who, faced with a whole array of different routes to salvation, *still* persist in choosing a deviant and mistaken path. Just as faced with a variety of goods, men may still choose evil, so faced with a variety of true religions men may still choose error and blasphemy.

Certainly, Locke was confidently of the opinion that most of the groups and sects he proposed to tolerate (such as Jews who disbelieved the New Testament and heathens who denied most of the Old as well) had got these matters objectively and evidently wrong. He was prepared to 'readily grant that these opinions are false and absurd' (p. 123). His argument, then, did not depend on any misgivings about contemporary orthodoxy (though in fact he did not support contemporary Anglicanism in all the details of its faith and liturgy); nor was it based on any suspicion, however slight, that at the last trump the sects that he proposed to tolerate might turn out to have been right all along. His position was rather that a false belief, even if it is objectively and demonstrably false, cannot be changed by a mere act of will on the part of its believer, and that it is therefore irrational to threaten penalties against the believer no matter how convinced we are of the falsity of his beliefs. Locke's view, then, is not like the main theme in J.S. Mill's essay *On Liberty* that persecution is irrational because it tends to suppress doctrines which may turn out to have been worth preserving (for one reason or another).[13] It is more like Mill's subordinate argument that the state of mind produced by coercive indoctrination is so far from genuine belief as to call in question the rationality of one who is trying to inculcate it.[14]

There is one line of argument present in the *Letter* which may make us think that Locke was taking a sceptical position on religious matters. Locke was very concerned by the fact that if a magistrate or a ruler were to require certain religious beliefs or practices of us, there would be no guarantee that the religion he favoured would be correct.

> Princes are born superior in power, but in nature equal to other mortals. Neither the right nor the art of ruling carries with it the certain knowledge of other things, and least of all true religion. For if it were so, how does it come about that the lords of the earth differ so vastly in religious matters?
>
> (p. 95)

But at most this is scepticism about the religious discernment of princes, not scepticism about religious matters as such. Locke maintains that 'a private man's study' is every bit as capable of revealing religious truth to him as the edicts of a magistrate (p. 93). He insists that each man is *individually* responsible for finding 'the narrow way and the strait gate that leads to heaven' (p. 71) and that God will excuse no man for a failure to discharge this responsibility on grounds of duress or obedience to orders. If the magistrate makes a mistake and I obey him, then I bear the responsibility and the cost I face may be everlasting perdition: 'What security can be given for the kingdom of heaven?' (p. 95). Locke adds one further point, which, in his view, 'absolutely determines this controversy' (p. 99) by distinguishing religious from other forms of paternalism:

> even if the magistrate's opinion in religion is sound … yet, if I am not thoroughly convinced of it in my own mind, it will not bring me salvation … I may grow rich by an art that I dislike, I may be cured of a disease by remedies I distrust; but I cannot be saved by a religion I distrust, or by worship I dislike. It is useless for an unbeliever to assume the outward appearance of morality; to please God he needs faith and inward sincerity. However likely and generally approved a medicine may be, it is administered in vain if the stomach rejects it as soon as it is taken, and it is wrong to force a remedy on an unwilling patient when his particular constitution will turn it to poison.
>
> (pp. 99–101)

One may be forced to be free, be healthy or to be rich, but 'a man cannot be forced to be saved' (p. 101). Religious truth must be left to individual conscience and individual discernment alone. So there are here certainly individualistic doubts about the abilities of princes; but none of these points is consistent with any more far-reaching doubts about truth or knowledge in matters of religion …

VII

[…] Locke's position is a *negative* one: toleration, as he says in his *Second Letter* on the subject, is nothing but the absence or 'removing' of force in matters of religion.[15] The argument is about the irrationality of coercive persecution and it entails nothing more than that sort of activity ought not to be undertaken. Nothing is entailed about the positive value of religious or moral diversity. Unlike Mill, Locke does not see anything to be gained from the existence of a plurality of views, or anything that might be lost in monolithic unanimity, in these matters. There is nothing in his argument to justify a policy of fostering religious pluralism or of providing people with a meaningful array of choices.

Even more important, we need to see that Locke's negative argument is directed not against coercion *as such*, but only against *coercion undertaken for certain reasons* and with certain ends in mind. The argument concerns the rationality of the would-be persecutor and his purposes; it is concerned about what happens to his rationality when he selects means evidently unfitted to his ends. Coercion, as we know, is in Locke's view unfitted to religious ends, but if it is being used for other ends to which it is not so unfitted (such as Hobbesian ends of public order), then there can be no objection on the basis of this argument, even if *incidentally* some church or religious sect is harmed. The religious liberty for which Locke argues is defined *not* by the actions permitted on the part of the person whose liberty is in question, but by the motivations it prohibits on the part of the person who is in a position to threaten the liberty. It is what Joseph Raz has called elsewhere 'a principle of restraint'.[16] Thus it is not a right to freedom of worship as such, but rather, and at most, a right not to have one's worship interfered with for religious ends.

This point is emphasized quite nicely by an example that Locke uses towards the end of the *Letter on Toleration*. In the course of considering various practices that heathen sects may engage in, Locke takes up the case of animal sacrifice. He begins by saying that if people want to get together and sacrifice a calf, 'I deny that should be forbidden by law' (p. 109). The owner of the calf is perfectly entitled to slaughter the animal at home and burn any bit of it he pleases. The magistrate cannot object when the slaughter takes on a religious character – for the element that makes it a religious *sacrifice* (and therefore an affront to God in the eyes of decent Anglicans) is precisely the internal aspect of belief which political power can never reach. *However*, Locke goes on, suppose the magistrate wants to prohibit the killing and burning of animals for non-religious reasons:

> if the state of affairs were such that the interest of the commonwealth required all slaughter of beasts to be forborne for a while, in order to increase the stock of cattle destroyed by some murrain; who does not see that in such a case the magistrate may forbid all his subjects to kill any calves for any use whatever? But in this case the law is made not about a religious but a political matter, and it is not the sacrifice but the slaughter of a calf that is prohibited.
>
> (p. 111)

But, of course, the *effect* of the economic ban on animal slaughter may be exactly the same as a ban that was religiously inspired. Perhaps in both cases the religious sect in question will wither and die out as its congregation, deprived of their favourite ceremony, drift off to other faiths. But what matters for Locke's purposes is not coercion as such or its effects, but the reasons that motivate it. If the reasons are religious, the coercion is irrational. But if the reasons are economic or political, then the argument for toleration gets no grip whatsoever despite the fact that the coercion may discriminate unequally in its consequences against a particular group. There may, of course, be other arguments against this sort of inequity, but they are not based on a Lockean principle of toleration …

VIII

Let us return now, finally, to the details of the Lockean argument. The nub of the case, you will recall, was his claim that there is an unbridgeable causal gap between coercive means and religious ends – the gap which, as I put it, is framed by these two propositions that 'Coercion works on the will' and 'Belief cannot be affected by the will.' So long as these two frames remain in place, the irrationality of using coercive means for religious ends is evident.

We have already seen one reason for questioning the first of these propositions. Coercion, or more generally force, may be applied to a person not in order to put pressure on his will but simply in order to punish him, retributively, for the wrong he has done, but it is with the second of the two propositions that I am now chiefly concerned …

Though a man with his eyes open cannot help but see, he can decide which objects to look at, which books to read and more generally which arguments to listen to, which people to take notice of and so on. In this sense, if not his beliefs then at least the sources of his beliefs are partly under his control.

All this is familiar and evidently true. But it opens up a first and fatal crack in the framework of Locke's argument for toleration. Suppose there are books and catechisms, gospels and treatises, capable of instructing men in the path of the true religion, if only they will read them. Then although the law cannot compel men coercively to believe this or that because it cannot compel the processes of the understanding, it can at least lead them to water and compel them to turn their attention in the direction of this material. A man may be compelled to learn a catechism on pain of death or to read the gospels every day to avoid discrimination. The effect of such threats and such discrimination may be to increase the number of people who eventually end up believing the orthodox faith. Since coercion may therefore be applied to religious ends by this indirect means, it can no longer be condemned as in all circumstances irrational.

The case is even stronger when we put it the other way round. Suppose the religious authorities know that there are certain books that would be sufficient, if read, to shake the faith of an otherwise orthodox population. Then, although again people's beliefs cannot be controlled directly by coercive means, those who wield political power can put it to work indirectly to reinforce belief by banning everyone on pain of death from reading or obtaining copies of these heretical tomes. Such means may well be efficacious even though they are intolerant and oppressive; and Locke, who is concerned only with the rationality of persecution, provides no argument against them.

Once we catch the drift of this criticism, we begin to see how the rest of Locke's case falls apart. His case depended on the Protestant importance he attached to sincere belief: 'All the life and power of true religion consists in the inward and full persuasion of the mind; and faith is not faith without believing'. So long as our attention is focused on the state of belief itself and *its* immunity from interference, Locke's argument is safe. But now we are starting to look at the epistemic apparatus that surrounds and supports belief – the apparatus of selection, attention, concentration and so on – which, although it does not generate belief directly, nevertheless plays a sufficient role in its genesis to provide a point of leverage. Even if belief is not under the control of one's will, the surrounding apparatus may be; and that will be the obvious point for a rational prosecutor to apply his pressure.

Perhaps the following sort of response may be made on Locke's behalf.[17] What matters for the purposes of true religion is genuine belief. But belief to be genuine must be based on the free and autonomous activity of the mind, choosing and selecting its own materials and its own evidence, uncoerced and undetermined by outside factors. Belief-like states generated in the mind of an individual on the basis of a coerced input of ideas are not genuine in this sense; they are more like the states of mind of an individual who has been brainwashed or subjected incessantly to propaganda. Such an individual may look like a believer from the outside – and he may even feel like a believer from the inside (he is not merely mouthing formulas to evade punishment) – but nevertheless, in virtue of the history of their causation, his beliefs do not count as genuine.[18] Since it is genuine belief that the religious authorities are interested in securing, it will therefore be irrational for them to resort even to the sort of indirect coercion I have been describing.

I have two worries about this line of argument. First, it is difficult to see why the 'free' input of ideas should *matter* so much in determining what counts as genuine belief. We have said already that it is not a phenomenological matter of whether beliefs generated in this way *feel* more genuine than beliefs generated on the basis of coercively determined input. So is the point rather that belief-like states which are not 'genuine' in this sense cannot perform some or all of the *functions* we expect beliefs to perform? Are they functionally deficient in some way? Are they, for example, like brainwashed 'beliefs', peculiarly resistant to logical pressure and to requirements of consistency? That, I suppose, is a possibility. But I find it hard to imagine what sort of epistemology or philosophy of mind could possibly connect the *external* conditions under which sensory input was acquired with the functional efficacy of the beliefs generated on the basis of that input. If I am forced at the point of a bayonet to look at the colour of snow, is my consequent belief that snow is white likely to function differently from the corresponding belief of someone who did not need to be forced to take notice of this fact?

Second, this approach appears to place such great demands on the notion of *genuine belief* as to lead us to doubt the genuineness of everything we normally count as a belief in ordinary life. In *most* cases (not just a few), the selection of sensory input for our understanding is a matter of upbringing, influence, accident or constraint; freedom (in any sense that might plausibly be important) and autonomy seem to play only minor roles. But if this yields the conclusion that most religious belief is not 'genuine' anyway, then we have offered the persecutors an easily defensible position: they can now say that their intention is not to inculcate 'genuine' belief (since that is impossible for most people anyway), but simply to generate in would-be heretics beliefs which are the same in content and status as those of the ordinary members of orthodox congregations. Against this proposal, it would seem, Locke has nothing to say.

We may attack the question of the relation between belief and *practice* in the constitution of religious faith in a similar sort of way. Locke is relying on the view that practice – outward conformity to certain forms of worship – by itself without genuine belief is nothing but empty hypocrisy which is likely to further imperil rather than promote the salvation of the souls of those forced into it. But this is to ignore the possibility that practice may stand in some sort of generative and supportive relation to belief – that it too may be part of the apparatus which surrounds, nurtures and sustains the sort of intellectual conviction of which true religion, in Locke's opinion, is composed. So here we have another point of leverage for the theocrat. A law requiring attendance at Matins every morning may, despite its inefficacy in the immediate coercion of belief, nevertheless be the best and most rational indirect way of avoiding a decline in genuine religious faith.

Some of these points were raised by Jonas Proast in a critique of Locke's *Letter*, to which the latter responded in his *Second* and subsequent *Letters Concerning Toleration*.[19] Proast had conceded Locke's point that beliefs could not be imposed or modified directly by coercive means, but he insisted that force applied 'indirectly and at a distance' might be of some service in concentrating the minds of recalcitrants and getting religious deviants to reflect on the content of the orthodox faith.[20] Force may be unable to inculcate truth directly, but it may remove the main obstacles to the reception of the truth, namely, 'negligence' and 'prejudice'.[21]

Despite the enormous amount of ink that he devoted to his response, Locke failed to provide any adequate answer to this point. He said that it would be difficult to distinguish sincere and reflective dissenters from those whose religious dissent was negligent, slothful or based on removable prejudice; and he insisted that it would certainly be wrong to use force indiscriminately on all dissenters when its proper object could only be a certain subset of them. This is undoubtedly correct. But now the case in principle against the use of force in religious matters has collapsed into a purely pragmatic argument: force *may* be serviceable, only it is likely to be difficult to tell *in which cases* it will be serviceable. In place of the knock-down argument against the use of political means for religious ends, we have now an argument to the effect that political means must not be used indiscriminately and without great care for religious ends. Because the in-principle argument has collapsed, the sharp functional distinction between church and state that Locke was arguing for goes with it. We can no longer say that the magistrate's power is *rationally inappropriate* in the service of true religion. Everything now depends on how sure the magistrate is that the deviants he is dealing with have prejudiced and negligent minds. It is impossible, therefore, to agree with J.D. Mabbott that Locke provides a 'complete and effective' response to Proast's critique.[22] On the contrary, the response he provides completely and effectively demolishes the substance of his position.

IX

I do not see any other way of reconstructing Locke's argument to meet the criticisms that I have outlined. Religious faith, and more generally moral commitment, are complex phenomena. Yet Locke has relied, for his indictment of the rationality of persecution, on a radical and distorted simplification of that complexity. A charge of irrationality based on that sort of simplification is likely to be returned with interest!

It is possible that the gist of Locke's position is correct. Perhaps at a very deep level, there *is* something irrational about intolerance and persecution; perhaps ultimately reason and liberal commitment do converge in this respect. But, on the face of it, it seems unlikely that this convergence is going to take place at the level of *instrumental* rationality. Censors, inquisitors and persecutors have usually known exactly what they were doing, and have had a fair and calculating idea of what they could hope to achieve. If our only charge against their enterprise was hopeless and instrumentally irrational from the start, then we perhaps betray only our ignorance of their methods and objectives, and the irrelevance of our liberalism to their concerns. If by their persistence they indicate that they *do* have a viable enterprise in mind, then there comes a point when the charge of instrumental irrationality must be dropped (on pain of misunderstanding), and a more direct challenge to their actions taken up.

At this point, what one misses above all in Locke's argument is a sense that there is anything *morally* wrong with intolerance, or a sense of any deep concern for the *victims* of persecution or the moral insult that is involved in the attempt to manipulate their faith. What gives Locke's argument its peculiar structure and narrowness is that it is, in the end, an argument about agency rather than an argument about consequences. It appeals to and is concerned with the interests of the persecutors and with the danger that, in undertaking intolerant action, they may exhibit a less than perfect rationality. Addressed as it is to the persecutors in *their* interests, the argument has nothing to do with the interests of the victims of persecution as such; rather those interests are addressed and protected only incidentally as a result of what is, in the last resort, prudential advice offered to those who are disposed to oppress them ...

NOTES

1   First page references in the text are to John Locke, *Epistola de Tolerantia: A Letter on Toleration*, edited by R. Klibansky and translated by J.W. Gough (Oxford, 1968).

2   For the development of Locke's views on toleration, see M. Cranston, *John Locke: A Biography* (London, 1957), pp. 44ff., 59–67, 111–13, 125–33, 314–21, 331ff. See also J.D. Mabbott, *John Locke* (London, 1973), pp. 171–5; and J.W. Gough, 'Introduction' to the Klibansky and Gough edition of the *Letter*, op. cit., pp. 1ff. For detailed accounts of the historical circumstances of the *Letter*'s composition, see R. Klibansky, 'Preface' to the Klibansky and Gough edition, op. cit.; and M. Montuori, 'Introduction' to *John Locke: A Letter Concerning Toleration*, edited by M. Montuori (The Hague, 1963).

3   It is of course controversial whether Locke's political arguments can be abstracted and deployed in this way. For the suggestion that there may be dangers here, see Q. Skinner, 'Meaning and understanding in the history of ideas', *History and Theory*, 8 (1969); and J. Dunn, *The Political Thought of John Locke: An Historical Account of the 'Two Treatises of Government'* (Cambridge,1969), Chapters 1 and 19. For a less pessimistic view, see D. Boucher, 'New histories of political thought for old', *Political Studies*, 31 (1983).

4   I use 'persecute' in its dictionary sense of 'to harass, afflict, hunt down, put to death, esp. for religious ... opinions' (Chambers Twentieth Century Dictionary, edited by A.M. MacDonald (London, 1977), p. 994) as a general term to cover all acts at variance with toleration. Jonathan Harrison pointed out to me that the word also has emotive and evaluative connotations. Clearly it would be wrong to rely on these for the purposes of argument: I do not intend to and I hope I have not done so.

5   J.S. Mill, *On Liberty* (1859), edited by C.V. Shields (Indianapolis and New York, 1956).

6   For modern theories of this kind, see especially J. Rawls, *A Theory of Justice* (Oxford, 1971), pp. 201–34, 325–32; R.M. Dworkin, 'Liberalism', in S. Hampshire (ed.), *Public and Private Morality* (Cambridge, 1978); and B. Ackerman, *Social Justice in the Liberal State* (New Haven and London, 1980).

7   For the reception of the *Letter*, see Cranston, op. cit., pp. 331ff. For the *Second*, *Third*, and *Fourth Letter Concerning Toleration*, see *The Works of John Locke*, 11th edn (London, 1812), vol. VI, pp. 59–274.

8   For a contrary view see Joseph Raz, 'Autonomy, toleration and the harm principle', in S. Mendus (ed.), *Justifying Toleration* (Cambridge, 1985), pp. 137–55.

9   For some interesting questions about this assumption, see Robert Nozick, *Philosophical Explanations* (Cambridge, Mass., 1981), pp. 405–9.

10 See, for example, R.M. Unger, *Knowledge and Politics* (New York and London 1976), p. 76: 'From the start, liberal political thought has been in revolt against the concept of objective value.' (Historically, of course, such a claim is utterly groundless.)

11 See the excellent argument by G. Harrison, 'Relativism and tolerance', in P. Laslett and J. Fishkin (eds), *Philosophy, Politics and Society*, 5th series (Oxford, 1979), p. 273.

12 See John Locke, *An Essay Concerning Human Understanding* (1690), edited by J. Yolton (London,1961), Book IV, chapters 3 (section 21) and 10.

13 Mill, op. cit., chapter 2.

14 Ibid., pp. 43, 49–50.

15 Locke defines it explicitly in these terms in the *Second Letter*, in *Works*, op. cit., vol. VI, p. 62.

16 J. Raz, 'Liberalism, autonomy and the politics of neutral concern', in P. French, T. Uehling and H. Wettstein (eds), *Midwest Studies in Philosophy VII: Social and Political Philosophy* (Minneapolis, 1982), pp. 90–1; see also C. L. Ten, *Mill on Liberty* (Oxford, 1980), p. 40.

17 I am grateful to Joseph Raz for suggesting this line of argument to me. He is not responsible for any inadequacies in its formulation here.

18 For an interesting discussion, see D. Dennett, 'Mechanism and responsibility', in Ted Honderich (ed.), *Essays on Freedom of Action* (London, 1973).

19 J. Proast, *The Argument of the Letter Concerning Toleration Briefly Considered and Answered* (Oxford, 1690). See 'Introduction' to the Klibansky and Gough edition of the *Letter*, op. cit., pp. 32ff; also Mabbott, op. cit., pp. 180–2.

20 Proast is quoted in these terms by Locke in the *Second Letter*, in *Works*, op. cit., vol. VI, p. 69.

21 Ibid., p. 74.

22 Mabbott, op. cit., p. 182.

3 'The place of liberty'

Jonathan Wolff

In this extract from his recent introductory book on political philosophy (1996, pp. 115–42), Jonathan Wolff examines and criticizes the main arguments for freedom used by John Stuart Mill in his *On Liberty*. The content of this reading overlaps significantly with the material covered in Chapters 3–5 of *Arguments for Freedom*. It is included here to provide an overview of the area and to provide a slightly different approach to the same subject matter. You may find it useful to re-read this essay as part of your revision of Mill's arguments.

MILL ON LIBERTY

The only purpose for which power can be rightfully exercised over any member of a civilized community, against his will, is to prevent harm to others. His own good, either physical or moral, is not a sufficient warrant.

(Mill 1962 edn, p. 135)

ONE SIMPLE PRINCIPLE

Once democracy is in place, what work is there left for the political philosopher? An optimistic view is that, as soon as we have a democratic decision-making procedure, the fundamental work of political philosophy is over. All decisions can now be left to the fair process of the electoral machine. Sadly ... even if democracy is the best system we can think of, it is not a cure-all. And Mill suggests it has its own dangers: the threat of the tyranny of the majority. It is naïve to think that the existence of democracy rules out injustice. The fact that 'the people' make the laws does not rule out the possibility that the majority will pass laws which oppress, or are otherwise unfair to, the minority. Somehow the minority must be protected.

Mill's way out of this problem may seem surprising. After arguing for the virtues of representative democracy, the next thing he proposes is that we should severely limit its powers. His work *On Liberty* (in fact, published earlier than *On Representative Government*) is concerned with the question of 'the nature and limits of the power which can be legitimately exercised by society over the individual' (*On Liberty*, p. 126). Mill argues that we should reserve considerable powers for the individual. There are limits to state intervention, and also limits to the proper use of public opinion as a way of moulding beliefs and behaviour.

How much power should the state have? ... [A] range of views is possible. At one extreme, the anarchist claims that the state has no justified power at all. This seems equivalent to the view that there is no acceptable limit to the liberty of the individual, or, at least, not a limit that the state may impose. At the other extreme, defenders of absolute government, such as Hobbes, argue that the state has no obligation to pay any regard at all to the liberties of its subjects. It may enforce whatever rules and restrictions it wishes.

Between these two poles, a spectrum of possibilities exists. Finding neither anarchy nor absolutism acceptable, Mill took it to be his task to define his position on this spectrum. Why, as a champion of liberty, did Mill reject anarchy, which many feel is the highest realization of individual liberty? ... Mill takes the view that if people are given complete freedom then some will surely abuse it, using the absence of government to exploit others. Hence he writes: 'All that makes existence valuable to any one depends on the enforcement of restraints upon the actions of other people' (*On Liberty*, p. 130). Anarchy means living without the law, and, according to Mill, our lives would then hardly be worth living. Mill takes it for granted that tyranny is no longer to be considered a serious option, and so sets out to determine the correct mix of freedom and authority.

On what grounds may the state interfere to prohibit people from acting as they wish, or force them to act against their wishes? Different societies, Mill observes, have 'solved' this problem in different ways. Some, for example, have prevented the practice of certain religions or even suppressed religion completely. Others have imposed censorship on the press and other media. Many have outlawed certain sexual practices. Homosexual acts between men were illegal until as recently as the 1960s in Great Britain, and while prostitution is not illegal in Britain, it remains against the law for a prostitute to solicit for customers. All these are limitations of people's liberty, carried out through the exercise of state power. But does the state have the right to interfere in people's lives and liberties in any of these ways?

Mill seeks a principle, or set of principles, that will allow us to decide each case on its real merits, rather than abandoning the matter to arbitrary custom and popular morality – Mill's greatest enemy. His answer is both radical and refreshingly simple. Mill's Liberty Principle (cited at the start of this [Reading]) announces that you may justifiably limit a person's freedom of action only if they threaten harm to another. To many modern readers this principle (also known as the 'Harm Principle') may seem blindingly obvious. But it has not been obvious through most of history. For centuries people have been persecuted for worshipping the wrong god, or for not worshipping at all. But what harm did they do to anyone, or anything, except perhaps to their own immortal souls? Mill's view should not even be obvious to us now. Suppose a friend is falling into drug addiction. May you forcibly interfere to stop her only if she is likely to cause harm to others? This example opens up serious issues regarding both the interpretation and plausibility of Mill's principle. Probably no society, past or present, has ever lived by the principle as Mill intended it to be understood. Indeed, as we shall also see, Mill himself shied away from some of its most unconventional consequences.

Before going any further, however, it is worth returning to one element in the statement of Mill's Liberty Principle. He says that it is to apply to 'any member of a civilized community'. So does he intend to accept restrictions on the liberty of the uncivilized? As a matter of fact, he does. He explicitly states that the principle is meant to apply only to people in 'the maturity of their faculties' (*On Liberty*, p. 135). Children and 'barbarians' are excluded, for 'Liberty, as a principle, has no application to any state of things anterior to the time when mankind have become capable of being improved through free and equal discussion' (*On Liberty*, p.136).

Mill's point here is that liberty is only valuable under certain conditions. If those conditions do not apply, then liberty can do a great deal of harm. Children should not be free to decide whether or not to learn to read, and Mill shared the Victorian view that certain peoples were 'backward' and thus should also be treated as children. What is important here is not whether Mill was right or wrong about barbarians, but the condition he laid down for the application of the Liberty Principle. Liberty is valuable as a means to improvement – moral progress. Under some circumstances liberty will, just as likely, have the opposite effect, and so progress will have to be effected by some other means. But Mill is in no doubt that when society is in its maturity – when we have progressed to a civilized level – state interference in individual action should be regulated by the Liberty Principle.

AN ILLUSTRATION: FREEDOM OF THOUGHT

One of Mill's most cherished beliefs was that there should be complete freedom of thought and discussion. He devotes almost a third of *On Liberty* to these vital freedoms, while accepting that there should sometimes be limits to what one is permitted to say in public. The first thing to note, for Mill, is that the fact a view is unpopular is no reason at all to silence it: 'If all mankind minus one were of one opinion, and only one person were of the contrary opinion, mankind would be no more justified in silencing that one person, than he, if he had the power, would be justified in silencing mankind' (*On Liberty*, p. 142). In fact, Mill argues, we have very good reason to welcome the advocacy even of unpopular views. To suppress them would be to 'rob the human race, posterity as well as the existing generation'. How so? Well, Mill argues that, whether the controversial view is true, false, or a mix of the two, we will never gain by refusing it a voice. If we suppress a true view (or one that is partially true) then we lose the chance to exchange error, whole or partial, for truth. But if we suppress a false view we lose in a different way: to challenge, reconsider, and perhaps reaffirm, our true views. So there is nothing to gain by suppression, whatever the truth of the view in question.

Is there really harm in suppressing a false view? We must first ask how we can be so sure that it is false. Even if the would-be censor claims to be certain of the truth of the customary opinion, there is quite a gulf, as Mill points out, between *our being certain of* a view, and *the view being certain*. Not to recognize this is to assume infallibility, but history provides enough evidence of how mistaken this assumption is. Many beliefs that were once held as certainties have been considered by later generations not only to be false, but to be absurd. Think, for example, of those people who now claim to hold the once widespread belief that the earth is flat.

More dramatically Mill reminds us of the cases of Socrates and Jesus, the first executed for impiety and immorality, the second for blasphemy. Both were tried by honest judges, acting in good faith. But both perished in societies where the assumption of infallibility led to laws prohibiting the advocacy of views contrary to established traditions. Of course, in western democracies we are unlikely to execute people for their views now. The point, however, is that the moral systems of both Socratic philosophy and Christianity were suppressed because they conflicted with established views 'known for certain' to be true. This illustrates the thought that the human race is capable of monumental error. Never, thinks Mill, have we the right to claim infallibility.

One further example may illustrate and extend Mill's point. The ancient Alexandrian library, one of the treasures of the ancient world, was reputed, at its height, to contain over 700,000 volumes. But in the year AD 640 Alexandria was captured by the Arabs, under the leadership of 'Amr, and this, according to the tale of the much later writer Abulfaragius (apparently a highly unreliable source) is what happened to the library:

> John the Grammarian, a famous Peripatetic philosopher, being in Alexandria at the time of its capture, and in high valour with 'Amr begged that he would give him the royal library. 'Amr told him that it was not in his power to grant such a request, but promised to write to the caliph for his consent. Mar, on hearing the request of his general, is said to have replied that if these books contained the same doctrine as the Koran, they could be of no use, since the Koran contained all necessary truths; but if they contained anything contrary to that book, they ought to be destroyed; and therefore, whatever their contents were, he ordered them to be burnt. Pursuant to this order, they were distributed among the public baths, of which there was a large number of the city, where, for six months, they served to supply the fires.
>
> (Quoted in *Encyclopaedia Britannica*, 11th edn, 1910–11, i–ii, p. 570)

It is a pity that the Arabs did not have *On Liberty* available to them, for they would have done well to take pause, and heed Mill's point that: 'There is the greatest difference between presuming an opinion to be true, because, with every opportunity for contesting it, it has not been refuted, and assuming its truth for the purpose of not permitting its refutation' (*On Liberty*, p. 145).

But before we feel too smug, we should note Rousseau's comments on the story of the library:

> [Omar's] reasoning has been cited by our men of letters as the height of absurdity; but if Gregory the Great had been in the place of Omar and the Gospel in the place of the [Koran], the library would still have been burnt, and it would have been perhaps the finest action of his life.
>
> (*Discourse on the Arts and Sciences*, p. 26n.)

The *Discourse on the Arts and Sciences* was written by Rousseau in 1750, for a competition set by the Academy of Dijon on the question 'Whether the restoration of the Sciences and the Arts has had a purifying effect on morals'. Why would book-burning have been the finest act of Gregory the Great's life? Rousseau reports that the truth on such matters came to him on the road between Paris and Vincennes, on the way to visit Diderot, who had been imprisoned for sedition. He realized, so he says, that developments in the arts and sciences, so far from aiding human progress, had caused more unhappiness than happiness, and, furthermore, had corrupted public morals. Unable to complete his journey, he sat down and scribbled out a draft of this highly controversial thesis, with which he won the prize. It is hard to imagine a view further from Mill's. Rousseau suggests that we offer up a prayer: 'Almighty God! Thou who holdest in Thy hand the minds of men, deliver us from the fatal arts and sciences – give us back ignorance, innocence, and poverty, which alone can make us happy and are precious in Thy sight' (*Discourse on the Arts and Sciences*, p. 27). Beneath Rousseau's rhetoric is a very serious objection to Mill's project. Can it be right to assume that it is always better to know the truth than to remain in ignorance? Mill's argument appears implicitly to assume that knowledge will lead to happiness, but why should we believe that? Just as an individual may sometimes lead a happier life in blissful ignorance of what his or her acquaintances really think of them, presumably there are times when society profits too by ignorance or false belief. Perhaps the truth is too hard to bear, or will dissolve the bonds of society. This is often said about belief in God and the afterlife. That is, so the argument goes, the reason why people should believe is not because there is a God and an afterlife – there may or may not be – but because unless these beliefs are widely held society will fall into selfishness and immorality. Therefore, we should not allow the propagation of atheism, for, if it catches on, society will disintegrate. Whether or not we accept that argument, it does not take much imagination to come to the conclusion that human beings would have been better off if we had never discovered certain scientific truths: those, for example, which led to the development of nuclear weapons.

Should we then sometimes oppose freedom of thought? The argument that we should rests not on the truth of the received opinion, but on its utility, its importance to society. On this view, we can have good reason to suppress an opinion even if it is true. This argument against freedom of thought seems very strong, but so is Mill's reply. Everything depends on the theory that a certain view is necessary for social peace, and that its contrary will be destructive of that peace. But what makes us so sure that, say, disbelief in God will lead society into dissolution? Or that knowing about the structure of the atom will lead to more harm than good? We are just as fallible on that issue as we are on any. As Mill puts the point:

> The usefulness of an opinion is itself matter of opinion: as disputable, as open to discussion, and requiring discussion as much as the opinion itself. There is the same need of an infallible judge of opinions to decide an opinion to be noxious as to decide it to be false.
>
> (Mill 1962 edn, p. 148)

Indeed, Mill reminds us, Christianity itself was suppressed by the Romans, on the grounds of the harm it would do to the preservation of society.

Still, the position is not quite as clear as Mill makes out. If we cannot know for certain whether believing the truth is more likely to lead to happiness or to harm, then we have no more reason, on this argument, to permit freedom of thought than to ban it. Thus Mill must be making the assumption that, in general at least, believing the truth is a way of achieving happiness.

If that is so, what harm can be done by suppressing a false view? In fact, there are very strong reasons against doing so, Mill argues, even if we could know it to be false. If we do not consider challenges to our opinion, then 'however true it may be, if it is not fully, frequently, and fearlessly discussed, it will be held as a dead dogma, not a living truth' (*On Liberty*, p. 161). As Mill says, we 'go to sleep at [the] post as soon as there is no enemy in the field' (*On Liberty*, p. 170). One danger here is that the real meaning of the view might be lost or enfeebled if it is not constantly challenged and defended, and so becomes 'deprived of its vital effect on the character and conduct, the dogma becoming a mere formal profession, inefficacious for good' (*On Liberty*, p. 181). But perhaps the great danger is that when challenged by a sparkling presentation of the opposite, false, view, the champions of the received truth will be unable to defend themselves. Not only will they look foolish, but the false view may gain a popularity it does not merit, sometimes with disastrous consequences.

This, according to some accounts, is what has happened to evolutionary theory in the United States. Believers in Darwinism, while realizing the theory has some apparent flaws, nevertheless did not take seriously the thought that any intelligent, scientifically trained person could fail to accept the broad truth of evolutionary theory in some form or other. Consequently, when well-organized and skilful religious fundamentalists started packaging and deliberately mixing up sophisticated and plausible objections to Darwinism with their own advocacy of 'creation science' – the literal belief in the Old Testament – the Darwinian establishment was not ready to meet the challenge. And so the creationists developed a following way out of proportion to the scientific merits (nil) of their theory. Many Americans – in certain southern states a majority – still believe that evolutionary theory should not be taught in schools.

Two types of case have been considered so far: where the new view is true and where it is false. In each case, allowing the expression of the view will do good, not harm. There is a third case where this is even more obvious: where there is partial truth on both sides of the issue. This is the most common case of all. The only way in which truth might finally emerge is by allowing full and free discussion of all sides of the issue. So, Mill concludes, in all cases mankind will benefit from the expression of views opposed to the current orthodoxy, and so there is never a case for censorship.

HARM TO OTHERS

While there is never a case for censorship, Mill accepts that there are occasions on which it is right to limit freedom of expression. An example he suggests is this:

> An opinion that corn-dealers are starvers of the poor, or that private property is robbery, ought to be unmolested when simply circulated through the press, but may justly incur punishment when delivered orally to an excited mob assembled before the house of a corn-dealer, or when handed about among the same mob in the form of a placard.
>
> (Mill 1962 edn, p. 184)

The fact that freedom of expression, in this case, is almost certain to lead to harm to others is enough, Mill thinks, to bring it within the scope of activities that can properly be regulated by governments.

Now we have seen that, according to Mill, we may interfere with the liberty of an adult only to prevent harm, or threat of harm, to others. In severe cases, we can, with justification, use the force of law, while in other cases social pressure is the more appropriate restraint. But what does Mill mean by 'harm'? Suppose that a group of people want to set up a new religion, and worship in private. Mill's view is that as long as they do not attempt to coerce anyone into membership, then the rest of society has no business interfering. Why not? Because this behaviour does no harm to anyone else. But immediately the zealot of another, established, religion will object: of course they are causing me harm. First, their heathen behaviour causes me great offence and anguish. Second, they are thwarting my plans to convert the whole world to my religion. It is simply not true that they do no harm.

This objection can be put another way. We can divide actions into two classes: purely self-regarding actions and other-regarding actions. Other-regarding actions affect or involve at least one other person. Purely self-regarding actions concern only the agent, or if they do involve others it is with their free consent. Mill's Liberty Principle, then, comes down to the claim that, while we may regulate and supervise other-regarding actions, we have no business interfering in self-regarding actions. So far so good. But now Mill's critic asks for an example of a purely self-regarding action to fall into this protected realm. And, pretty much whatever we offer, the critic will be able to find some third party affected by the action. For example, whether I decide to wear black shoes or brown shoes today looks like a self-regarding action, if any action is. But then the makers of brown shoe-polish would clearly prefer me to wear brown shoes. Furthermore, my friends of highly refined sensibilities might suffer distress and embarrassment on my behalf if it turns out I am wearing the wrong shoes for the occasion. So even a trivial example like this seems to turn out to be other-regarding. If we try very hard we might find some examples of purely self-regarding action. For example, if I live alone it is perhaps hard to see how my decision whether to sleep on my front or my back could affect anyone else (although the pillow-making industry may have an opinion, as may the health service if I am more likely to avoid back pain one way or another). But if we have to resort to such examples then Mill is lost. If we interpret the Liberty Principle as giving the individual freedom, but only over self-regarding actions understood this way, then it is left without a serious range of application.

Thus it is clear that Mill could not have intended to be understood in this manner. He was determined that the sphere of liberty was not to be left to the 'likings and dislikings' of society. So it is obvious that he must distinguish between those actions which society, or its members, dislike, or find annoying or offensive, and those actions which cause *harm*. Mere offence, or dislike, for Mill, is no harm. So what did Mill mean by harm?

Mill often uses the terminology of 'interests' in his statements of the Liberty Principle. So, for example, he says that his view authorizes 'the subjection of individual spontaneity to external control, only in respect to those actions of each, which concern the interest of other people' (*On Liberty*, p. 136). Harm, then, is sometimes read as 'damage to interests'. Understood in this way, the Liberty Principle essentially reads 'act as you like, so long as you do not harm the interests of another person'.

This gives us some help, but unfortunately no one seems to have been able to give an adequate definition of 'interests' in this sense. The term is most commonly used in connection with financial interests. If someone has a financial interest in a scheme, then they stand to gain or lose money depending on the success of that venture. However, Mill was not exclusively concerned with people's financial well-being, and so we must add that individuals have, at least, an interest in their personal safety and security. Therefore murder, assault, rape, theft, and fraud would all count as actions which harm the interests of the person attacked or defrauded. The Liberty Principle then would, quite rightly, allow us to restrict individuals' freedom of action to prevent them carrying out such acts.

But we must be careful here. Mill does not say that society may rightly interfere with someone's freedom of action whenever he or she threatens to harm your interests. We have already seen an example which illustrates this. My decision to wear black shoes may, in some small way, harm the interests of the brown shoe-polish manufacturers, but Mill gives them no right to intervene. In fact Mill himself points out many much more serious examples of this: 'whoever succeeds in an overcrowded profession, or in a competitive examination; whoever is preferred to another in any contest for an object which both desire, reaps benefit from the loss of others, from their wasted exertion and their disappointment' (*On Liberty*, p. 227). Mill intends that none of these forms of competition will be ruled out by the Liberty Principle, despite the fact that they are capable of doing severe harm to the interests of the losers. Clearly, then, we have not yet got to the bottom of the Liberty Principle. In Mill's view, harming another's interests is not enough (not a sufficient condition) to justify constraint. Indeed, we will later see reason to question whether Mill even thinks it is a necessary condition. To make further progress we must broaden our view.

JUSTIFYING THE LIBERTY PRINCIPLE

> [Each person] should be bound to observe a certain line of conduct towards the rest. This conduct consists ... in not injuring the interests of one another, or rather certain interests which, either by express legal provision or by tacit understanding, ought to be considered as rights.
>
> (Mill 1962 edn, p. 205)

LIBERTY, RIGHTS, AND UTILITY

In the passage just quoted Mill appeals to a new idea: interests which ought to be considered as rights, or 'rights-based interests'. Perhaps this can help us understand the Liberty Principle. For example, while there are laws which enforce my right to keep my property against your attempts to take it by force, I have no similar right to be protected against economic competition. Indeed there are many interests which do not normally seem to give rise to claims of right. When my rich aunt strikes me out of her will, my interest may suffer, but she does not infringe my rights.

This may seem a promising approach, but there are two serious matters to consider. First how do we know what rights we have? Suppose I claim a right for my business to be protected against competitors. What can Mill say to show me that I have no such right? Second, it is very odd to see Mill using the concept of rights at such a crucial point in the argument. For early in the essay he writes (or should we say boasts?): 'It is proper to state that I forego any advantage which could be derived to my argument from the idea of abstract right, as a thing independent of utility' (*On Liberty*, p. 136). But how is this consistent with the appeal to the idea of 'rights-based interest'? This statement of intent apparently contradicts the explicit appeal to rights in the passage just noted.

Perhaps it will be thought that the most charitable thing to do would be simply to ignore Mill's statement that he will refrain from appeal to the notion of an 'abstract right'. But this would not really do. Mill has very good reasons for making this statement, as we can see if we look, for a moment, at the idea of a right.

Within liberal circles it is often taken as a fundamental axiom that people have certain basic rights. Normally included are the right to life, free speech, free assembly, and freedom of movement, together with rights to vote and stand for office. Some theorists, although not all, add rights to a decent standard of living (shelter, food, and health-care). Most often these rights would now be collected together under the name of 'human rights' or 'universal human rights'. In the past they would have been called 'the rights of man' or 'natural rights'. Anything – particularly any action by a government – that violates a human or natural right is morally wrong, and should be remedied. It is a familiar and comforting notion that we all have rights, and that these must be respected. Countries which ignore the rights of their citizens are often the subject of intense international criticism.

Nevertheless, the idea of a natural right is highly problematic. In fact, one of the features which makes a theory of natural rights initially so attractive turns out to be one of its main weaknesses. That is, the theory claims that natural rights are basic, fundamental, or axiomatic: they are the ultimate ground of all further decisions. This is attractive because it makes the theory seem so rigorous and principled. But the disadvantage is that we are left with nothing more fundamental to say in defence of these rights. Suppose an opponent doubts that there are any natural rights. How can we reply? Short of saying that the opponent must be insincere or confused, there seems nowhere left to turn. Using the terminology of natural rights may be a successful tactic in disputes between those who agree that there are such things, but otherwise it seems to leave us dangling and exposed.

A further, related, difficulty is that, if natural rights have a fundamental status, and so are not arrived at on the basis of some other argument, how do we know what rights we have? This difficulty was exploited by Bentham, who pointed out that if it is 'self-evident' that people have natural rights, why do different theorists have different ideas about what those rights should be? There are major inconsistencies between the accounts given by different political philosophers. This raises not only the question of how to adjudicate between different accounts, but also leads to the troubling thought that a statement of what natural rights we have often seems little more than one person's opinion.

Bentham's best-known attack on the idea of natural rights starts with the observation that a right seems to be a legal idea. We think of rights and duties as being distributed by laws. The laws give you rights to vote, to receive welfare benefits, to protection by the police, and so on. In Bentham's view this is all there is to a right: 'Right is with me the child of law – A natural right is a son that never had a father' (*Anarchical Fallacies*, p. 73). If this is correct then it makes the idea of a natural right – a right independent of the law of the land – 'nonsense on stilts' (*Anarchical Fallacies*, p. 53). There just cannot be such a thing.

Of course not everyone will accept Bentham's argument. Theorists like Locke simply deny Bentham's major assumption: that rights can only be created by legal decree. But Mill favoured Bentham's view, and was very suspicious of the idea of natural rights. This is what he means by saying that he intends to make no use of the idea of abstract right. But how, then, can he use the notion of rights-based interests? Does he mean 'those interests *already respected* by the law as rights'? A moment's thought is enough to dismiss this idea. After all, Mill saw himself as putting forward a doctrine with radical, reforming consequences, critical of the current state of affairs. To accept the present system of rights would be to put oneself back into the hands of custom and prejudice, and this is precisely what Mill wanted to avoid.

If Mill can neither accept natural rights nor rely on conventional rights, then what is left for him? The answer lies in how he completes the passage where he declares his opposition to abstract rights, partially cited above. After saying that he will make no use of the idea of abstract right, as a 'thing independent of utility', he adds: 'I regard utility as the ultimate appeal on all ethical questions; but it must be utility in the largest sense, grounded on the permanent interests of a man as a progressive being' (*On Liberty*, p. 136).

Mill intends to defend a view of rights which makes them not natural or fundamental, nor a simple echo of whatever happen to be the laws of the land, but derived from the theory of utilitarianism … Mill explains and defends the utilitarian system in his work *Utilitarianism*. As he defines it, utilitarianism is the theory which: 'holds that actions are right in proportion as they tend to promote happiness, wrong as they tend to produce the reverse of happiness. By happiness is intended pleasure and the absence of pain; by unhappiness pain and the privation of pleasure' (*Utilitarianism*, p. 257). Broadly we might summarize the view as saying that utilitarianism requires us to maximize the sum total of happiness or pleasure in the world. (This will not quite do as a summary of Mill's view, as he claims that some pleasures – of the intellect, for example – are qualitatively more valuable than other more bodily pleasures. But we can ignore this complication.)

How can we connect the idea of a right with utility? This connection is made explicit in *Utilitarianism*: 'To have a right, then, is I conceive, to have something which society ought to defend me in the possession of. If the objector goes on to ask, why it ought? I can give him no other reason than general utility' (*Utilitarianism*, p. 309).

In brief, the basic idea is to lay out a system of rights which will maximize the general happiness. That is, we grant people certain rights so that more happiness can be achieved within the structure of those rights than would be possible under any alternative system. Perhaps the best way of thinking about this is to put yourself in the position of a utilitarian legislator. Suppose you are responsible for setting out the legal system, and you want to set it up in such a way that laws maximize happiness. Naïvely, it might be thought that under such circumstances you should make just one law: 'Act to maximize happiness.' But this is not so obvious.

[…] A direct utilitarian believes that an individual should perform an action whenever that action will lead to more happiness than any available alternative. On this view … it is sometimes said that it is acceptable to punish someone who is innocent if that will placate an angry mob and defuse a potentially disastrous situation. The direct utilitarian must weigh up the distress to the innocent victim, the likelihood that the deception will become public, the likely effects of allowing the mob to try to find the guilty party, and any other factors that might affect the balance of pain and pleasure that will flow from the situation. If the sums say that we will maximize happiness by punishing the innocent, then this is what we should do.

The indirect utilitarian follows a more subtle strategy. On this view, it is accepted that the goal of law and morality is that happiness should be maximized, but it is claimed that this goal will not be achieved by allowing individuals to seek to maximize happiness themselves. Consider the last example. Suppose it is true that utility is sometimes advanced by making some people scapegoats. Suppose, too, that everyone knows this. Everyone, then, realizes that there is a possibility that they will be picked on and victimized. Knowing this is likely to cause an atmosphere of anxiety and gloom. The possibility of scapegoating would be detrimental to the general happiness. Therefore the indirect utilitarian might calculate that the general happiness will best be served by ensuring that no one is punished unless they are proved guilty. Although there might be a few, very special, occasions when we might profit from scapegoating, in the long term we do much better in utilitarian terms by giving everyone immunity – a right – against victimization. This, then, is a sketch of how to derive a utilitarian theory of rights. While it is true that, in the short term, we might do better to violate a right, when we take long-term effects into account utilitarianism suggests that rights are to be obeyed.

Indeed indirect utilitarianism can be taken one step further, although Mill did not do this himself. Henry Sidgwick (1838–1900), the most thoughtful and sophisticated of the early utilitarians, suggested that, while utilitarianism is the correct moral theory, it might sometimes be better if this were kept secret. Perhaps most people should be given some very straightforward, simple maxims to follow: do not lie, do not murder, do not cheat, and so on. His reason for this is that, should ordinary people know the truth of utilitarianism, they would be likely to attempt to calculate in direct utilitarian terms. Not only would this be a bad thing for the reasons already given; most people would also make poor calculations through lack of care, or ability, or through the magnification of their own interests … It is much better, thought Sidgwick, to keep utilitarianism as an esoteric doctrine, revealed only to the enlightened élite. (This view has been called 'government house utilitarianism' by its opponents. It treats citizens in the patronizing fashion that European powers treated their colonial subjects in the days of empire.)

As I said, Mill did not go this far, and, it is true, his own indirect utilitarianism is implicit in his view rather than explicitly stated. But once we have appreciated the idea of indirect utilitarianism, we have seen how a utilitarian theory of rights is possible. This, then will inform the utilitarian legislator. The insight of indirect utilitarianism is to note that, instead of setting out a single law – maximize happiness – the utilitarian legislator might do much better, in terms of the general happiness, to set out a larger body of law, which guarantees and respects secure rights of individuals. Indeed, it may well be that Bentham and Mill thought of themselves as primarily addressing law-makers, rather than the public. After all, Bentham's major book on the topic is called *An Introduction to the Principles of Morals and Legislation*.

And now we can begin to see how the pieces fit together. According to Mill, the greatest happiness will be achieved by giving people a private sphere of interest where no intervention is permitted, while allowing a public sphere where intervention is possible; but only on utilitarian grounds.

How does this solve the question of where to draw the line between the private and public spheres? Mill himself is not explicit, but there is a ready answer. First we acknowledge that the private sphere is identified with the sphere of 'rights-based interests'. Then we raise the difficult question of what makes the difference between rights-based interests (my interest in personal safety) and other interests (my interest in not being struck out of my aunt's will)? The answer to this question is given by the theory of utilitarianism. It will serve the general happiness if we pass a law which protects people's interests in walking down the street free from attack, but it will diminish general happiness if we set out restrictions about whether aunts can or cannot strike their nephews out of their wills.

Other examples might help to make this clearer. As we saw in detail, Mill wants to protect freedom of thought. Why? Because this is most likely to achieve the truth, and (Mill implies) knowledge of the truth increases happiness. So we are assumed to have a rights-based interest in freedom of thought. But Mill does not want to protect an individual's business against fair competition. Why not? Because according to Mill the utilitarian advantages of free trade mean that no other system can advance happiness to the same extent. (The feudal system, for example, in which individuals purchased licences to be the monopoly supplier of a particular good, led to enormous inefficiencies.) Therefore people are to be given rights to compete in business, not rights which protect their financial interests against competition. The position is somewhat complex, because, of course, Mill accepts that we have to have certain rights in our property which protects it from theft and fraud. But indirect utilitarianism, in Mill's view, does not extend to protection against economic competition.

This utilitarian defence of the Liberty Principle seems very plausible. The utilitarian theory of rights supplies exactly what is missing: a doctrine of rights which does not rest on the false foundation of natural rights theory, nor on the shifting sands of convention. It appears to allow us to make perfect sense of Mill's proposal. Yet the idea that a utilitarian defence can be given of Mill's Liberty Principle has met with strong criticism. And it is not difficult to find examples where utility and liberty seem to conflict. As one critic has said: 'A drug addict who has successfully kicked the habit is thoroughly justified on utilitarian grounds in stopping some incautious young experimenter from taking the first steps down a road which may prove to have no turning' (R.P. Wolff, *The Poverty of Liberalism*, p. 29). In other words, utilitarianism would seem to encourage exactly the type of paternalistic intervention that the Liberty Principle expressly rules out: remember that the Liberty Principle does not permit anyone to interfere with another even for their own good. So, it is thought, liberal rights cannot be justified in utilitarian terms.

This objection brings out that even if it is possible to construct a utilitarian theory of rights, it does not yet follow that the utilitarian theory would be a liberal theory. Why should we think that, in the long term, there would be more happiness in Mill's society than in the society, governed by customary morality, that he sought to replace? Or in some other society in which enlightened, experienced elders are given the right to direct the lives of its younger members?

To appreciate Mill's response to this problem we need to take yet another look at the wording of the passage in *On Liberty* where Mill declares his allegiance to utility: 'I regard utility as the ultimate appeal on all ethical questions; but it must be utility in the largest sense, grounded on the permanent interests of a man as a progressive being' (*On Liberty*, p. 136). 'Utility in the largest sense' presumably means that we should include all sorts of pleasures and forms of happiness – intellectual and emotional as well as bodily – in the calculation. But why does he add 'grounded on the permanent interests of a man as a progressive being'? There are some further aspects of Mill's view that we will have to understand before everything falls into place.

INDIVIDUALITY AND PROGRESS

The key to solving this problem lies in chapter 3 of *On Liberty*, entitled 'On Individuality, as one of the Elements of Well-being'. It is here that Mill tries to show that the general happiness will be best advanced by assigning people a large private sphere of rights to non-interference. In this chapter Mill argues that freedom is essential to originality and individuality of character. And, Mill claims, 'the free development of individuality is one of the leading essentials of well-being' (*On Liberty*, p. 185). Here Mill wants to make several points, and it may be helpful to set them in the context of a criticism made by one of Mill's earliest and more impressive critics, James Fitzjames Stephen (1829–94), in his book *Liberty, Equality, Fraternity*, first published in 1873.

Stephen argued that it is absurd to think that liberty is always good in itself. Rather, he claims, it is like fire. It would be irrational to ask whether fire is good in itself; it all depends on the purpose to which it is put. And Stephen has chosen his analogy well. Controlled fire has given us many of our most important technological achievements – the internal combustion engine, for example – but uncontrolled fire is a great fear and, often, a great disaster. This, supposes Stephen, is the case for liberty too.

Mill is prepared to accept that liberty does not always lead to 'improvement'. But he stresses, 'the only unfailing and permanent source of improvement is liberty' (*On Liberty*, p. 200). Advancing liberty contributes much more to human happiness than any other possible competing policy might. Mill has several reasons for saying this.

First, he argues that, even though people do make mistakes, individuals are still *more likely* to be right about what would make them happy than anyone else. After all, they pay more attention to the issue, and give it more thought than anyone else is likely to. Nevertheless, Mill recognizes that people could exercise liberty far more than they do at present, for he notes that people commonly abuse this power, and before acting ask: 'what is suitable to my position? what is usually done by persons of my station and pecuniary circumstances? or (worse still) what is usually done by persons of a station and circumstances superior to mine?' (*On Liberty*, p. 190). Independence of judgement, Mill claims, will surely lead to superior consequences. But he does not mean that no one should ever try to influence other people's behaviour. On the contrary, he is keen to emphasize that each of us has a duty to try to convince others of their mistakes, if we feel that they are embarking on foolish or damaging courses of action. We may reason and plead with people. But this is all we may do. Force is out of the question:

> Considerations to aid [another's] judgement, exhortations to strengthen his will, may be offered to him, even obtruded on him, by others: but he himself is the final judge. All errors which he is likely to commit against advice and warning are far outweighed by the evil of allowing others to constrain him to what they deem his good.
>
> (Mill 1962 edn, p. 207)

Such measures must, in Mill's view, nevertheless fall short of concerted social pressure, although how in practice we can draw this distinction he does not make clear. But overall Mill's position is that leaving people to themselves will tend to make them happier than if we insist that they follow society's recommendations.

A second reason for liberty is that it will not only lead to better decisions in the long run, but also that the exercise of freedom of choice is itself vital to the full development of human nature. Those who are slaves to custom, Mill suggests, will never develop into rounded, flourishing individuals; not necessarily because they will be unhappy, but because they will fail to develop one of their most distinctively human capacities, the capacity for choice.

Mill's third – and most important – reason for championing liberty and individuality is this:

> As it is useful that while mankind are imperfect there should be different opinions, so it is that there should be different experiments of living; that free scope should be given to varieties of character, short of injury to others; and that the worth of different models of life should be proved partially ... [This is] quite the chief ingredient of individual and social progress.
>
> (Mill 1962 edn, p. 185)

Thus, Mill claims: 'In proportion to the development of his individuality, each person becomes more valuable to himself, and is therefore capable of being more valuable to others' (*On Liberty*, p. 192). Mill's idea is that human progress is best served by giving individuals the licence to engage in 'experiments of living'. Those who take up this opportunity may well conduct 'successful' experiments, and so arrive at styles of life which others can choose to follow. In other words, role models can show others how to live (or not to live) their own lives, and from these role models the less creative can take up various new possibilities for themselves.

It is at this point that we see Mill at perhaps his most optimistic and we see the point of his appeal to 'utility in the largest sense, grounded on the permanent interests of a man as a progressive being'. Mill's view is that mankind is progressive, in the sense that human beings are capable of learning from experience, to the long-term benefit of all. Through the experiments of some individuals we may learn things of great value, for the permanent benefit of mankind. Those of us too timid to conduct experiments of our own may nevertheless learn from the more adventurous. It is by observing, and trying out, the various possibilities that we are presented with that mankind will be able to learn what sorts of lives will lead to genuine human flourishing. Liberty is vital as a condition of experimentation. This, it seems, is the primary reason why Mill is convinced that liberty will – in the long run – secure the greatest possible happiness for human kind.

Is Mill too optimistic? That was certainly the opinion of James Fitzjames Stephen. His immediate criticism is that Mill was wrong to think that giving people liberty is likely to lead to vigorous experimentation. Freedom from the interference of others is just as likely to lead to idleness, and lack of interest in life. But a deeper point can also be made, one far more threatening to Mill's project.

In the interpretation of Mill I have presented, the great weight of his position comes down on his assumption that human beings are progressive, capable of learning from experience. Does the experience of the twentieth century give the lie to this view? If so, then the heart drops out of Mill's position. Humankind keeps on repeating its mistakes. If people will not learn from others' experience, then we lose Mill's reason for encouraging experiments in living. What is the point of other people demonstrating new lifestyles to us, if we are not prepared to learn? Without some such defence of experiments of living, there is far less justification for individuality and liberty, on the arguments Mill gives. Indeed some have said that human beings, generally, are in the state Mill reserved for 'children and barbarians': incapable of being improved by free and equal discussion. And, as Mill himself argues, such people are not fit recipients of liberty, at least, not according to the utilitarian calculus. Perhaps this pessimism about the possibility of human improvement is a great exaggeration. But if the truth lies somewhere in the middle, if humans are less capable of improvement than Mill imagines, the utilitarian case for liberty is correspondingly weakened. Progress is the cornerstone of Mill's doctrine.

LIBERTY AS AN INTRINSIC GOOD

Could it be that Mill was wrong to attempt to defend the Liberty Principle in utilitarian terms? In effect Mill has presented liberty as *instrumentally* valuable: it is valuable as a way of achieving the greatest possible happiness for society. But perhaps he should have argued that liberty is intrinsically good, good in itself. If we take such a view, as many contemporary liberals claim to, then we avoid the problem that maximizing happiness perhaps requires a non-liberal society. Liberty is valuable, whatever its consequences.

Some will object that there are no intrinsic goods: everything is valued for something else, rather than for itself. But note that even Mill must accept that there is at least one intrinsic good: happiness. Utilitarians claim that happiness is the only intrinsic good. Everything must be justified in terms of its contribution to the total sum of happiness. But then, why shouldn't we say that there are *two* (or more) intrinsic goods, happiness and liberty? In fact, some commentators have been tempted to say that this is Mill's real view, even though he denied it!

Mill would reject this interpretation of his views. He is clear that liberty is good primarily as a means to improvement, and where it fails to have that effect – in the case of children and barbarians – there is no case for liberty. Liberty is intrinsically good only when it adds to our happiness, but then it is 'part of happiness' rather than an independent value. Furthermore, unconstrained liberty would lead to anarchy. Utilitarianism provides an account of what liberties we should have, and which we should not have. For example, Mill argues that we should be free to compete in trade, but not free to use another's property without their consent. Thus his position allows us to set out limits to liberty, while paying it great respect.

This is not a conclusive argument for Mill's approach. It is not true that only utilitarianism can set out restrictions to liberty: perhaps liberty can be restricted for the sake of liberty, or fairness. And there are other ways of defending liberty without relying on utilitarianism … Thus Mill's argument is only one way of trying to defend liberalism. Yet the Liberty Principle gives us a reasonable, if problematic, statement of a liberal political philosophy. Is it one we should accept? Not everyone thinks so.

PROBLEMS WITH LIBERALISM

Euthanasia or the killing of another at his own request, suicide, attempted suicide and suicide pacts, duelling, abortion, incest between brother and sister, are all acts which can be done in private and without offence to others and need not involve the corruption or exploitation of others.

(Devlin 1963/83, p. 7)

POISON, DRUNKENNESS, AND INDECENCY

What would life be like if we tried to regulate society according to the Liberty Principle? As I mentioned early on in this chapter, Mill himself falls short of endorsing some of the most shocking implications of his view. In his final chapter Mill sets out some of the 'obvious limitations' of the Liberty Principle. One limitation concerns certain restrictions on liberty that are justifiable to prevent crime. So, for example, Mill argues that if the only reason why people bought poison was to commit murder, then society would be entirely justified in banning its production and sale. The fact is, however, that most poisons have other functions too, and so Mill recommends that the law should require chemists to keep a register, recording full details of sales, including the name of the purchaser, and their declared purpose. Accordingly if someone is later found poisoned, the police will already have a list of prime suspects. Strictly, a purchaser, with innocent intent, might complain that this arrangement is intrusive, and in violation of personal liberty. But Mill's view is that the violation is trivial in the light of the benefits of the system, and so this is an obvious exception to the generality of the Liberty Principle.

Another exception is that, while drunkenness, ordinarily, is no crime, anyone who has been convicted of violence to others when drunk should, according to Mill, be prohibited from drinking. Here, for Mill, the danger of harm outweighs an individual's right to drink alcohol.

Although certain liberals might worry that these cases – particularly the latter one – are overly restrictive of human liberty, Mill's point is that restrictions are justified to ward off serious harm, even if that harm is a fairly remote possibility. A further example, however, raises much more serious issues of principle:

there are many acts which, being directly injurious only to the agents themselves, ought not to be legally interdicted, but which, if done publicly, are a violation of good manners, and coming thus within the category of offences against others, may rightly be prohibited. Of this kind are offences against decency: on which it is unnecessary to dwell, the rather as they are only connected indirectly with our subject, the objection to publicity being equally strong in the case of many actions not in themselves condemnable, nor supposed to be.

(Mill 1962 edn, pp. 230–1)

Mill's prose, on this delicate subject, does not have its usual clarity, but the intention of the passage is clear. Certain actions – sexual intercourse between husband and wife, for example – would be condemned by no moral code if performed in private, but would be acceptable to very few people (and certainly not to Mill) if performed publicly.

But how can Mill make this view consistent with the Liberty Principle? What harm does 'public indecency' do? After all, Mill insists that mere offence is no harm. Here Mill, without being explicit, seems to allow customary morality to override his adherence to the Liberty Principle. Few, perhaps, would criticize his choice of policy. But it is hard to see how he can render this consistent with his other views: indeed, he appears to make no serious attempt to do so.

Once we begin to consider examples of this kind we begin to understand that following Mill's 'one simple principle' would lead to a society of a kind never seen before, and, perhaps, one which we would never wish to see. Some of the apparent inconsistencies in the liberal position were brought out very well by Lord Justice Devlin, in his essay 'Morals and the Criminal Law', published partly as a response to the Wolfenden Report of 1957, which recommended the decriminalization of homosexual acts between consenting adults. The Wolfenden Report also argued that prostitution should not be made illegal. These recommendations seem fully in accord with the Liberty Principle. Yet, as Devlin observes, many of the laws of contemporary societies are very hard to defend in terms of the Liberty Principle. Some examples are laws against duelling, incest between siblings, and euthanasia.

To make his point, Devlin focuses on the question of prostitution. Why is the liberal prepared to permit it to exist? The standard answer might be that it is simply none of the law's business: prostitution is a matter of concern only for the prostitute and the customer. But then, asks Devlin:

> If prostitution is ... not the law's business, what concern has the law with the ponce or the brothel-keeper ... ? The Report recommends that the laws which make these activities criminal offences should be maintained ... and brings them ... under the head of exploitation ... But in general a ponce exploits a prostitute no more than an impresario exploits an actress.
>
> (Devlin 1963/83, p. 52)

Devlin's own view is that we can understand these matters only by assuming that society holds certain moral principles, which it enforces through the criminal law. If anyone breaks these principles they are thought of as offending society as a whole.

While Mill would certainly deny Devlin's claim that the law ought always to uphold customary morality, there is no doubt that he would have felt uncomfortable if faced with Devlin's examples. This is not to say that liberals like Mill could never find grounds for objecting to euthanasia or brothel-keeping. The real question is that, if the Liberty Principle is intended as seriously as Mill suggests, why should the liberal be concerned if it comes into conflict with customary morality? Mill's pretended adherence to 'one simple principle' does not reflect how complicated his beliefs really are.

4 'Law, morality and the freedom of expression'

Bernard Williams et al.

This is an extract from the report of the Committee on Obscenity and Film Censorship, first published in 1979. The Committee was chaired by the philosopher Bernard Williams and its brief was 'to review the laws concerning obscenity, indecency and violence in publications, displays and entertainments in England and Wales, except in the field of broadcasting, and to review the arrangements for film censorship in England and Wales; and to make recommendations' (p. 1). This extract (from Bernard Williams (ed.) *Obscenity and Film Censorship*, Cambridge University Press, 1981) concentrates on the notion of harm in the context of debates about freedom of expression. Some of John Stuart Mill's arguments from *On Liberty* are shown to be of continuing relevance, in particular his linking of the value of freedom of expression with the open future of human development. This extract also includes a discussion of the disagreements between Lord Devlin and Professor Hart; their arguments are treated at greater length in Chapter 5.

5.1 What sorts of conduct may the law properly seek to suppress? An answer to that question which is widely accepted in our society, as in many other modern societies, is that no conduct should be suppressed by law unless it can be shown to harm someone. It is one sign of how many people now accept this answer and the condition which it imposes on legislation – it may be called the *harm condition* – that almost without exception the evidence we received, insofar as it touched on these matters of principle, stated something like this condition or took it for granted. Submissions to us differed, very obviously, about what harms, if any, publications and films might cause. They differed also about what might count as a harm. Those who favoured the abolition or limitation of legal restraint tended, not surprisingly, to define 'harm' in a narrower and more determinate way, while those who supported greater legal control admitted more generalized and less identifiable harms. Virtually everyone, however, whatever their suggestions, used the language of 'harm' and accepted, so it seemed, the harm condition.

5.2 We accept the harm condition. As the variety of views in the submissions to us shows, however, that leaves many basic questions still to be answered.

LAW AND MORALITY

5.3 The harm condition has been very much discussed in recent years in the context of debates on the question whether prevailing morality should be made into law: that is to say, whether the fact that many people in society think something morally wrong is a good enough reason for there being a law against it. If the harm condition for legislation is accepted, then the answer to this question will be 'no', since there are acts which are morally disapproved but are not harmful, and it will follow from the harm condition that there should be no law against these.

5.4 Some people hold that if society held correct moral views, this question should not arise, since even *moral* judgement should, correctly, be controlled by the harm condition. They will say that if certain conduct does no harm, then not only should there not be a law against it, but it should not be the object of any moral reactions either: if someone's behaviour does no harm, then it is nobody's business but his own, and no question of morality comes into it. This is clearly a liberal and tolerant outlook, and can be a beneficent one, but it does involve a very narrow view of morality. It tends to imply that everything that does not involve harm is simply a matter of taste or preference, as some people like spinach or detective stories and others do not. This is simply not true to the depth and complexity of one's possible reactions to other people's behaviour and to social phenomena. People can be distressed or contemptuous, admiring or impressed, more variously and more seriously than this model allows, and in ways which they think it important, for instance, to impart to their children. They still, following the harm condition, may not think that the matters which arouse these reactions are matters for the law, but they do care about them, and properly so, at a level which is not catered for by making 'harm' the only notion relevant to morality.

5.5 In the matter of pornography, there exists real disagreement about how serious a matter it is, even among those who think that it does little identifiable harm. Some do, after serious consideration, think that it is entirely a matter of preference: some people like it, some people do not. Others think that it is, at any rate, a deeper matter than that and whatever one might think about the case of an individual person, the fact that a society was extensively given to the consumption of pornography would tell one something about it, and something discouraging. It would not be merely like learning, for instance, that a certain society had a tendency to consume an unusually large amount of pasta. At the individual level as well, some would take a similar view. There are many of our witnesses who might not perhaps react to those with a taste for pornography with 'moral disapproval', but who nevertheless would regard such a person's state as a matter for ethical concern (if one may so put it) and think that such a person was in respect of his character and personality not as people desirably should be;

and that we all had good reason to hope that our children would not develop into such a state, and to discourage them from doing so.

5.6 There is, then, a view that wants to apply the harm condition to both morality and the law. An opposed view, associated in recent years with arguments advanced by Lord Devlin,[1] agrees with us that what is of serious moral concern can range more widely than the harm condition, but argues from this that even legislation should not be tied by the harm condition and can properly go wider, to express and affirm morality.

5.7 The shortest argument for the harm condition is simply that there is a presumption in favour of individual freedom: that the incursions of government into that freedom have to be justified; that the proper sphere of government is the protection of the interests of citizens; and so what is justifiably curbed by government is only what harms the interest of some citizens. But there is of course more to society than a collection of individuals under a set of rules which harmonize and collectively promote their self-interest. Society involves shared history, culture, and values, and there is more to being "at home" in it than knowing the language (that is already a lot) and remembering the way to the market. It is from this truth that Lord Devlin argued that the harm condition was not correct. Since a society rests on moral consensus, he claimed, what threatens moral consensus threatens society. But it is the business of the law to protect society; hence it can properly be used to protect the moral consensus.

5.8 As Professor Hart[2] and other critics have argued, however, the conclusion that Lord Devlin wanted does not follow. One immediate point is that his position seems not so much to abandon the harm condition as to urge another and wider category of harms, those associated with society's moral disintegration; and indeed … many of our witnesses did urge on us the existence and importance of harms of this very general type, supposedly associated with pornography and violent publications. Such witnesses were undoubtedly arguing in the terms of the harm condition. With Lord Devlin's argument, however, and the issues of principles it raises, there is an important, if perhaps rather fine, distinction to be made. On his view, there will be kinds of act which are not necessarily harmful in themselves, but are morally disapproved by (let us suppose) a majority of citizens. He argues, roughly, that if these acts are not discouraged by the law, certain harms will follow, of social and moral disintegration. On Lord Devlin's argument, however, those harms follow not simply from that type of act, but from that type of act when, in addition, it is morally disapproved by the citizens: in a society with a different moral fabric, containing no moral opinion against those acts, it is possible that no harms would follow from there not being laws against them. That kind of harm would not be admitted (except perhaps in extreme cases) by those who believe that legislation should be restricted by the harm condition. They are concerned with the harms that follow from the kind of act itself, leaving aside the citizens' moral opinion of those acts. They would say that to allow citizens' opinions to determine the matter in this way, is to sacrifice people's rights to do things that are otherwise harmless totally to majority prejudice. So even though Lord Devlin speaks in terms of harms, the harms of social disintegration, there is a difference between those who believe in the harm condition, and Lord Devlin or anyone else who believes, in the celebrated words of Lord Mansfield, referred to approvingly by a Law Lord in 1962:[3]

> Whatever is *contra bonos mores et decorum* the principles of our laws prohibit, and the King's Court as the general censor and guardian of the public morals is bound to restrain and punish.

5.9 A substantial point against Lord Devlin's view is that it exaggerates the identity and extent of the moral consensus required by a society, and hence over-states the harms that supposedly follow if moral opinion is not made into law. Certainly society requires some degree of moral consensus, but moral opinion can, and does, change without the disintegration of society. One thing that can happen is that the society moves to a new consensus; another is that it supports, in some particular area, a real degree of variety and pluralism.

5.10 Of course, there are many people who would prefer, or believe that they would prefer, a society less pluralistic than modern capitalist societies, and embodying a stronger moral consensus and a higher level of moral conviction. This yearning for a morally more homogeneous society takes many different forms, belonging, in political terms, both to the Right and to the Left. Some seek the recovery of a consensus which they believe once existed, others look to a new society yet to emerge.

5.11 We have been impressed by the extent to which submissions that we have received against pornography and obscene publications have been very obvi-ously moved by sentiments not just about these phenomena themselves, but about certain underlying features of the modern world, and express in some cases nostalgia, in others an aspiration, for a world where not just sexuality but human relations more generally were controlled by a firmer and more effective morality. Some of these views, naturally enough, ascribe present evils to the decline of Christian belief.

5.12 Many of these submissions are evidently deeply sincere, some of them indeed speak more for 'the party of humanity' than does a certain kind of 'liberal' evidence which we have received, which complacently extols the high task of furthering enlightenment and human fulfilment which, it claims, is sustained by the more literate kind of porno magazine. Any Committee enquiring into this kind of subject is likely to encounter a certain amount of humbug. Perhaps the most striking example of it that came our way was the pretence that present day commercial pornography represents some fulfilment of liberal and progressive hopes.

5.13 Leaving aside those with a commercial interest in it, few but the incur-ably complacent are likely to be pleased by the present scene in parts of Soho, for instance. The distaste for that scene indeed goes beyond those who pine for a more extensive moral consensus, and is felt by many who want a very individu-alist society containing many different images of life.

5.14 There is indeed a question of how deeply significant, as opposed to distasteful, these phenomena are. But even if such things as obscene publications are significant expressions, as some of our witnesses passionately believe, of things wrong with our society, there would still remain another question of whether laws directed to suppressing those publications would be either justified or effective. To be the identifiable cause of harms is one thing, to be the expression of underlying ills in society is another.

FREEDOM OF EXPRESSION

5.15 A particularly eloquent and influential advocate of the harm condition was John Stuart Mill, and he and his work *On Liberty* (1859), have been several times cited in submissions to us. Mill applied the harm condition to all proposals to coerce people's actions. He held, however, that where the actions in question were those of publishing a book or expressing oneself in speech or writing, there were special reasons against coercion and in favour of liberty. The freedom of expression is not for him just one more example of freedom from coercion but is a very special and fundamental form of freedom. It is clear that many of our witnesses share this view, some of them for Mill's own reasons, and we think it important to give those reasons some attention. Some of Mill's reasons we believe to be still very relevant today. Some of his arguments, however, were always flimsy and are yet more so in modern conditions. His basic thought was that human beings have no infallible source of knowledge about human nature or how human affairs may develop, and do not know in advance what arrangements or forms of life may make people happy or enable them to be, as Mill passionately wanted them to be, original, tolerant and uncowed individuals. Since we do not know in advance, we do not know what new proposals, ideas or forms of expression may contribute to the development of man and society.

5.16 From this Mill drew the conclusion that we have no basis for suppressing or censoring any of them. He did so, in particular, because he thought (and many others have shared this view) that the only way the truth could emerge was by a form of natural selection in a 'free market' of ideas: if all ideas were allowed expression, good ideas would multiply, bad ideas would die out. This conception, if sound, would have very powerful consequences. It is important, for instance, that it would tell almost as much against restricting a publication as against suppressing it, since any constraint on a work's availability will reduce the chance of its message being heard. However, we do not find Mill's conception entirely convincing, anyway, and it is also far from clear how it applies (as it has been applied) to the sort of material which is the subject of our enquiry.

5.17 If the 'survival of the true' notion applies to anything, it applies to publications which indeed contain *ideas*, which may be true or false. It can be extended more widely – to works of serious literature, for instance, the expressive powers of which contribute in their own way to the formation of images of men and of human possibilities. It is hard to see, however, how the argument can be extended to everything that is published. In particular it is hard to see how it applies to such things as standard photographic pornography, and we find it a rather ironical comment on the survival power of good ideas that some submissions to us have put forward in defence of the most vacant and inexpressive pornographic material the formulations which Mill hoped would assist in furthering ' … the permanent interests of man as a progressive being'.

5.18 It is interesting in this connection that the Supreme Court of the United

States has for a long time followed a line – though both unclearly and controversially – of arguing that the First Amendment to the United States Constitution, which says that 'Congress shall make no law ... abridging the freedom of speech ... ', does not protect hard-core pornography (at least), on the ground that such pornography is not, in a constitutional sense, 'speech': the idea being that it lacks communicative content.[4] This is not an issue which, happily, we are under any obligation to pursue, but the fact that this argument can be influentially sustained does illustrate the point that there is something open to question in calling on the 'market-place of truth' argument in defence of such items as standard photographic pornography.

5.19 Even in the area of ideas, the notion of a 'free market' has to be regarded with some scepticism, and the faith in *laissez-faire* shown by the nineteenth century and earlier does not altogether meet modern conditions. If everyone talks at once, truth will not prevail, since no one can be heard and nothing will prevail: and falsehood indeed may prevail, if powerful agencies can gain an undue hold on the market. Even in natural science, which Mill regarded as the paradigm, he neglected the importance of scientific institutions and the filter against cranks which is operated, and necessarily operated, by expert opinion, excluding for serious consideration what it sees as incompetence. Against the principle that truth is strong and (given the chance) will prevail, must be set Gresham's Law, that bad money drives out good, which has some application in matters of culture and which predicts that it will not necessarily be the most interesting ideas or the most valuable works of art that survive in competition – above all, in commercial competition.

5.20 Thus we cannot entirely agree that 'the Truth certainly would do well enough if she were left to fend for herself';[5] she may need more of a chance than that. This point can surely justify intervention. Intervention, however, need not be and should not be negative intervention: it can take the form of such things as state subventions for the arts, or policies of refusing to design television programmes solely on the basis of ratings, or subsidising institutions of critical enquiry. This is not just a point about the rights of minorities; it involves Mill's own basic idea (though differently applied) that progress involves a belief or a value being first a minority belief or value, which must be preserved if it is ever to reach further.

5.21 The fact that the market-place model is an inadequate basis for the value of free expression does not mean that one replaces the market with monopoly, and institutes a censorship by the State or by worthy citizens. There is certainly no reason to think that that would do better in the detection of error or the advance of enlightenment. The more basic idea, to which Mill attached the market-place model, remains a correct and profound idea: that we do not know in advance what social, moral or intellectual developments will turn out to be possible, necessary or desirable for human beings and for their future, and free expression, intellectual and artistic – something which may need to be fostered and protected as well as merely permitted – is essential to human development, as a process which does not merely happen (in some form or another, it will happen anyway), but so far as possible is rationally understood. It is essential to it, moreover, not just as a means to it, but as part of it. Since human beings are not just subject to their history but aspire to be conscious of it, the development of human individuals, of society and of humanity in general, is a process itself properly constituted in part by free expression and the exchange of human communication.

5.22 We realize that some may disagree with this basic idea because they think that fundamental human moral truths have been laid down unchangeably for all time, for instance in religious terms. Mill, certainly, thought that there was no such revealed truth, and his arguments for freedom of expression and those of people who think like him are to that extent an expression of religious scepticism. We would suggest, however, that even those who believe that there are revealed truths of morality and religion should attend very anxiously to the argument for freedom of expression. First, the barest facts of cultural history show that any set of supposed revealed truths which have survived have received constantly new applications and interpretations, to which new moral perceptions have contributed. Second, every believer in some set of moral certainties has to share the world with other believers in some different set of moral certainties. If they share the same society, at least, and even if they could come to do so, they have some common interest in not accepting principles which would allow someone else's certainty to persecute their own. Third, many religious believers in moral certainties also believe that human beings have been created not just to obey or mirror those certainties, but freely to live by them, and that institutions of free expression can be in fact a more developed representation of the religious consciousness itself than authoritarian institutions. We have thus not been surprised, though we have been impressed, by the constructive concern for freedom of expression which has been shown by many of the submissions we have received from religious bodies, disturbed though most of them have been by the present situation.

5.23 Because we believe that the value of the freedom of expression is connected with the open future of human development, we do find a difficulty with certain proposals for obscenity law we have received, which both admit the fact of changing standards, and also invoke present standards to justify the actual suppression of certain publications. The Nationwide Festival of Light and others, following a formulation of Lord Longford's Committee, have recommended the suppression of what grossly affronts 'contemporary standards of decency or humanity accepted by the public at large'. But while some such provision might ground, as we shall ourselves suggest, a *restriction* of some material, to prevent its offending the public at large, the position of trying to justify suppression – which, if successful, is permanent – on the basis of what are acknowledged to be contemporary standards, seems to us to make, more than is justified, present views the determinant of the future.

5.24 We come back to the total emptiness of almost all the material we are concerned with. These arguments, it will be said, are all very well for serious works of art or for writings of intellectual content, but it is absurd to apply them to everyday, in particular pictorial, pornography. We do not claim that, directly, they do apply. But here we must stress two very fundamental points: first, that what the argument grounds is a general presumption in favour of free expression, and second, that censorship is in its nature a blunt and treacherous instrument.

The value of free expression does not lie solely in its consequences, such that it turns out on the whole to be more efficient to have it rather than not. It is rather that there is a right to free expression, a presumption in favour of it, and weighty considerations in terms of harms have to be advanced by those who seek to curtail it. Methods of control, moreover, bring their own harms, and can readily involve other violations of rights. Once one has left on one side the suppression of what produces the most immediate and obvious and gross harms, it is quite unrealistic to suppose that institutions of censorship can be guaranteed not to take on a repressive and distorting character, whether simply in the interests of some powerful or influential group or in opposition to new perceptions and ideas. Most of what is in our field of discussion contains no new perception and no idea at all, old or new, and that cannot seriously be disputed. But even if there were a case for suppressing that material, it must never be forgotten that no one has invented, or in our opinion could invent, an instrument which would suppress only that, and could not be turned against something which might reasonably be argued to be of a more creative kind. The Obscene Publications Acts sought to avoid this danger by the 'public good defence', to prevent conviction of material which was creatively valuable. We have already given an account of its sad history; we shall later argue that such a device is misconceived in principle.

5.25 The 'slippery slope' difficulty, the vagueness of any test, is inherent in any proposals for legislation about obscene publications, and indeed for any censorship at all, and this itself constitutes an argument against attempts at suppression. We shall argue later that rather different considerations apply to the less drastic course of restricting, without suppressing, certain publications. In that connection we shall also argue that there are reasons for treating the printed word differently from pictorial matter, and considerations drawn from the present area of discussion also support that conclusion, since (without entering on the troubled waters of the Supreme Court's definition of 'speech' to which we have already referred) there is no doubt that it is to the printed word that the argument about the survival of new ideas and perceptions applies most directly.

HARMS

5.26 The presumption in favour of freedom of expression is strong, but it is a presumption, and it can be overruled by considerations of harms which the speech or publication in question may cause. The first question that arises is, harms to whom? (In this chapter, as elsewhere, we will speak generally of harms to persons, though sometimes it might be more natural to speak of harms to their interests.) In particular, in the case of publications, there is the question whether supposed harm to consumers – i.e. those who voluntarily choose to read the material – is, just in itself, to count. Mill and many others who advance what we have called the 'harm condition' for coercing behaviour would say that it did not. They say this because they accept the principle that, if one is dealing with adult persons, it is best to assume that each person is the best judge of whether he or she is being harmed. This additional principle makes an important difference. The harm condition by itself would not necessarily produce very liberal results. One might agree that laws should only suppress what does harm but think that disgusting books should be suppressed by law because their readers (though those readers would not themselves agree) are in fact harmed by them. With this other principle added, however, such paternalist laws would be ruled out.

5.27 Most people would admit some paternalistic principles – with regard to harmful drugs, for instance. Some would like to apply similar ideas to people's reading habits, and regard 'harmful' publications in much the same light as dangerous drugs.

It is worth noting that the very strong resistance from liberal opinion that this kind of analogy meets is not just due to the uncertainty that surrounds the 'effects' in question, and whether literature produces them. It is also that in this case, but not (for the most part) in the case of drugs, there is a real question about 'who is to judge' what counts as harm; since it is a question of moral harm, there is room for disagreement about what such harms are, and there is a danger that the moral opinions of some group, presumably some rather conservative group, should be made authoritative for the moral health of readers. In the proceedings against *Lady Chatterley's Lover* in 1960, the prosecuting counsel in his opening speech invited the jury to ask themselves 'Is it a book that you would even wish your wife or your servants to read?', and this ingenuous and unfor-gotten remark has served for twenty years to remind people that questions of what one should read cannot be regarded just as questions of health, on which there are experts as there are experts on drug addiction, but are closely connected with issues of power and authority in society.

5.28 An important point connected with the issue of paternalism is whether there is some *independent* test of whether a given activity produces harm. The effects of drug taking are a bad physical and mental condition, and this condition would be bad even if it were caused by something other than drugs. But if the bad effects of reading dirty books were alleged to lie only in the fact that they produced a deplorable state of mind manifested just in wanting to read dirty books, that would not be much of an argument; though if the state produced were that of compulsively reading dirty books, against one's will (as one witness has claimed to us happened to him), that would be more of an argument.

5.29 In fact a lot of the argument about harm supposedly caused by publica-tions lies in the area of claims that they cause harms not to consumers, or merely to consumers, but to those affected by consumers. The harms cited in these argu-ments are usually the kind of thing that is indisputably a harm. In evidence put to us it was claimed, for example, that crimes, particularly sexual crimes, are caused by exposure to pornographic or violent films or publications. There were other arguments about individual behaviour being modified or conditioned by what was read or seen in ways that were less specifically antisocial but which conflicted with perceived standards of morality or with the expectations of society. Some emphasized the aspects of pornography which degrade women in that much material is not only offensive, but encourages a view of women as subservient and as properly the object of, or even desirous of, sexual subjugation or assault. Others emphasized the exploitation of those who participate in the production of pornography and the damaging effects this was believed to have. At a rather more general level, some people saw certain kinds of material, in presenting a distorted view of human experience, as damaging to human relationships by hindering the full development of the human personality or corrupting the imagination. So we heard arguments about pornography leading to sex crimes, and violence in the media engendering crimes of violence, about pornography leading to marital breakdown by encouraging unusual and sometimes abhorrent sexual demands (usually by husbands of their wives) and arousing false expectations of sexual fulfilment, about the encouragement of promiscuity and sexual deviation, about the promotion of self-gratification and a contempt for discipline, about the engendering of hate and aggression, about the risk to the normal sexual development of the young, about people becoming desensitized or callous through a diet of violence.

5.30 ... Besides these, however, harms of a less definite and more pervasive kind have been alleged, which relate to general effects on society of pornography and violent publications and films, and which can best be summed up, perhaps, under the phrase, used by several witnesses, 'cultural pollution'. Such phrases certainly refer to something, and we take seriously what they refer to. In the case of such descriptions, however, there is often a real difficulty in identifying what the harmful effect of the material is supposed to be, and whether indeed it is really an *effect* of the materials circulating that is in question, rather than the circulation itself which is regarded as intrinsically an objectionable thing; as we have already mentioned, it may be an expression, rather than a cause, of an undesirable state of society.

5.31 In the next chapter [not included] we shall try to evaluate some claims that have been made about these various harms and their association with pornography. In evaluating these claims, there are two general principles that we think it important to bear in mind. One is the requirement, for legal purposes, that the causation of the harm should lie 'beyond reasonable doubt'.

5.32 Restrictions on freedom of publication in connections other than obscenity are, of course, accepted by every legislature: with respect to libel, for instance, or sedition. It is significant, however, that in such cases liberal states require that the harms in question should be of a clear and immediate kind. So in the law of the United States in respect of seditious matter, where Mr Justice Holmes in a Supreme Court decision of 1919 produced the famous formula

> ... The question in every case is whether the words used are used in such circumstances and are of such a nature as to create a clear and present danger that they will bring about the substantive evils that Congress has a right to prevent. It is a question of proximity and degree ... [6]

At least one United States Judge did attempt to apply the same test to the alleged effects of obscene publications. Judge Bok, of Philadelphia, dismissing in 1948 a case against a number of books that included Faulkner's *Sanctuary* and Caldwell's *God's Little Acre*, stressed the impossibility of 'even reasonable precision' in assessing a reader's reactions to a book, and sought to establish the principle that no book should be suppressed unless it could be shown that there was a clear and present danger of the commission of a crime as a result of its publication.[7]

Superior Courts upheld his judgement of the case, and his reasoning in other respects, but not this suggested principle.

5.33 The causal concept of obscenity, in terms of doing harm, has in legal practice proved very resistant to being given the precise application, and submitting to the canons of proof, required in general by the law; and, as we have already said in an earlier chapter, the courts seem often in fact to have been proceeding on a basis altogether different from that of the publications supposedly causing harm.

5.34 The second principle that should be borne in mind is the requirement that if a certain class of publications, say pornographic publications, is to be legally banned, then harms have to be ascribable to that class of publications. No one can reasonably say – though one or two of our witnesses have incautiously said it – that no pornographic book has ever harmed anyone. But that is not the point. It may well be that reading the Bible, for instance, has harmed someone. The question is whether pornography constitutes a class of publications to which, as such, there belongs a tendency to cause harms ...

5.35 We must not forget at the same time that arguments about the effects of pornography have also been advanced in the opposite direction, suggesting that sexual and violent material has positive benefits in the opportunity it offers for the release of sexual or aggressive tensions, for the removal of ignorance, fear, guilt, and inhibition, for the relief and comfort of lonely, handicapped or frustrated people and for members of society as a whole to gain a more open acceptance of sex as a natural part of life.

NOTES

1 E.g. in *The Enforcement of Morals*, Oxford, 1959.
2 H.L.A. Hart, *Law, Liberty and Morality*, Oxford, 1963.
3 For references, see Hart 1963, pp. 7–9. Lord Mansfield's dictum dates from 1774.
4 See F. Schauer: 'Speech and "Speech" – Obscenity and "Obscenity": An Exercise in the Interpretation of Constitutional Language': *Georgetown Law Journal* 67, (1979) 899–933, which defends the argument. We are grateful to Professor Schauer for discussion and for information about US law.
5 A remark made, but perhaps not totally endorsed, by John Locke: see his *Letter Concerning Toleration*, ed. Gough (1948), p. 151.
6 Schenck v. United States, 249 US 47.
7 Commonwealth v. Gordon, 66 Pa.D. and C. 101 (Phila. 1949).

5 'Liberty and pornography'

Ronald Dworkin

In this essay (originally published in the *New York Review of Books*, 1991, reprinted in Sontag (ed.) *Best American Essays 1992*, Ticknor and Fields, 1992) Ronald Dworkin examines a recent attempt to justify limiting freedom of expression in the name of negative freedom: the claim that some forms of pornography effectively silence women's attempts to be heard and so should themselves be silenced. Using Berlin's 'Two Concepts of Liberty' to provide a framework for his discussion, Dworkin shows that this sort of argument involves confusion: there may be arguments for silencing some sorts of expression, but these cannot be arguments based on the concept of negative freedom. They must be based on some other value given a greater weighting, such as equality or fairness or justice. It is worth noting in passing that in setting out Berlin's notion of positive freedom, Dworkin emphasizes the notion of collective rather than individual self-mastery; in Chapter 1 above I lay greater stress on the notion of individual self-mastery. Both are important aspects of Berlin's concept of positive freedom.

When Isaiah Berlin delivered his famous inaugural lecture as Chichele Professor of Social and Political Theory at Oxford, in 1958, he felt it necessary to acknowledge that politics did not attract the professional attention of most serious philosophers in Britain and America. They thought philosophy had no place in politics, and vice versa; that political philosophy could be nothing more than a parade of the theorist's own preferences and allegiances with no supporting arguments of any rigour or respectability. That gloomy picture is unrecognizable now. Political philosophy thrives as a mature industry; it dominates many distinguished philosophy departments and attracts a large share of the best graduate students almost everywhere.

Berlin's lecture, 'Two Concepts of Liberty', played an important and distinctive role in this renaissance. It provoked immediate, continuing, heated, and mainly illuminating controversy. It became, almost at once, a staple of graduate and undergraduate reading lists, as it still is. Its scope and erudition, its historical sweep and evident contemporary force, its sheer interest, made political ideas suddenly seem exciting and fun. Its main polemical message – that it is fatally dangerous for philosophers to ignore either the complexity or the power of those ideas – was both compelling and overdue. But chiefly, or so I think, its importance lay in the force of its central argument. For though Berlin began by conceding to the disdaining philosophers that political philosophy could not match logic or the philosophy of language as a theatre for 'radical discoveries', in which 'talent for minute analyses is likely to be rewarded', he continued by analysing subtle distinctions that, as it happens, are even more important now, in the Western democracies at least, than when he first called our attention to them.

I must try to describe two central features of his argument, though for reasons of space I shall have to leave out much that is important to them. The first is the celebrated distinction described in the lecture's title: between two (closely allied) senses of liberty. Negative liberty (as Berlin came later to restate it) means not being obstructed by others in doing what one might wish to do. We count some negative liberties – like the freedom to speak our minds without censorship – as very important and others – like driving at very fast speeds – as trivial. But they are both instances of negative freedom, and though a state may be justified in imposing speed limits, for example, on grounds of safety and convenience, that is nevertheless an instance of restricting negative liberty.

Positive liberty, on the other hand, is the power to control or participate in public decisions, including the decision how far to curtail negative liberty. In an ideal democracy – whatever that is – the people govern themselves. Each is master to the same degree, and positive liberty is secured for all.

In his inaugural lecture Berlin described the historical corruption of the idea of positive liberty, a corruption that began in the idea that someone's true liberty lies in control by his rational self rather than his empirical self, that is, in control that aims at securing goals other than those the person himself recognizes. Freedom, on that conception, is possible only when people are governed, ruthlessly if necessary, by rulers who know their true, metaphysical will. Only then are people truly free, albeit against their will. That deeply confused and dangerous, but nevertheless potent, chain of argument had in many parts of the world turned positive liberty into the most terrible tyranny. Of course, by calling attention to this corruption of positive liberty, Berlin did not mean that negative liberty was an unalloyed blessing, and should be protected in all its forms in all circumstances at all costs. He said later that on the contrary, the vices of excessive and indiscriminate negative liberty were so evident, particularly in the form of savage economic inequality, that he had not thought it necessary to describe them in much detail.

The second feature of Berlin's argument that I have in mind is a theme repeated throughout his writing on political topics. He insists on the complexity of political value, and the fallacy of supposing that all the political virtues that are attractive in themselves can be realized in a single political structure. The ancient Platonic ideal of some master accommodation of all attractive virtues and goals, combined in institutions satisfying each in the right proportion and sacrificing none, is in Berlin's view, for all its imaginative power and historical influence, only a seductive myth. He later summed this up:

> One freedom may abort another; one freedom may obstruct or fail to create conditions which make other freedoms, or a larger degree of freedom, or freedom for more persons, possible; positive and negative freedom may collide; the freedom of the individual or the group may not be fully compatible with a full degree of participation in a common life, with its demands for co-operation, solidarity, fraternity. But beyond all these there is an acuter issue: the paramount need to satisfy the claims of other, no less ultimate, values: justice, happiness, love, the realization of capacities to create new things and experiences and ideas, the discovery of the truth. Nothing is gained by identifying freedom proper, in either of its senses, with these values, or with the conditions of freedom, or by confounding types of freedom with one another.[1]

Berlin's warnings about conflating positive and negative liberty, and liberty itself, with other values seemed, to students of political philosophy in the great Western democracies in the 1950s, to provide important lessons about authoritarian regimes in other times and places. Though cherished liberties were very much under attack in both America and Britain in that decade, the attack was not grounded in or defended through either form of confusion. The enemies of negative liberty were powerful, but they were also crude and undisguised. Joseph McCarthy and his allies did not rely on any Kantian or Hegelian or Marxist concept of metaphysical selves to justify censorship or blacklists. They distinguished liberty not from itself, but from security; they claimed that too much free speech made us vulnerable to spies and intellectual saboteurs and ultimately to conquest.

In both Britain and America, in spite of limited reforms, the state still sought to enforce conventional sexual morality about pornography, contraception, prostitution, and homosexuality. Conservatives who defended these invasions of negative liberty appealed not to some higher or different sense of freedom, however, but to values that were plainly distinct from, and in conflict with, freedom: religion, true morality, and traditional and proper family values. The wars over liberty were fought, or so it seemed, by clearly divided armies.

Liberals were for liberty, except, in some circumstances, for the negative liberty of economic entrepreneurs. Conservatives were for that liberty, but against other forms when these collided with security or their view of decency and morality.

But now the political maps have radically changed and some forms of negative liberty have acquired new opponents. Both in America and in Britain, though in different ways, conflicts over race and gender have transformed old alliances and divisions. Speech that expresses racial hatred, or a degrading attitude toward women, has come to seem intolerable to many people whose convictions are otherwise traditionally liberal. It is hardly surprising that they should try to reduce the conflict between their old liberal ideals and their new acceptance of censorship by adopting some new definition of what liberty, properly understood, really is. It is hardly surprising, but the result is dangerous confusion, and Berlin's warnings, framed with different problems in mind, are directly in point.

I shall try to illustrate that point with a single example: a lawsuit arising out of the attempt by certain feminist groups in America to outlaw what they consider a particularly objectionable form of pornography. I select this example not because pornography is more important or dangerous or objectionable than racist invective or other highly distasteful kinds of speech, but because the debate over pornography has been the subject of the fullest and most comprehensive scholarly discussion.

Through the efforts of Catharine MacKinnon, a professor of law at the University of Michigan, and other prominent feminists, Indianapolis, Indiana, enacted an antipornography ordinance. The ordinance defined pornography as 'the graphic sexually explicit subordination of women, whether in pictures or words … ' and it specified, as among pornographic materials falling within that definition, those that present women as enjoying pain or humiliation or rape, or as degraded or tortured or filthy, bruised or bleeding, or in postures of servility or submission or display. It included no exception for literary or artistic value, and opponents claimed that applied literally it would outlaw James Joyce's *Ulysses*, John Cleland's *Memoirs of a Woman of Pleasure*, various works of D.H. Lawrence, and even Yeats's 'Leda and the Swan'. But the groups who sponsored the ordinance were anxious to establish that their objection was not to obscenity or indecency as such, but to the consequences for women of a particular kind of pornography, and they presumably thought that an exception for artistic value would undermine that claim.[2]

The ordinance did not simply regulate the display of pornography so defined, or restrict its sale or distribution to particular areas, or guard against the exhibition of pornography to children. Regulation for those purposes does restrain negative liberty, but if reasonable it does so in a way compatible with free speech. Zoning and display regulations may make pornography more expensive or inconvenient to obtain, but they do not offend the principle that no one must be prevented from publishing or reading what he or she wishes on the ground that its content is immoral or offensive.[3] The Indianapolis ordinance, on the other hand, prohibited any 'production, sale, exhibition, or distribution' whatever of the material it defined as pornographic.

Publishers and members of the public who claimed a desire to read the banned material arranged a prompt constitutional challenge. The federal district court held that the ordinance was unconstitutional because it violated the First Amendment to the United States Constitution, which guarantees the negative liberty of free speech.[4] The Circuit Court for the Seventh Circuit upheld the district court's decision,[5] and the Supreme Court of the United States declined to review that holding. The Circuit Court's decision, in an opinion by Judge Easterbrook, noticed that the ordinance did not outlaw obscene or indecent material generally but only material reflecting the opinion that women are submissive, or enjoy being dominated, or should be treated as if they did. Easterbrook said that the central point of the First Amendment was exactly to protect speech from content-based regulation of that sort. Censorship may on some occasions be permitted if it aims to prohibit directly dangerous speech – crying fire in a crowded theatre or inciting a crowd to violence, for example – or speech particularly and unnecessarily inconvenient – broadcasting from sound trucks patrolling residential streets at night, for instance. But nothing must be censored, Easterbrook wrote, because the message it seeks to deliver is a bad one, or because it expresses ideas that should not be heard at all.

It is by no means universally agreed that censorship should never be based on content. The British Race Relations Act, for example, forbids speech of racial hatred, not only when it is likely to lead to violence, but generally, on the grounds that members of minority races should be protected from racial insults. In America, however, it is a fixed principle of constitutional law that such regulation is unconstitutional unless some compelling necessity, not just official or majority disapproval of the message, requires it. Pornography is often grotesquely offensive; it is insulting, not only to women but to men as well. But we cannot consider that a sufficient reason for banning it without destroying the principle that the speech we hate is as much entitled to protection as any other. The essence of negative liberty is freedom to offend, and that applies to the tawdry as well as the heroic.

Lawyers who defend the Indianapolis ordinance argue that society does have a further justification for outlawing pornography: that it causes great harm as well as offence to women. But their arguments mix together claims about different types or kinds of harm, and it is necessary to distinguish these. They argue, first, that some forms of pornography significantly increase the danger that women will be raped or physically assaulted. If that were true, and the danger were clear and present, then it would indeed justify censorship of those forms, unless less stringent methods of control, such as restricting pornography's audience, would be feasible, appropriate, and effective. In fact, however, though there is some evidence that exposure to pornography weakens people's critical attitudes toward sexual violence, there is no persuasive evidence that it causes more actual incidents of assault. The Seventh Circuit cited a variety of studies (including that of the Williams' Commission in Britain in 1979), all of which concluded, the court said, 'that it is not possible to demonstrate a direct link between obscenity and rape ... '[6] A recent report based on a year's research in Britain said: 'The evidence does not point to pornography as a cause of deviant sexual orientation in offenders. Rather, it seems to be used as part of that deviant sexual orientation.'[7]

Some feminist groups argue, however, that pornography causes not just physical violence but a more general and endemic subordination of women. In that way, they say, pornography makes for inequality. But even if it could be shown, as a matter of causal connection, that pornography is in part responsible for the economic structure in which few women attain top jobs or equal pay for the same work, that would not justify censorship under the Constitution. It would plainly be unconstitutional to ban speech directly *advocating* that women occupy inferior roles, or none at all, in commerce and the professions, even if that speech fell on willing male ears and achieved its goals. So it cannot be a reason for banning pornography that it contributes to an unequal economic or social structure, even if we think that it does.

But the most imaginative feminist literature for censorship makes a further and different argument: that negative liberty for pornographers conflicts not just with equality but with positive liberty as well, because pornography leads to women's *political* as well as economic or social subordination. Of course pornography does not take the vote from women, or somehow make their votes count less. But it produces a climate, according to this argument, in which women cannot have genuine political power or authority because they are perceived and understood unauthentically – that is, they are made over by male fantasy into people very different from, and of much less consequence than, the people they really are. Consider, for example, these remarks from the work of the principal sponsor of the Indianapolis ordinance. '[Pornography] institutionalizes the sexuality of male supremacy, fusing the eroticization of dominance and submission with the social construction of male and female ... Men treat women as who they see women as being. Pornography constructs who that is. Men's power over women means that the way men see women defines who women can be.'[8]

Pornography, on this view, denies the positive liberty of women; it denies them the right to be their own masters by recreating them, for politics and society, in the shapes of male fantasy. That is a powerful argument, even in constitutional terms, because it asserts a conflict not just between liberty and equality but within liberty itself, that is a conflict that cannot be resolved simply on the ground that liberty must be sovereign. What shall we make of the argument understood that way? We must notice, first, that it remains a causal argument. It claims not that pornography is a consequence or symptom or symbol of how the identity of women has been reconstructed by men, but an important cause or vehicle of that reconstruction.

That seems strikingly implausible. Sadistic pornography is revolting, but it is not in general circulation, except for its milder, soft-porn manifestations. It seems unlikely that it has remotely the influence over how women's sexuality or character or talents are conceived by men, and indeed by women, that commercial advertising and soap operas have. Television and other parts of popular culture use sexual display and sexual innuendo to sell virtually everything, and they often show women as experts in domestic detail and unreasoned intuition and nothing else. The images they create are subtle and ubiquitous, and it would not be surprising to learn, through whatever research might establish this, that they indeed do great damage to the way women are understood and allowed to be influential in politics. Sadistic pornography, though much more offensive and disturbing, is greatly overshadowed by these dismal cultural influences as a causal force.

Judge Easterbrook's opinion for the Seventh Circuit assumed, for the sake of argument, however, that pornography did have the consequences the defenders of the ordinance claimed. He said that the argument nevertheless failed because the point of free speech is precisely to allow ideas to have whatever consequences follow from their dissemination, including undesirable consequences for positive liberty. 'Under the First Amendment,' he said, 'the government must leave to the people the evaluation of ideas. Bald or subtle, an idea is as powerful as the audience allows it to be ... [The assumed result] simply demonstrates the power of pornography as speech. All of these unhappy effects depend on mental intermediation.'

That is right as a matter of American constitutional law. The Ku Klux Klan and the American Nazi party are allowed to propagate their ideas in America, and the

British Race Relations Act, so far as it forbids abstract speech of racial hatred, would be unconstitutional in the US. But does the American attitude represent the kind of Platonic absolutism Berlin warned against? No, because there is an important difference between the idea he thinks absurd, that all ideals attractive in themselves can be perfectly reconciled within a single utopian political order, and the different idea he thought essential, that we must, as individuals and nations, choose, among possible combinations of ideals, a coherent, even though inevitably and regrettably limited, set of these to define our own individual or national way of life. Freedom of speech, conceived and protected as a funda-mental negative liberty, is the core of the choice modern democracies have made, a choice we must now honour in finding our own ways to combat the shaming inequalities women still suffer.

This reply depends, however, on seeing the alleged conflict within liberty as a conflict between the negative and positive senses of that virtue. We must consider yet another argument which, if successful, could not be met in the same way, because it claims that pornography presents a conflict within the negative liberty of speech itself. Berlin said that the character, at least, of negative liberty was reasonably clear, that although excessive claims of negative liberty were dangerous, they could at least always be seen for what they were. But the argu-ment I have in mind, which has been offered by, among others, Frank Michelman of the Harvard Law School, expands the idea of negative liberty in an unantici-pated way. He argues that some speech, including pornography, may be itself 'silencing', so that its effect is to prevent other people from exercising their negative freedom to speak.

Of course it is fully recognized in First Amendment jurisprudence that some speech has the effect of silencing others. Government must indeed balance nega-tive liberties when it prevents heckling or other demonstrative speech designed to stop others from speaking or being heard. But Michelman has something different in mind. He says that a woman's speech may be silenced not just by noise intended to drown her out but also by argument and images that change her audience's perceptions of her character, needs, desires, and standing, and also, perhaps, change her own sense of who she is and what she wants. Speech with that consequence silences her, Michelman supposes, by making it impossible for her effectively to contribute to the process Judge Easterbrook said the First Amendment protected, the process through which ideas battle for the public's favour. '[It] is a highly plausible claim,' Michelman writes, '[that] pornography [is] a cause of women's subordination and silencing ... It is a fair and obvious ques-tion why our society's openness to challenge does not need protection against repressive private as well as public action.'[9]

He argues that if our commitment to negative freedom of speech is conse-quentialist – if we want free speech in order to have a society in which no idea is barred from entry – then we must censor some ideas in order to make entry possible for other ones. He protests that the distinction that American constitu-tional law makes between the suppression of ideas by the effect of public criminal law and by the consequences of private speech is arbitrary, and that a sound concern for openness would be equally worried about both forms of control. But the distinction the law makes is not between public and private power as such, but between negative liberty and other virtues, including positive liberty. It would indeed be contradictory for a constitution to prohibit official censorship while protecting the right of private citizens physically to prevent other citizens from publishing or broadcasting specified ideas. That would allow private citizens to violate the negative liberty of other citizens by preventing them from saying what they wish.

But there is no contradiction in insisting that every idea must be allowed to be heard, even those whose consequence is that other ideas will be misunderstood, or given little consideration, or even not be spoken at all because those who might speak them are not in control of their own public identities and therefore cannot be understood as they wish to be. These are very bad consequences, and they must be resisted by whatever means our Constitution permits. But acts that have these consequences do not, for that reason, deprive others of their negative liberty to speak, and the distinction, as Berlin insisted, is very far from arbitrary or inconsequential.

It is of course understandable why Michelman and others should want to expand the idea of negative liberty in the way they try to do. Only by characterizing certain ideas as themselves 'silencing' ideas – only by supposing that censoring pornography is the same thing as stopping people from drowning out other speakers – can they hope to justify censorship within the constitutional scheme that assigns a pre-eminent place to free speech. But the assimilation is nevertheless a confusion, exactly the kind of confusion Berlin warned against in his original lecture, because it obscures the true political choice that must be made. I return to Berlin's lecture, which put the point with that striking combination of clarity and sweep I have been celebrating:

> I should be guilt-stricken, and rightly so, if I were not, in some circumstances, ready to make [some] sacrifice [of freedom]. But a sacrifice is not an increase in what is being sacrificed, namely freedom, however great the moral need or the compensation for it. Everything is what it is: liberty is liberty, not equality or fairness or justice or culture, or human happiness or a quiet conscience.

NOTES

1   Isaiah Berlin, *Four Essays on Liberty*, Oxford University Press, 1968, p. lvi.
2   McKinnon explained that 'if a woman is subjected, why should it matter that the work has other value?' See her article 'Pornography, Civil Rights, and Speech', in *Harvard Civil Rights – Civil Liberties Law Review*, Vol. 28, p. 21.
3   See my article 'Do We Have a Right to Pornography?' reprinted as Chapter 17 in my book *A Matter of Principle*, Harvard University Press, 1985.
4   American Booksellers Association, Inc. *et al*. v. William H. Hudnit, III, Mayor, City of Indianapolis, *et al*., 598 F. Supp. 1316 (S.D. Ind. 1984).
5   771 F. 2d 232 (US Court of Appeals, Seventh Circuit).
6   That court, in a confused passage, said that it nevertheless accepted 'the premises of this legislation', which included the claims about a causal connection with sexual violence. But it seemed to mean that it was accepting the rather different causal claim considered in the next paragraph, about subordination. In any case, it said that it accepted those premises only for the sake of argument, since it thought it had no authority to reject decisions of Indianapolis based on its interpretation of empirical evidence.
7   See the *Daily Telegraph*, December 23, 1990. Of course further studies might contradict this assumption. But it seems very unlikely that pornography will be found to stimulate physical

violence to the overall extent that non-pornographic depictions of violence, which are much more pervasive in our media and culture, do.

8   See MacKinnon's article cited in footnote 2.

9   Frank Michelman, 'Conceptions of Democracy in American Constitutional Argument: The Case of Pornography Regulation', *Tennessee Law Review*, Vol. 56, No. 291 (1989), pp. 303–4.

6 'Immorality and treason'

H.L.A. Hart

In this article, which originally appeared in 1959 (reprinted in Wasserstrom [ed.] *Morality and the Law*, Wadsworth, 1971 and in R.M. Dworkin [ed.] *The Philosophy of Law*, Oxford University Press, 1977, pp. 83–8), H.L.A. Hart, who was Professor of Jurisprudence at Oxford University, responds to Patrick Devlin's claim that there is a strong analogy between immoral acts, even if performed in private, and acts of treason. Hart attacks this analogy, and in the process undermines Devlin's idea that popular feelings of intolerance, indignation and disgust should determine which activities are made illegal. The fact that something makes the man on the Clapham omnibus feel sick is not sufficient on its own to justify making a change to the criminal law.

The most remarkable feature of Sir Patrick's lecture is his view of the nature of morality – the morality which the criminal law may enforce. Most previous thinkers who have repudiated the liberal point of view have done so because they thought that morality consisted either of divine commands or of rational principles of human conduct discoverable by human reason. Since morality for them had this elevated divine or rational status as the law of God or reason, it seemed obvious that the state should enforce it, and that the function of human law should not be merely to provide men with the opportunity for leading a good life, but actually to see that they lead it. Sir Patrick does not rest his repudiation of the liberal point of view on these religious or rationalist conceptions. Indeed much that he writes reads like an abjuration of the notion that reasoning or thinking has much to do with morality. English popular morality has no doubt its historical connection with the Christian religion: 'That,' says Sir Patrick, 'is how it got there.' But it does not owe its present status or social significance to religion any more than to reason.

What, then, is it? According to Sir Patrick it is primarily a matter of feeling. 'Every moral judgement,' he says, 'is a feeling that no right-minded man could act in any other way without admitting that he was doing wrong.' Who then must feel this way if we are to have what Sir Patrick calls a public morality? He tells us that it is 'the man in the street,' 'the man in the jury box,' or (to use the phrase so familiar to English lawyers) 'the man on the Clapham omnibus'. For the moral judgements of society so far as the law is concerned are to be ascertained by the standards of the reasonable man, and he is not to be confused with the rational man. Indeed, Sir Patrick says 'he is not expected to reason about anything and his judgement may be largely a matter of feeling'.

INTOLERANCE, INDIGNATION, AND DISGUST

But what precisely are the relevant feelings, the feelings which may justify use of the criminal law? Here the argument becomes a little complex. Widespread dislike of a practice is not enough. There must, says Sir Patrick, be 'a real feeling of reprobation'. Disgust is not enough either. What is crucial is a combination of intolerance, indignation, and disgust. These three are the forces behind the moral law, without which it is not 'weighty enough to deprive the individual of freedom of choice'. Hence there is, in Sir Patrick's outlook, a crucial difference between the mere adverse moral judgement of society and one which is inspired by feeling raised to the concert pitch of intolerance, indignation, and disgust.

This distinction is novel and also very important. For on it depends the weight to be given to the fact that when morality is enforced individual liberty is necessarily cut down. Though Sir Patrick's abstract formulation of his views on this point is hard to follow, his examples make his position fairly clear. We can see it best in the contrasting things he says about fornication and homosexuality. In regard to fornication, public feeling in most societies is not now of the concert-pitch intensity. We may feel that it is tolerable if confined: only its spread might be gravely injurious. In such cases the question whether individual liberty should be restricted is for Sir Patrick a question of balance between the danger to society in the one scale, and the restriction of the individual in the other. But if, as may be the case with homosexuality, public feeling is up to concert pitch, if it expresses a 'deliberate judgement' that a practice as such is injurious to society, if there is 'a genuine feeling that it is a vice so abominable that its mere presence is an offence', then it is beyond the limits of tolerance, and society may eradicate it. In this case, it seems, no further balancing of the claims of individual liberty is to be done, though as a matter of prudence the legislator should remember that the popular limits of tolerance may shift: the concert pitch feeling may subside. This may produce a dilemma for the law; for the law may then be left without the full moral backing that it needs, yet it cannot be altered without giving the impression that the moral judgement is being weakened.

A SHARED MORALITY

If this is what morality is — a compound of indignation, intolerance, and disgust — we may well ask what justification there is for taking it, and turning it as such, into criminal law with all the misery which criminal punishment entails. Here Sir Patrick's answer is very clear and simple. A collection of individuals is not a society; what makes them into a society is among other things a shared or public morality. This is as necessary to its existence as an organized government. So society may use the law to preserve its morality like anything else essential to it. 'The suppression of vice is as much the law's business as the suppression of subversive activities.' The liberal point of view which denies this is guilty of 'an error in jurisprudence': for it is no more possible to define an area of private morality than an area of private subversive activity. There can be no 'theoretical limits' to legislation against immorality just as there are no such limits to the power of the state to legislate against treason and sedition.

Surely all this, ingenious as it is, is misleading. Mill's formulation of the liberal point of view may well be too simple. The grounds for interfering with human liberty are more various than the single criterion of 'harm to others' suggests: cruelty to animals or organizing prostitution for gain do not, as Mill himself saw, fall easily under the description of harm to others. Conversely, even where there is harm to others in the most literal sense, there may well be other principles limiting the extent to which harmful activities should be repressed by law. So there are multiple criteria, not a single criterion, determining when human liberty may be restricted. Perhaps this is what Sir Patrick means by a curious distinction which he often stresses between theoretical and practical limits. But with all its simplicities the liberal point of view is a better guide than Sir Patrick to clear thought on the proper relation of morality to the criminal law: for it stresses what he obscures – namely, the points at which thought is needed before we turn popular morality into criminal law.

SOCIETY AND MORAL OPINION

No doubt we would all agree that a consensus of moral opinion on certain matters is essential if society is to be worth living in. Laws against murder, theft, and much else would be of little use if they were not supported by a widely diffused conviction that what these laws forbid is also immoral. So much is obvious. But it does not follow that everything to which the moral vetoes of accepted morality attach is of equal importance to society; nor is there the slightest reason for thinking of morality as a seamless web: one which will fall to pieces carrying society with it, unless all its emphatic vetoes are enforced by law. Surely even in the face of the moral feeling that is up to concert pitch – the trio of intolerance, indignation, and disgust – we must pause to think. We must ask a question at two different levels which Sir Patrick never clearly enough identifies or separates. First, we must ask whether a practice which offends moral feeling is harmful, independently of its repercussion on the general moral code. Secondly, what about repercussion on the moral code? Is it really true that failure to translate this item of general morality into criminal law will jeopardize the whole fabric of morality and so of society?

We cannot escape thinking about these two different questions merely by repeating to ourselves the vague nostrum: 'This is part of public morality and public morality must be preserved if society is to exist.' Sometimes Sir Patrick seems to admit this, for he says in words which both Mill and the Wolfenden Report might have used, that there must be the maximum respect for individual liberty consistent with the integrity of society. Yet this, as his contrasting examples of fornication and homosexuality show, turns out to mean only that the immorality which the law may punish must be generally felt to be intolerable. This plainly is no adequate substitute for a reasoned estimate of the damage to the fabric of society likely to ensure if it is not suppressed.

Nothing perhaps shows more clearly the inadequacy of Sir Patrick's approach to this problem than his comparison between the suppression of sexual immorality and the suppression of treason or subversive activity. Private subversive activity is, of course, a contradiction in terms because 'subversion' means overthrowing government, which is a public thing. But it is grotesque, even where moral feeling against homosexuality is up to concert pitch, to think of the homosexual behaviour of two adults in private as in any way like treason or sedition either in intention or effect. We can make it seem like treason only if we assume that deviation from a general moral code is bound to affect that code, and to lead not merely to its modification but to its destruction. The analogy could begin to be plausible only if it was clear that offending against this item of morality was likely to jeopardise the whole structure. But we have ample evidence for believing that people will not abandon morality, will not think any better of murder, cruelty, and dishonesty, merely because some private sexual practice which they abominate is not punished by the law.

Because this is so the analogy with treason is absurd. Of course 'No man is an island': what one man does in private, if it is known, may affect others in many different ways. Indeed it may be that deviation from general sexual morality by those whose lives, like the lives of many homosexuals, are noble ones and in all other ways exemplary will lead to what Sir Patrick calls the shifting of the limits of tolerance. But if this has any analogy in the sphere of government it is not the overthrow of ordered government, but a peaceful change in its form. So we may listen to the prompting of common sense and of logic, and say that though there could not logically be a sphere of private treason there is a sphere of private morality and immorality.

Sir Patrick's doctrine is also open to a wider, perhaps a deeper, criticism. In his reaction against a rationalist morality and his stress on feeling, he has I think thrown out the baby and kept the bath water; and the bath water may turn out to be very dirty indeed. When Sir Patrick's lecture was first delivered *The Times* greeted it with these words: 'There is a moving and welcome humility in the conception that society should not be asked to give its reason for refusing to tolerate what in its heart it feels intolerable'. This drew from a correspondent in Cambridge the retort: 'I am afraid that we are less humble than we used to be. We once burnt old women because, without giving our reasons, we felt in our hearts that witchcraft was intolerable.'

This retort is a bitter one, yet its bitterness is salutary. We are not, I suppose, likely, in England, to take again to the burning of old women for witchcraft or to punishing people for associating with those of a different race or colour, or to punishing people again for adultery. Yet if these things were viewed with intolerance, indignation, and disgust, as the second of them still is in some countries, it seems that on Sir Patrick's principles no rational criticism could be opposed to the claim that they should be punished by law. We could only pray, in his words, that the limits of tolerance might shift.

CURIOUS LOGIC

It is impossible to see what curious logic has led Sir Patrick to this result. For him a practice is immoral if the thought of it makes the man on the Clapham omnibus sick. So be it. Still, why should we not summon all the resources of our reason, sympathetic understanding, as well as critical intelligence, and insist that before general moral feeling is turned into criminal law it is submitted to scrutiny of a different kind from Sir Patrick's? Surely, the legislator should ask whether the general morality is based on ignorance, superstition, or misunderstanding; whether there is a false conception that those who practise what it condemns are in other ways dangerous or hostile to society; and whether the misery to many parties, the blackmail and the other evil consequences of criminal punishment, especially for sexual offences, are well understood. It is surely extraordinary that among the things which Sir Patrick says are to be considered before we legislate against immorality these appear nowhere: not even as 'practical considerations,' let alone 'theoretical limits.' To any theory which, like this one, asserts that the criminal law may be used on the vague ground that the preservation of morality is essential to society and yet omits to stress the need for critical scrutiny, our reply should be: 'Morality, what crimes may be committed in thy name!'

As Mill saw, and de Tocqueville showed in detail long ago in his critical but sympathetic study of democracy, it is fatally easy to confuse the democratic principle that power should be in the hands of the majority with the utterly different claim that the majority, with power in their hands, need respect no limits. Certainly there is a special risk in a democracy that the majority may dictate how all should live. This is the risk we run, and should gladly run; for it is the price of all that is so good in democratic rule. But loyalty to democratic principles does not require us to maximize this risk: yet this is what we shall do if we mount the man in the street on the top of the Clapham omnibus and tell him that if only he feels sick enough about what other people do in private to demand its suppression by law no theoretical criticism can be made of his demand.

7 'Philosophical approaches to criminalization: consent and the harm principle'

In this extract from a Law Commission consultation paper (Appendix C to Law Commission Consultation Paper 139, *Consent in the Criminal Law*, HMSO, 1995) the author gives a clear summary of some of the philosophical implications of the notions of harm and consent. In particular, he shows how those who place a high value on autonomy (the ability to make choices about one's own life), will advocate minimal state interference in people's lives, the limits on this being set by the harm principle. On this liberal view, if two or more people have given genuine and fully informed consent to an activity which may result in injury then they should be immune from prosecution under the criminal law. However, there are many forms of apparent consent which fall short of genuine consent.

CONSENT AND THE CRIMINAL LAW

LIBERAL IDEALS AND VALUES

C.34 Liberalism has as its central value 'liberty' or, in its more modern expression, 'autonomy'.[1] The autonomous life that liberals cherish is the life that can be characterized as (in part) self-determined, self-authored or self-created. The autonomous person is self-possessed, independent, self-reliant and self-disciplined, but not to the extent that these virtues become vices through excess. Autonomy makes a person the sovereign authority over her life. She must choose and develop her own preferences, principles and commitments, live faithfully according to her choices and be responsible for the life she makes for herself. The liberal vision is not of a once-and-for-all career choice compulsively pursued.

Instead, life is seen as an on-going project in which a person may defer decision-making ('keep her options open'), rethink her direction or even change course in mid-stream. It is essential to the liberal's conception of the good life that people should be free to choose, follow and revise their own life projects, to have the opportunity to develop their talents and to indulge their tastes, and to be given the chance of living out a good and fulfilling life.[2] For the liberal, the act of choosing is not a thing of value in itself; somebody with ten choices is not twice as well off as somebody with only five choices. A choice is only valuable in itself if one chooses well. The liberal values the *opportunity* to choose because this is an essential component of a person's goals, projects and achievements being authentically her own. An important aspect of a good and successful life is that she should freely choose her projects and goals and then pursue them herself. The achievement would be greatly diminished if she were forced by someone else to live out that life against her will. It would also be greatly diminish if another person were to choose her life projects and goals on her behalf, unless and until she came to embrace them as her own.[3]

C.35 Describing the ideal of autonomy in this way might give the impression that it is an obsessively individualistic, atomistic or even selfish ideal, which it is not. Its leading advocates, such as Professor Feinberg and Professor Raz, are at pains to emphasize that human existence is a thoroughly social existence.[4] The autonomous life is fashioned from the cultural materials that provide each of us with our horizons of meaning and value, as well as from individual biology and the exercise of free will. People make their own lives, but not in the conditions of their own choosing.

C.36 For the liberal, autonomy is an essential component of living well. However, since individual choice is integral to an autonomous life there is never any guarantee that any particular person will in fact lead an autonomous life: this is up to each individual to choose for her or himself. Any attempt to compel someone else to live autonomously would by that very act betray the ideal of autonomy. To be presented with the opportunity for genuine success implies the possibility of failure:

> One way of caring for the well-being of others is to allow them the opportunity to fail, for therein lies the opportunity to succeed ... In a society built on social, occupational, and geographical mobility, failure is regarded as itself potentially rewarding and enriching. It is part of the process of maturation, growing self-awareness and self-control.[5]

C.37 Most conceivable life choices and projects, particularly those that are the most valuable and worthwhile, carry with them the risk of pain, loss and suffering. Yet the risk of being hurt cannot be eliminated without effacing much or all of what is valuable in that feature of life and, as a result, the value of choosing it:

> [A]nguish, frustration, and even suffering are often part and parcel of rewarding activities and experiences, which depend on the suffering, etc., for their meaning, and therefore for their value as well. The same can be said, to a more limited extent, of pain ... [S]ome contemporary cultures dedicate much effort to the elimination and minimization of pain

and suffering. This has a devastatingly flattening effect on human life, not only eliminating much which is of value in our culture, but also making the generation of deeply rewarding forms of life, relationships, and activities impossible.[6]

C.38 Given these elementary features of our lives and the place of value in them, the necessity for genuine choice between an adequate range of valuable options entails that an autonomous person must have the opportunity to choose wisely or badly, to choose between good and evil.

LIBERALISM AND CRIMINALIZATION

C.39 The centrality of autonomy in the liberal's scheme of values gives him a preference for minimal state intervention in people's lives. The liberal is particularly hostile to state intervention through the mechanism of criminal prohibition and regulation, for the obvious reason that criminalization is the state's most coercive form of social control.[7] What could be more invasive of personal autonomy than a system of prohibitions backed by sanctions, including fines, community service and incarceration, administered and enforced by full-time professional investigators, prosecutors, judges and prison officers? As Raz observes:

> [C]oercion by criminal penalties is a global and indiscriminate invasion of autonomy. Imprisoning a person prevents him from almost all autonomous pursuits. Other forms of coercion may be less severe, but they all invade autonomy, and they all, at least in this world, do it in a fairly indiscriminate way. That is, there is no practical way of ensuring that the coercion will restrict the victims' choice of repugnant options but will not interfere with their other choices.[8]

C.40 The criminal law places direct limits on individual freedom which the liberal wants to keep to a minimum. But that there *must be* limits to individual freedom is implicit in the liberal's own position, for the absolute autonomy of one is incompatible with the autonomy of any others. Brown's freedom to punch Green in the face is clearly at odds with Green's freedom to go about his business without suffering violent assault. The liberal does not value absolute liberty ('licence'), but rather the maximum individual liberty that is compatible with similar liberty for all. That is, the liberal supports the harm and offence principles, as elaborated and augmented for example by Feinberg, but she cannot countenance criminalization on any other basis. For the liberal the harm and offence principles exhaust the moral limits of the criminal law.

C.41 The criminalization of harm to others has a strong intuitive appeal, as was noted above, but it is necessary to say something more at this point about the criminalization of offence. Liberals support the offence principle because some forms of offence can be so extreme and protracted that they unacceptably infringe the autonomy of unwilling observers and are therefore, on liberal principles, legitimate candidates for criminalization.[9] The liberal is, however, extremely cautious in using the criminal law to this end and will only endorse an offence principle that is properly qualified and carefully circumscribed. The reason is clear; since just about every conceivable activity might give offence to *somebody*, *everybody's* autonomy would be severely and unacceptably curtailed if the criminal law routinely targeted offensive conduct. This point is deployed with particular force in response to the argument that conduct should be criminalized solely on the basis that people are repelled by the mere thought of it going on in private. In most cases, people who use this argument are not really claiming that they are *offended* by the conduct, but rather that it is evil and should be stopped. This is a legal moralist argument, to which no liberal would subscribe. But suppose that someone really was offended by the mere thought of, say, consensual 'unnatural sexual intercourse' taking place behind locked doors and closed shutters, to such an extent that his obsession with the thought of it dominated and disrupted his life to a seriously detrimental extent. How would the liberal (or anybody else) deal with this situation? We would surely say that the cause of that person's malady is his own abnormal sensitivity. We might set about helping him to deal with his illness, but we would not pass criminal laws which indiscriminately restrict the freedom of other people with normal sensibilities. The liberal, at any rate, will only countenance criminalizing offence which is extreme and unavoidable, and this can never be said of activity which takes place in private.

CONSENT AND THE HARM PRINCIPLE

C.42 It follows from the fact that liberalism will only countenance interference with individual liberty in order to prevent harm or serious offence to others that it is inconsistent with liberal principles to criminalize self-injury. Self-injury may be in the actor's interests and contribute to his well-being overall, as where a man cuts off his finger to prevent the spread of infection, but the liberal will not interfere with his determination to injure himself even where injury is not in his interests. This man chooses, perversely we may think, to set back his own interests, but he does not wrong himself. From the liberal perspective, his conduct is not within the legitimate province of the criminal law. Moreover, a person who genuinely consents to being harmed by another cannot be said to be wronged in the relevant sense either, as Feinberg explains:

> The harm principle will not justify the prohibition of consensual activities even when they are likely to harm the interests of the consenting parties; its aim is to prevent only those harms that are wrongs.[10]

C.43 Feinberg poses the question whether a person can ever be wronged by conduct to which he has fully consented, and then proceeds to answer it:

> There is a principle of law which emphatically answers this question in the negative: *Volenti non fit injuria* ('To one who has consented no wrong is done'). This ancient maxim is found in the Roman Law and has a central place in all modern legal systems. Perhaps the earliest arguments for it are found in Aristotle's *Nicomachean Ethics*. One person wrongs another, according to Aristotle, when he inflicts harm on him voluntarily, and a harmful infliction is voluntary when it is not the result of compulsion, and is performed in full awareness of all the relevant circumstances including the fact that the action is contrary to the wish of the

person acted upon. Therefore it is impossible for a person to consent to being treated unjustly (wronged) by another, for this would be to consent to being-treated-contrary-to-one's-wishes, which is absurd.[11]

C.44 The liberal position on criminalization and the effect of consent can be derived directly from the principles contained in the last quotation:

It follows from these premises that no one can rightly intervene to prevent a responsible adult from voluntarily doing something that will harm only himself (for such a harm is not a 'wrong'), and also that one person cannot properly be prevented from doing something that will harm another when the latter has voluntarily assumed the risk of harm himself through his free and informed consent.[12]

[F]ully valid consent ought to be a defence to all the crimes that are defined in terms of individuals acting on other individuals, including battery, [serious injury] and murder ... Collaborative behaviour ought never to be criminal when the collaboration is fully voluntary on both sides and no interests other than those of the collaborative parties are directly or substantially affected. (The latter position excludes as proper crimes sodomy, bigamy, adult incest, prostitution, and mutual fighting, among other things.)[13]

CONSENT AND ITS COUNTERFEITS

C.45 There is, however, one thing that needs to be made clear. The liberal position does not entail the assertion that *any* expression of assent on the part of an injured person negates the wrongfulness of the harmful act and thereby precludes the intervention of the criminal law. From the liberal perspective, some real expressions of consent are not legally effective, and some apparent expressions of consent are not real consent at all.

C.46 In particular, some categories of people are not capable of giving valid consent. These include children and young people and those who are mentally or physically disabled. To deny legal effect to the consent of members of these groups (if in fact they are physically capable of indicating their assent) is not incompatible with liberal principles. The liberal ideal of individual autonomy assumes a person who is sufficiently mature and has adequate intellectual capacity to lead an autonomous life.

C.47 Children are thought not to have sufficiently developed characters or to have enough experience of the world to make drastically life-altering choices. Their parents or other legal guardians may therefore make choices on their behalf, in their child's best interests and even against his or her stated preferences, where these are in conflict. Similar considerations apply to the severely incapacitated. But in every case the nature of the choice and the extent of the incapacity are paramount, since children and those who are severely incapacitated must, like everybody else, enjoy the maximum autonomy that is consistent with their condition. Their consent to matters which promote their interests, or are neutral in their effect, should be respected. On the other hand, they are deemed incapable ('incompetent') of giving an effective consent to serious interferences with their interests.

C.48 Another example is provided by the man who is physically incapable of giving his consent. It is consistent with liberal principles for a surgeon to operate on the comatose patient who requires emergency surgery to treat a life-threatening condition because in this case there is no question of the surgeon overriding the patient's revealed preferences.[14] The patient is in no condition either to consent or to withhold consent to the treatment, so that in the absence of indications to the contrary the surgeon proceeds on the safest assumption: that the patient would consent to what is in his best interests were he able to do so. (This assumption does not *supply* consent. It is an alternative basis, consistent with liberal principles, for justifying interference with personal autonomy.) If there are in fact indications to the contrary the situation is very different. If there is reliable information that the patient refuses to have blood transfusions on religious grounds and would choose to die rather than undergo surgery involving a transfusion, he should be left to die. Most people may think that this is not in his best interests, but it is the only way to respect his autonomy.

C.49 A second important consideration is that the conditions under which an apparent consent is given may invalidate that consent, or at least give rise to the strong suspicion that the consent is not genuine. It is consistent with liberal principles for the criminal law to intervene in these cases, because intervention does not in fact override any genuine, voluntary consent to harm. It therefore does not impinge upon individual autonomy.

C.50 Circumstances which reduce or obliterate voluntariness and may invalidate consent include (literal) compulsion (i.e. physical force), coercive threats or offers ('duress') and defective beliefs induced by fraud or mistake.

C.51 The 'perfectly voluntary choice' is an illusion because in the real world choices are never 'perfectly' voluntary. We always choose under a complex of pressures which vary in form and intensity. Of these the irreducible minimum derive from the pressures of personal competence, talents and preferences (which are not the product of our 'perfectly' free choice either). The relevant question is therefore always: is the choice *sufficiently* voluntary to be effective, given its context and the purpose of our inquiry. The judgement 'voluntary enough' is irreducibly context-specific and value-laden, as Feinberg explains:

> [T]he validity of an expression of assent cannot simply be read off the facts or derived from an analysis of the concepts of voluntariness and coercion. How much voluntariness is required for a valid (legally effective) act of consent is at least partly a matter of policy, to be decided by reference to a rule itself justified by the usual legislative reasons of utility and social justice.[15]

C.52 It follows that the voluntariness of consent cannot be gauged by reference to a general rule of universal application. Fact-situations must be investigated in their own terms in order to arrive at tailor-made solutions for the particular problems to which each gives rise.

C.53 This brief survey shows that liberal arguments to justify criminalization are not defeated by any and every expression of apparent consent. An expression of consent might be ineffective due to incapacity or invalidated by coercion. Liberals can give endorsement to provisions of the criminal law that are designed to check on the pedigree and authenticity of apparent consent. But once the true status of the consent is established, the liberal cannot give endorsement to coercive interference with the competent adult's voluntary choice, even where he or she chooses to consent to a setback to his interests.

NOTES

1 See generally, J. Feinberg, *MLCL*, vol. 3, ch. 18 and pp. 206–14; J. Raz, *The Morality of Freedom* (1986), chs 13 and 14.

2 'To form, to revise, and rationally to pursue a conception of the good', in John Rawls's famous formulation. See J. Rawls, 'Kantian Constructivism in Moral Theory', *Journal of Philosophy*, 77 (1980) pp. 517, 525.

3 Professor Will Kymlicka puts it this way: 'no life goes better by being led from the outside according to values the person doesn't endorse. My life only goes better if I'm leading it from the inside, according to my beliefs about value. Praying to God may be a valuable activity, but you have to believe that it's a worthwhile thing to do. You can coerce someone into going to church and making the right physical movements, but you won't make someone's life better that way.' W. Kymlicka, *Liberalism, Community and Culture* (1989), p. 12.

4 J. Feinberg, *MLCL*, vol. 4, ch. 29A; J. Raz, *The Morality of Freedom* (1986), pp. 307–13.

5 J. Raz, *Ethics in the Public Domain* (1994), pp. 14–15.

6 Ibid., p. 19.

7 It should not be thought, however, that the liberal is unconcerned about more subtle forms of coercion. Mill, amongst others, recognized the potential for autonomy to be unjustifiably restricted by the 'tyranny of public opinion': see J. Schonsheck, *On Criminalization: An Essay in the Philosophy of the Criminal Law* (1994), pp. 44–6, 56–9.

8 J. Raz, *The Morality of Freedom* (1986), pp. 418–19.

9 Feinberg offers a list containing amusing and repellent examples of serious offence at *MLCL*, vol. 2, pp.10–13.

10 J. Feinberg, *MLCL*, vol. 1, pp. 35–6.

11 Ibid., p. 115 (footnotes omitted).

12 Ibid., p. 116.

13 J. Feinberg, *MLCL*, vol. 4, p. 165.

14 See para 1.18, n. 42 of the original report.

15 J. Feinberg, *MLCL*, vol. 3, p. 261.

8 'What's wrong with negative liberty'

Charles Taylor

In this article, the full text of which is printed here, the philosopher
Charles Taylor presents some powerful arguments against the idea that a
pure opportunity-concept of freedom is adequate.

Charles M. Taylor, 'What's wrong with negative liberty', in The Idea of Freedom, *ed. A. Ryan (Oxford: Oxford University Press, 1979), 175–93. Reprinted by permission of the author.*

This is an attempt to resolve one of the issues that separate 'positive' and 'negative' theories of freedom, as these have been distinguished in Isaiah Berlin's seminal essay, 'Two Concepts of Liberty'.[1] Although one can discuss almost endlessly the detailed formulation of the distinction, I believe it is undeniable that there are two such families of conceptions of political freedom abroad in our civilization.

Thus there clearly are theories, widely canvassed in liberal society, which want to define freedom exclusively in terms of the independence of the individual from interference by others, be these governments, corporations, or private persons; and equally clearly these theories are challenged by those who believe that freedom resides at least in part in collective control over the common life. We unproblematically recognize theories descended from Rousseau and Marx as fitting in this category.

There is quite a gamut of views in each category. And this is worth bearing in mind, because it is too easy in the course of polemic to fix on the extreme, almost caricatural variants of each family. When people attack positive theories of freedom, they generally have some Left totalitarian theory in mind, according which freedom resides exclusively in exercising collective control over one's destiny in a classless society, the kind of theory which underlies, for instance, official Communism. This view, in its caricaturally extreme form, refuses to recognize the freedoms guaranteed in other societies as genuine. The destruction of 'bourgeois freedoms' is no real loss of freedom, and coercion can be justified in the name of freedom if it is needed to bring into existence the classless society in which alone men are properly free. Men can, in short, be forced to be free.

Even as applied to official Communism, this portrait is a little extreme, although it undoubtedly expresses the inner logic of this kind of theory. But it is an absurd caricature if applied to the whole family of positive conceptions. This includes all those views of modern political life which owe something to the ancient republican tradition, according to which men's ruling themselves is seen as an activity valuable in itself, and not only for instrumental reasons. It includes in its scope thinkers like Tocqueville, and even arguably the J.S. Mill of *On Representative Government*. It has no necessary connection with the view that freedom consists *purely and simply* in the collective control over the common life, or that there is no freedom worth the name outside a context of collective control. And it does not therefore generate necessarily a doctrine that men can be forced to be free.

On the other side, there is a corresponding caricatural version of negative freedom which tends to come to the fore. This is the tough-minded version, going back to Hobbes, or in another way to Bentham, which sees freedom simply as the absence of external physical or legal obstacles. This view will have no truck with other less immediately obvious obstacles to freedom, for instance, lack of awareness, or false consciousness, or repression, or other inner factors of this kind. It holds firmly to the view that to speak for instance of someone's being less free because of false consciousness, is to abuse words. The only clear meaning which can be given to freedom is that of the absence of external obstacles.

I call this view caricatural as a representative portrait of the negative view, because it rules out of court one of the most powerful motives behind the modern defence of freedom as individual independence, viz., the post-Romantic idea that each person's form of self-realization is original to him/her, and can therefore only be worked out independently. This is one of the reasons for the defence of individual liberty by among others J.S. Mill (this time in his *On Liberty*). But if we think of freedom as including something like the freedom of self-fulfilment, or self-realization according to our own pattern, then we plainly have something which can fail for inner reasons as well as because of external obstacles. We can fail to achieve our own self-realization through inner fears, or false consciousness, as well as because of external coercion. Thus the modern notion of negative freedom which gives weight to the securing of each person's right to realize him/herself in his/her own way cannot make do with the Hobbes/Bentham notion of freedom. The moral psychology of these authors is too simple, or perhaps we should say too crude, for its purposes.

Now there is a strange asymmetry here. The extreme caricatural views tend to come to the fore in the polemic, as I mentioned above. But whereas the extreme 'forced-to-be-free' view is one which the opponents of positive liberty try to pin on them as one would expect in the heat of the argument, the proponents of negative liberty themselves often seem anxious to espouse their extreme, Hobbesian view. Thus even Isaiah Berlin, in his eloquent exposition of the two concepts of liberty, seems to quote Bentham[2] approvingly and Hobbes[3] as well. Why is this?

To see this we have to examine more closely what is at stake between the two views. The negative theories, as we saw, want to define freedom in terms of individual independence from others; the positive also want to identify freedom with collective self-government. But behind this lie some deeper differences of doctrines.

Isaiah Berlin points out that negative theories are concerned with the area in which the subject should be left without interference, whereas the positive doctrines are concerned with who or what controls. I should like to put the point behind this in a slightly different way. Doctrines of positive freedom are concerned with a view of freedom which involves essentially the exercising of control over one's life. On this view, one is free only to the extent that one has effectively determined oneself and the shape of one's life. The concept of freedom here is an exercise-concept.

By contrast, negative theories can rely simply on an opportunity-concept, where being free is a matter of what we can do, of what it is open to us to do, whether or not we do anything to exercise these options. This certainly is the case of the crude, original Hobbesian concept. Freedom consists just in there being no obstacle. It is a sufficient condition of one's being free that nothing stand in the way.

But we have to say that negative theories can rely on an opportunity-concept, rather than that they necessarily do so rely, for we have to allow for that part of the gamut of negative theories mentioned above which incorporates some notion of self-realization. Plainly this kind of view can't rely simply on an opportunity-concept. We can't say that someone is free, on a self-realization view, if he is totally unrealized, if for instance he is totally unaware of his potential, if fulfilling it has never even arisen as a question for him, or if he is paralysed by the fear of breaking with some norm which he has internalized but which does not authentically reflect him. Within this conceptual scheme, some degree of exercise is necessary for a man to be thought free. Or if we want to think of the internal bars to freedom as obstacles on all fours with the external ones, then being in a position to exercise freedom, having the opportunity, involves removing the internal barriers; and this is not possible without having to some extent realized myself. So that with the freedom of self-realization, having the opportunity to be free requires that I already be exercising freedom. A pure opportunity-concept is impossible here.

But if negative theories can be grounded on either an opportunity- or exercise-concept, the same is not true of positive theories. The view that freedom involves at least partially collective self-rule is essentially grounded on an exercise-concept. For this view (at least partly) identifies freedom with self-direction, i.e. the actual exercise of directing control over one's life.

But this already gives us a hint towards illuminating the above paradox, that while the extreme variant of positive freedom is usually pinned on its protagonists by their opponents, negative theorists seem prone to embrace the crudest versions of their theory themselves. For if an opportunity-concept is incombinable with a positive theory, but either it or its alternative can suit a negative theory, then one way of ruling out positive theories in principle is by firmly espousing an opportunity-concept. One cuts off the positive theories by the root, as it were, even though one may also pay a price in the atrophy of a wide range of negative theories as well. At least by taking one's stand firmly on the crude side of the negative range, where only opportunity concepts are recognized, one leaves no place for a positive theory to grow.

Taking one's stand here has the advantage that one is holding the line around a very simple and basic issue of principle, and one where the negative view seems to have some backing in common sense. The basic intuition here is that freedom is a matter of being able to do something or other, of not having obstacles in one's way, rather than being a capacity that we have to realise. It naturally seems more prudent to fight the Totalitarian Menace at this last-ditch position, digging in behind the natural frontier of this simple issue, rather than engaging the enemy on the open terrain of exercise-concepts, where one will have to fight to discriminate the good from the bad among such concepts; fight , for instance, for a view of individual self-realization against various notions of collective self-realization, of a nation, or a class. It seems easier and safer to cut all the nonsense off at the start by declaring all self-realization views to be metaphysical hog-wash. Freedom should just be tough-mindedly defined as the absence of external obstacles.

Of course, there are independent reasons for wanting to define freedom tough-mindedly. In particular there is the immense influence of the anti-meta-physical, materialist, natural-science-orientated temper of thought in our civilization. Something of this spirit at its inception induced Hobbes to take the line that he did, and the same spirit goes marching on today. Indeed, it is because of the prevalence of this spirit that the line is so easy to defend, forensically speaking, in our society.

Nevertheless, I think that one of the strongest motives for defending the crude Hobbes–Bentham concept, that freedom is the absence of external obstacles, physical or legal, is the strategic one above. For most of those who take this line thereby abandon many of their own intuitions, sharing as they do with the rest of us in a post-Romantic civilization which puts great value on self-realization, and values freedom largely because of this. It is fear of the Totalitarian Menace, I would argue, which has led them to abandon this terrain to the enemy.

I want to argue that this not only robs their eventual forensic victory of much of its value, since they become incapable of defending liberalism in the form we in fact value it, but I want to make the stronger claim that this Maginot Line mentality actually ensures defeat, as is often the case with Maginot Line mentalities. The Hobbes–Bentham view, I want to argue, is indefensible as a view of freedom.

To see this, let's examine the line more closely, and the temptation to stand on it. The advantage of the view that freedom is the absence of external obstacles is its simplicity. It allows us to say that freedom is being able to do what you want, where what you want is unproblematically understood as what the agent can identify as his desires. By contrast an exercise-concept of freedom requires that we discriminate among motivations. If we are free in the exercise of certain capacities, then we are not free, or less free, when these capacities are in some way unfulfilled or blocked. But the obstacles can be internal as well as external.

And this must be so, for the capacities relevant to freedom must involve some self-awareness, self-understanding, moral discrimination, and self-control, otherwise their exercise couldn't amount to freedom in the sense of self-direction; and this being so, we can fail to be free because these internal conditions are not realized. But where this happens, where, for example, we are quite self-deceived, or utterly fail to discriminate properly the ends we seek, or have lost self-control, we can quite easily be doing what we want in the sense of what we can identify as our wants, without being free; indeed, we can be further entrenching our unfreedom.

Once one adopts a self-realization view, or indeed, any exercise-concept of freedom, then being able to do what one wants can no longer be accepted as a sufficient condition of being free. For this view puts certain conditions on one's motivation. You are not free if you are motivated, through fear, inauthentically internalized standards, or false consciousness, to thwart your self-realization. This is sometimes put by saying that for a self-realization view, you have to be able to do what you really want, or to follow your real will, or to fulfil the desires of your own true self. But these formulas, particularly the last, may mislead, by making us think that exercise-concepts of freedom are tied to some particular metaphysic, in particular that of a higher and lower self. We shall see below that this is far from being the case, and that there is a much wider range of bases for discriminating authentic and inauthentic desires.

In any case, the point for our discussion here is that for any exercise-concept of freedom, being free can't just be a question of doing what you want in the unproblematic sense. It must also be that what you want doesn't run against the grain of your basic purposes, or your self-realization. Or to put the issue in another way, which converges on the same point, the subject himself can't be the final authority on the question whether his desires are authentic, whether they do or do not frustrate his purposes.

To put the issue in this second way is to make more palpable the temptation for defenders of the negative view to hold their Maginot Line. For once we admit that the agent himself is not the final authority on his own freedom, do we not open the way to totalitarian manipulation? Do we not legitimate others, supposedly wiser about his purposes than himself, redirecting his feet on the right path, perhaps even by force, and all this in the name of freedom?

The answer is that of course we don't. Not by this concession alone. For there may be good reasons for holding that others are not likely to be in a better position to understand his real purposes. This indeed plausibly follows from the post-Romantic view above that each person has his/her own original form of realization. Some others, who know us intimately, and who surpass us in wisdom, are undoubtedly in a position to advise us, but no official body can possess a doctrine or a technique whereby they could know how to put us on the rails, because such a doctrine or technique cannot in principle exist if human beings really differ in their self-realization.

Or again, we may hold a self-realization view of freedom, and hence believe that there are certain conditions on my motivation necessary to my being free, but also believe that there are other necessary conditions which rule out my being forcibly led towards some definition of my self-realization by external authority. Indeed, in these last two paragraphs I have given a portrait of what I think is a very widely held view in liberal society, a view which values self-realization, and accepts that it can fail for internal reasons, but which believes that no valid guidance can be provided in principle by social authority, because of human diversity and originality, and holds that the attempt to impose such guidance will destroy other necessary conditions of freedom.

It is however true that totalitarian theories of positive freedom do build on a conception which involves discriminating between motivations. Indeed, one can represent the path from the negative to the positive conceptions of freedom as consisting of two steps: the first moves us from a notion of freedom as doing what one wants to a notion which discriminates motivations and equates freedom with doing what we really want, or obeying our real will, or truly directing our lives. The second step introduces some doctrine purporting to show that we cannot do what we really want or obeying our real will, or truly directing our lives. The second step introduces some doctrine purporting to show that we cannot do what we really want, or follow our real will, outside of a society of a certain canonical form, incorporating true self-government. It follows that we can only be free in such a society, and that being free *is* governing ourselves collectively according to this canonical form.

We might see an example of this second step in Rousseau's view that only a social contract society in which all give themselves totally to the whole preserves us from other-dependence and ensures that we obey only ourselves; or in Marx's doctrine of man as a species-being who realizes his potential in a mode of social production, and who must thus take control of this mode collectively.

Faced with this two-step process, it seems safer and easier to stop it at the first step, to insist firmly that freedom is just a matter of the absence of external obstacles, that it therefore involves no discrimination of motivation and permits in principle no second-guessing of the subject by any one else. This is the essence of the Maginot Line strategy. It is very tempting. But I want to claim that it is wrong. I want to argue that we cannot defend a view of freedom which doesn't involve at least some qualitative discrimination as to motive, i.e. which doesn't put some restrictions on motivations among the necessary conditions of freedom, and hence which could rule out second-guessing in principle.

There are some considerations one can put forward straight off to show that the pure Hobbesian concept won't work, that there are some discriminations among motivations which are essential to the concept of freedom as we use it. Even where we think of freedom as the absence of external obstacles, it is not the absence of such obstacles *simpliciter*. For we make discriminations between obstacles as representing more or less serious infringements of freedom. And we do this, because we deploy the concept against a background understanding that certain goals and activities are more significant than others.

Thus we could say that my freedom is restricted if the local authority puts up a new traffic light at an intersection close to my home; so that where previously I could cross as I liked, consistently with avoiding collision with other cars, now I have to wait until the light is green. In a philosophical argument, we might call this a restriction of freedom, but not in a serious political debate. The reason is that it is too trivial, the activity and purposes inhibited here are not really significant. It is not just a matter of our having made a trade-off and considered that a small loss of liberty was worth fewer traffic accidents, or less danger for the children; we are reluctant to speak here of a loss of liberty at all; what we feel we are trading off is convenience against safety.

By contrast a law which forbids me from worshipping according to the form I believe in is a serious blow to liberty; even a law which tried to restrict this to certain times (as the traffic light restricts my crossing of the intersection to certain times) would be seen as a serious restriction. Why this difference between the two cases? Because we have a background understanding, too obvious to spell out, of some activities and goals as highly significant for human beings and others as less so. One's religious belief is recognized, even by atheists, as supremely important, because it is that by which the believer defines himself as a moral being. By contrast my rhythm of movement through the city traffic is trivial. We don't want to speak of these two in the same breath. We don't even readily admit that liberty is at stake in the traffic light case. For *de minimis non curat libertas*.

But this recourse to significance takes us beyond a Hobbesian scheme. Freedom is no longer just the absence of external obstacle *tout court*, but the absence of external obstacle to significant action, to what is important to man. There are discriminations to be made; some restrictions are more serious than others, some are utterly trivial. About many, there is of course controversy. But what the judgement turns on is some sense of what is significant for human life. Restricting the expression of people's religious and ethical convictions is more significant than restricting their movement around uninhabited parts of the country; and both are more significant than the trivia of traffic control.

But the Hobbesian scheme has no place for the notion of significance. It will allow only for purely quantitative judgements. On the toughest-minded version of his conception, where Hobbes seems to be about to define liberty in terms of the absence of physical obstacles, one is presented with the vertiginous prospect of human freedom being measurable in the same way as the degrees of freedom of some physical object, say a lever. Later we see that this won't do, because we have to take account of legal obstacles to my action. But in any case, such a quantitative conception of freedom is a non-starter.

Consider the following diabolical defence of Albania as a free country. We recognize that religion has been abolished in Albania, whereas it hasn't been in Britain. But on the other hand there are probably far fewer traffic lights per head in Tirana than in London. (I haven't checked for myself, but this is a very plausible assumption.) Suppose an apologist for Albanian Socialism were nevertheless to claim that this country was freer than Britain, because the number of acts restricted was far smaller. After all, only a minority of Londoners practise some religion in public places, but all have to negotiate their way through traffic. Those who do practise a religion generally do so on one day of the week, while they are held up at traffic lights every day. In sheer quantitative terms, the number of acts restricted by traffic lights must be greater than that restricted by a ban on public religious practice. So if Britain is considered a free society, why not Albania?

So the application even of our negative notion of freedom requires a background conception of what is significant, according to which some restrictions are seen to be without relevance for freedom altogether, and others are judged as being of greater and lesser importance. So some discrimination among motivations seems essential to our concept of freedom. A minute's reflection shows why this must be so. Freedom is important to us because we are purposive beings. But then there must be distinctions in the significance of different kinds of freedom based on the distinction in the significance of different purposes.

But of course, this still doesn't involve the kind of discrimination mentioned above, the kind which would allow us to say that someone who was doing what he wanted (in the unproblematic sense) wasn't really free, the kind of discrimination which allows us to put conditions on people's motivations necessary to their being free, and hence to second-guess them. All we have shown is that we make discriminations between more or less significant freedoms, based on discriminations among the purposes people have.

This creates some embarrassment for the crude negative theory, but it can cope with it by simply adding a recognition that we make judgements of significance. Its central claim that freedom just is the absence of external obstacles seems untouched, as also its view of freedom as an opportunity-concept. It is just that we now have to admit that not all opportunities are equal.

But there is more trouble in store for the crude view when we examine further what these qualitative discriminations are based on. What lies behind our judging certain purposes/feelings as more significant than others? One might think that there was room here again for another quantitative theory; that the more significant purposes are those we want more. But this account is either vacuous or false.

It is true but vacuous if we take wanting more just to mean being more significant. It is false as soon as we try to give wanting more an independent criterion, such as for instance, the urgency or force of a desire, or the prevalence of one desire over another, because it is a matter of the most banal experience that the purposes we know to be more significant are not always those which we desire with the greatest urgency to encompass, nor the ones that actually always win out in cases of conflict of desires.

When we reflect on this kind of significance, we come up against what I have called elsewhere the fact of strong evaluation, the fact that we human subjects are not only subjects of first-order desires, but of second-order desires, desires about desires. We experience our desires and purposes as qualitatively discriminated, as higher or lower, noble or base, integrated or fragmented, significant or trivial, good and bad. This means that we experience some of our desires and goals as intrinsically more significant than others: some passing comfort is less important than the fulfilment of our lifetime vocation, our *amour propre* less important than a love relationship; while we experience some others as bad, not just comparatively, but absolutely: we desire not to be moved by spite, or some childish desire to impress at all costs. And these judgements of significance are quite independent of the strength of the respective desires: the craving for comfort may be overwhelming at this moment, we may be obsessed with our *amour propre*, but the judgement of significance stands.

But then the question arises whether this fact of strong evaluation doesn't have other consequences for our notion of freedom, than just that it permits us to rank freedoms in importance. Is freedom not at stake when we find ourselves carried away by a less significant goal to override a highly significant one? Or when we are led to act out of a motive we consider bad or despicable?

The answer is that we sometimes do speak in this way. Suppose I have some irrational fear, which is preventing me from doing something I very much want to do. Say the fear of public speaking is preventing me from taking up a career that I should find very fulfilling, and that I should be quite good at, if I could just get over this 'hang-up'. It is clear that we experience this fear as an obstacle, and that we feel we are less than we would be if we could overcome it.

Or again, consider the case where I am very attached to comfort. To go on short rations, and to miss my creature comforts for a time, makes me very depressed. I find myself making a big thing of this. Because of this reaction I can't do certain things that I should like very much to do, such as going on an expedition over the Andes, or a canoe trip in the Yukon. Once again, it is quite understandable if I experience this attachment as an obstacle, and feel that I should be freer without it.

Or I could find that my spiteful feelings and reactions which I almost can't inhibit are undermining a relationship which is terribly important to me. At times, I feel as though I am almost assisting as a helpless witness at my own destructive behaviour, as I lash out again with my unbridled tongue at her. I long to be able not to feel this spite. As long as I feel it, even control is not an option, because it just builds up inside until it either bursts out, or else the feeling somehow communicates itself, and queers things between us. I long to be free of this feeling.

These are quite understandable cases, where we can speak of freedom or its absence without strain. What I have called strong evaluation is essentially involved here. For these are not just cases of conflict, even cases of painful conflict. If the conflict is between two desires with which I have no trouble identifying, there can be no talk of lesser freedom, no matter how painful or fateful. Thus if what is breaking up my relationship is my finding fulfilment in a job which, say, takes me away from home a lot, I have indeed a terrible conflict, but I would have no temptation to speak of myself as less free.

Even seeing a great difference in the significance of the two terms doesn't seem to be a sufficient condition of my wanting to speak of freedom and its absence. Thus my marriage may be breaking because I like going to the pub and playing cards on Saturday nights with the boys. I may feel quite unequivocally that my marriage is much more important than the release and comradeship of the Saturday night bash. But nevertheless I wouldn't want to talk of my being freer if I could slough off this desire.

The difference seems to be that in this case, unlike the ones above, I still identify with the less important desire, I still see it is as expressive of myself, so that I couldn't lose it without altering who I am, losing something of my personality. Whereas my irrational fear, my being quite distressed by discomfort, my spite – these are all things which I can easily see myself losing without any loss whatsoever to what I am. This is why I can see them as obstacles to my purposes, and hence to my freedom, even though they are in a sense unquestionably desires and feelings of mine.

Before exploring further what's involved in this, let's go back and keep score. It would seem that these cases make a bigger breach in the crude negative theory. For they seem to be cases in which the obstacles to freedom are internal; and if this is so, then freedom can't simply be interpreted as the absence of external obstacles; and the fact that I'm doing what I want, in the sense of following my strongest desire, isn't sufficient to establish that I'm free. On the contrary, we have to make discriminations among motivations, and accept that acting out of some motivations, for example irrational fear or spite, or this too great need for comfort, is not freedom, is even a negation of freedom.

But although the crude negative theory can't be sustained in the face of these examples, perhaps something which springs from the same concerns can be reconstructed. For although we have to admit that there are internal, motivational, necessary conditions for freedom, we can perhaps still avoid any legitimation of what I called above the second-guessing of the subject. If our negative theory allows for strong evaluation, allows that some goals are really important to us, and that other desires are seen as not fully ours, then can it not retain the thesis that freedom is being able to do what I want, that is, what I can identify myself as wanting, where this means not just what I identify as my strongest desire, but what I identify as my true, authentic desire or purpose? The subject would still be the final arbiter of his being free/unfree, as indeed he is clearly capable of discerning this in the examples above, where I relied precisely on the subject's own experience of constraint, of motives with which he can't identify. We should have sloughed off the untenable Hobbesian reductive-materialist metaphysics, according to which only external obstacles count, as though action were just movement, and there could be no internal, motivational obstacles to our deeper purposes. But we would be retaining the basic concern of the negative theory, that the subject is still the final authority as to what his freedom consists in, and cannot be second-guessed by external authority. Freedom would be modified to read: the absence of internal or external obstacle to what I truly or authentically want. But we would still be holding the Maginot Line. Or would we?

I think not, in fact. I think that this hybrid or middle position is untenable, where we are willing to admit that we can speak of what we truly want, as against what we most strongly desire, and of some desires as obstacles to our freedom, while we still will not allow for second-guessing. For to rule this out in principle is to rule out in principle that the subject can ever be wrong about what he truly wants. And how can he never, in principle, be wrong, unless there is nothing to be wrong about in this matter?

That in fact is the thesis our negative theorist will have to defend. And it is a plausible one for the same intellectual (reductive-empiricist) tradition from which the crude negative theory springs. On this view, our feelings are brute facts about us; that is, it is a fact about us that we are affected in such and such a way, but our feelings can't themselves be understood as involving some perception or sense of what they relate to, and hence as potentially veridical or illusory, authentic or inauthentic. On this scheme, the fact that a certain desire represented one of our fundamental purposes, and another a mere force with which we cannot identify, would concern merely the brute quality of the affect in both cases. It would be a matter of the raw feel of these two desires that this was their respective status.

In such circumstances, the subject's own classification would be incorrigible. There is no such thing as an imperceptible raw feel. If the subject failed to experience a certain desire as fundamental, and if what we meant by 'fundamental' applied to the desire was that the felt experience of it has a certain quality, then the desire couldn't be fundamental. We can see this if we look at those feelings which we can agree are brute in this sense: for instance, the stab of pain I feel when the dentist jabs into my tooth, or the crawling unease when someone runs his fingernail along the blackboard. There can be no question of misperception here. If I fail to 'perceive' the pain, I am not in pain. Might it not be so with our fundamental desires, and those which we repudiate?

The answer is clearly no. For first of all, many of our feelings and desires, including the relevant ones for these kinds of conflicts, are not brute. By contrast with pain and the fingernail-on-blackboard sensation, shame and fear, for instance, are emotions which involve our experiencing the situation as bearing a certain import for us, as being dangerous or shameful. This is why shame and fear can be inappropriate, or even irrational, where pain and a *frisson* cannot. Thus we can be in error in feeling shame or fear. We can even be consciously aware of the unfounded nature of our feelings, and this is when we castigate them as irrational.

Thus the notion that we can understand all our feelings and desires as brute, in the above sense, is not on. But more, the idea that we could discriminate our fundamental desires, or those which we want to repudiate, by the quality of brute affect is grotesque. When I am convinced that some career, or an expedition in the Andes, or a love relationship, is of fundamental importance to me (to recur to the above examples), it cannot be just because of the throbs, *élans*, or tremors I feel; I must also have some sense that these are of great significance for me, meet important, long-lasting needs, represent a fulfilment of something central to me, will bring me closer to what I really am, or something of the sort. The whole notion of our identity, whereby we recognize that some goals, desires, allegiances are central to what we are, while others are not or are less so, can make sense only against a background of desires and feelings which are not brute, but what I shall call import-attributing, to invent a term of art for the occasion.

Thus we have to see our emotional life as made up largely of import-attributing desires and feelings, that is, desires and feelings which we can experience mistakenly. And not only can we be mistaken in this, we clearly must accept, in cases like the above where we want to repudiate certain desires, that we are mistaken.

For let us consider the distinction mentioned above between conflicts where we feel fettered by one desire, and those where we do not, where, for instance, in the example mentioned above, a man is torn between his career and his marriage. What made the difference was that in the case of genuine conflict both desires are the agent's, whereas in the cases where he feels fettered by one, this desire is one he wants to repudiate.

But what is it to feel that a desire is not truly mine? Presumably, I feel that I should be better off without it, that I don't lose anything in getting rid of it, I remain quite complete without it. What could lie behind this sense?

Well, one could imagine feeling this about a brute desire. I may feel this about my addiction to smoking, for instance – wish I could get rid of it, experience it as a fetter, and believe that I should be well rid of it. But addictions are a special case; we understand them to be unnatural, externally induced desires. We couldn't say in general that we are ready to envisage losing our brute desires without a sense of diminution. On the contrary, to lose my desire for, and hence delectation in, oysters, mushroom pizza, or Peking duck would be a terrible deprivation. I should fight against such a change with all the strength at my disposal.

So being brute is not what makes desires repudiable. And besides, in the above examples the repudiated desires aren't brute. In the first case, I am chained by unreasoning fear, an import-attributing emotion, in which the fact of being mistaken is already recognized when I identify the fear as irrational or unrea-soning. Spite, too, which moves me in the third case, is an import-attributing emotion. To feel spite is to see oneself and the target of one's resentment in a certain light; it is to feel in some way wounded, or damaged, by his success or good fortune, and the more hurt the more he is fortunate. To overcome feelings of spite, as against just holding them in, is to come to see self and other in a different light, in particular, to set aside self-pity, and the sense of being person-ally wounded by what the other does and is.

(I should also like to claim that the obstacle in the third example, the too great attachment to comfort, while not itself import-attributing is also bound up with the way we see things. The problem is here not just that we dislike discomfort, but that we are too easily depressed by it; and this is something which we over-come only by sensing a different order of priorities, whereby small discomforts matter less. But if this is thought too dubious, we can concentrate on the other two examples.)

Now how can we feel that an import-attributing desire is not truly ours? We can do this only if we see it as mistaken, that is, the import or the good it suppos-edly gives us a sense of is not a genuine import or good. The irrational fear is a fetter, because it is irrational; spite is a fetter because it is rooted in a self-absorp-tion which distorts our perspective on everything, and the pleasures of venting it preclude any genuine satisfaction. Losing these desires we lose nothing, because their loss deprives us of no genuine good or pleasure or satisfaction. In this they are quite different from my love of oysters, mushroom pizza, and Peking duck.

It would appear from this that to see our desires as brute gives us no clue as to why some of them are repudiable. On the contrary it is precisely their not being brute which can explain this. It is because they are import-attributing desires which are mistaken that we can feel that we would lose nothing in sloughing them off. Everything which is truly important to us would be safeguarded. If they were just brute desires, we couldn't feel this unequivocally, as we certainly do not when it comes to the pleasures of the palate. True, we also feel that our desire to smoke is repudiable, but there is a special explanation here, which is not available in the case of spite.

Thus we can experience some desires as fetters, because we can experience them as not ours. And we can experience them as not ours because we see them as incorporating a quite erroneous appreciation of our situation and of what matters to us. We can see this again if we contrast the case of spite with that of another emotion which partly overlaps, and which is highly considered in some societies, the desire for revenge. In certain traditional societies, this is far from being considered a despicable emotion. On the contrary, it is a duty of honour on a male relative to avenge a man's death. We might imagine that this too might give rise to conflict. It might conflict with the attempts of a new regime to bring some order to the land. The government would have to stop people taking vengeance, in the name of peace.

But short of a conversion to a new ethical outlook, this would be seen as a trade-off, the sacrifice of one legitimate goal for the sake of another. And it would seem monstrous were one to propose reconditioning people so that they no longer felt the desire to avenge their kin. This would be to unman them.[4]

Why do we feel so different about spite (and for that matter also revenge)? Because the desire for revenge for an ancient Icelander was his sense of a real obligation incumbent on him, something it would be dishonourable to repudiate; while for us, spite is the child of a distorted perspective on things.

We cannot therefore understand our desires and emotions as all brute, and in particular we cannot make sense of our discrimination of some desires as more important and fundamental, or of our repudiation of others, unless we understand our feelings to be import-attributing. This is essential to there being what we have called strong evaluation. Consequently the half-way position which admits strong evaluation, admits therefore that there may be inner obstacles to freedom, and yet will not admit that the subject may be wrong or mistaken about these purposes – this position doesn't seem tenable. For the only way to make the subject's assessment incorrigible in principle would be to claim that there was nothing to be right or wrong about here; and that could only be so if experiencing a given feeling were a matter of the qualities of brute feeling. But this it cannot be if we are to make sense of the whole background of strong evaluation, more significant goals, and aims that we repudiate. This whole scheme requires that we understand the emotions concerned as import-attributing as, indeed, it is clear that we must do on other grounds as well.

But once we admit that our feelings are import-attributing, then we admit the possibility of error, or false appreciation. And indeed, we have to admit a kind of false appreciation which the agent himself detects in order to make sense of the cases where we experience our own desires as fetters. How can we exclude in principle that there may be other false appreciations which the agent does not detect? That he may be profoundly in error, that is have a very distorted sense of his fundamental purposes? Who can say that such people can't exist? All cases are, of course, controversial; but I should nominate Charles Manson and Andreas Baader for this category, among others. I pick them out as people with a strong sense of some purposes and goals as incomparably more fundamental than others, or at least with a propensity to act the having such a sense so as to take in even themselves a good part of the time, but whose sense of fundamental purpose was shot through with confusion and error. And once we recognize such extreme cases, how avoid admitting that many of the rest of mankind can suffer to a lesser degree from the same disabilities?

What has this got to do with freedom? Well, to resume what we have seen:

our attributions of freedom make sense against a background sense of more and less significant purposes, for the question of freedom/unfreedom is bound up with the frustration/fulfilment of our purposes. Further, our significant purposes can be frustrated by our own desires, and where these are sufficiently based on misappreciation, we consider them as not really ours, and experience them as fetters. A man's freedom can therefore be hemmed in by internal, motivational obstacles, as well as external ones. A man who is driven by spite to jeopardize his most important relationships, in spite of himself, as it were, or who is prevented by unreasoning fear from taking up the career he truly wants, is not really made more free if one lifts the external obstacles to his venting his spite or acting on his fear. Or at best he is liberated into a very impoverished freedom.

If through linguistic/ideological purism one wants to stick to the crude definition, and insist that men are equally freed for whom the same external obstacles are lifted, regardless of their motivational state, then one will just have to introduce some other term to mark the distinction, and say that one man is capable of taking proper advantage of his freedom, and the other (the one in the grip of spite, or fear) is not. This is because in the meaningful sense of 'free', that for which we value it, in the sense of being able to act on one's important purposes, the internally fettered man is not free. If we choose to give 'free' a special (Hobbesian) sense which avoids this issue, we'll just have to introduce another term to deal with it.

Moreover since we have already seen that we are always making judgements of degrees of freedom, based on the significance of the activities or purposes which are left unfettered, how can we deny that the man, externally free but still stymied by his repudiated desires, is less free than one who has no such inner obstacles?

But if this is so, then can we not say of the man with a highly distorted view of his fundamental purpose, the Manson or Baader of my discussion above, that he may not be significantly freer when we lift even the internal barriers to his doing what is in line with this purpose, or at best may be liberated into a very impoverished freedom? Should a Manson overcome his last remaining compunction against sending his minions to kill on caprice, so that he could act unchecked, would we consider him freer, as we should undoubtedly consider the man who had done away with spite or unreasoning fear? Hardly, and certainly not to the same degree. For what he sees as his purpose here partakes so much of the nature of spite and unreasoning fear in the other cases, that is, it is an aspiration largely shaped by confusion, illusion, and distorted perspective.

Once we see that we make distinctions of degree and significance in freedoms depending on the significance of the purpose fettered/enabled, how can we deny that it makes a difference to the degree of freedom not only whether one of my basic purposes is frustrated by my own desires but also whether I have grievously misidentified this purpose? The only way to avoid this would be to hold that there is no such thing as getting it wrong, that your basic purpose is just what you feel it to be. But there is such a thing as getting it wrong, as we have seen, and the very distinctions of significance depend on this fact.

But if this is so, then the crude negative view of freedom, the Hobbesian definition, is untenable. Freedom can't just be the absence of external obstacles, for there may also be internal ones. And nor may the internal obstacles be just confined to those that the subject identifies as such, so that he is the final arbiter; for he may be profoundly mistaken about his purposes and about what he wants to repudiate. And if so, he is less capable of freedom in the meaningful sense of the word. Hence we cannot maintain the incorrigibility of the subject's judgements about his freedom, or rule out second-guessing, as we put it above. And at the same time, we are forced to abandon the pure opportunity-concept of freedom.

For freedom now involves my being able to recognize adequately my more important purposes, and my being able to overcome or at least neutralize my motivational fetters, as well as my way being free of external obstacles. But clearly the first condition (and, I would argue, also the second) require me to have become something, to have achieved a certain condition of self-clairvoyance and self-understanding. I must be actually exercising self-understanding in order to be truly or fully free. I can no longer understand freedom just as an opportunity-concept.

In all these three formulations of the issue – opportunity- versus exercise-concept; whether freedom requires that we discriminate among motivations; whether it allows of second-guessing the subject – the extreme negative view shows up as wrong. The idea of holding the Maginot Line before this Hobbesian concept is misguided not only because it involves abandoning some of the most inspiring terrain of liberalism, which is concerned with individual self-realization, but also because the line turns out to be untenable. The first step from the Hobbesian definition to a positive notion, to a view of freedom as the ability to fulfil my purposes, is one we cannot help taking. Whether we must also take the second step, to a view of freedom which sees it as realizable or fully realizable only within a certain form of society; and whether in taking a step of this kind one is necessarily committed to justifying the excesses of totalitarian oppression in the name of liberty; these are questions which must now be addressed. What is certain is that they cannot simply be evaded by a philistine definition of freedom which relegates them by fiat to the limbo of metaphysical pseudo-questions. This is altogether too quick a way with them.

NOTES

1   *Four Essays on Liberty* (Oxford, 1969), pp. 118–72.
2   *Four Essays*, p. 148 n.1.
3   Ibid., p. 164.
4   Compare the unease we feel at the reconditioning of the hero of Anthony Burgess's *A Clockwork Orange*.

Appendix: Reasoning

This appendix provides an introduction to argument structure and provides some answers to the question 'What is philosophy?'

ARGUMENT STRUCTURE

ARGUMENT

First of all it's important to establish what philosophers mean when they talk about arguments. An argument provides reasons or evidence in support of a conclusion. Arguments are very different from mere assertions. It is probably easiest to demonstrate this with some examples.

Here is an assertion:

'God doesn't exist'

This is the sort of statement you might hear in ordinary conversation, one that can have profound significance for how you choose to live. But why should anyone believe it? As it stands it is simply an unsupported declaration of one person's belief: it may even be a prejudice, a view the speaker has arrived at without bothering to consider reasons or evidence for or against it. The obvious question to ask is 'Why?', 'Why do you believe that God doesn't exist?' As soon as the speaker provides some reasons in support of the view, it ceases to be mere assertion and becomes part of an argument, though not necessarily a good one. Our speaker might back up the initial assertion in this way:

'Because if God did exist, then children wouldn't ever die of incurable diseases.'

This statement alone does not lead to the conclusion 'God does not exist'. But in most contexts it would be fairly obvious that the speaker meant you to realize that some children do actually die of incurable diseases. This belief about children dying is unstated, or implicit. If we make it explicit, then we get:

1   If God did exist, then children wouldn't ever die of incurable diseases.
2   Some children do die of incurable diseases.
3   So God doesn't exist.

(1) and (2) are premises from which the conclusion (3) is supposed to follow. Premises are the building blocks of arguments.

So, if we assume for the sake of argument that it is true that if God existed, then children wouldn't die of incurable diseases, *and* that some children do in fact die in this way, does it follow that God doesn't exist? Logically it *does* follow: *if* these two premises are true, then the conclusion (that God doesn't exist) *must* be true. This is one version of what is traditionally known as the Problem of Evil: the problem of how a kind and all-powerful God could allow human suffering given that He, She or It would want to eliminate suffering and also would have the power to do so.

It's important to realize that I'm not saying that God doesn't exist. I'm merely saying that if the two premises are true, then the conclusion that God doesn't exist must be true. You may well believe that the first premise ('If God did exist, then children wouldn't ever die of incurable diseases') is simply false. And if this is what you believe, then there are many people who share this belief. There may be an explanation of why God allows children to die in this way; certainly philosophers of religion have devoted a great deal of energy to finding such an explanation. But what we are doing here is separating the content of the argument from its structure or form. *When analysing the structure of an argument, we put on one side for the time being the question of whether or not the premises are true. Instead we concentrate on the question of whether or not the conclusion really follows from the premises given.*

Notice that the conclusion 'So God doesn't exist' was the first rather than the last thing said. The word 'conclusion' can be slightly confusing because it suggests that it should come at the end, like the conclusion of a story. But in fact, in ordinary discussion, conclusions are often given before the reasons that support them, and are sometimes sandwiched between reasons. When analysing an argument, however, it is a good idea to rearrange premises and conclusion so that their relationship can be seen clearly.

CONTENT AND FORM

Perhaps it's easier to understand the distinction between content and form of arguments if you consider another argument with the same underlying form as the one above:

If the thief had escaped through your garden, there'd be footprints in the flower-bed.
There are no footprints in the flower-bed.

So the thief did not escape through your garden.

Like the previous argument, if the premises are true, then the conclusion must be true. You can question whether or not the premises are true (for instance, you might think that the thief *could* have got away through your garden without leaving any footprints in the flower-bed). But if they are true, then the structure of the argument is such that it follows that it's true that the thief did not escape through your garden.

Sometimes a conclusion is indicated by words such as 'therefore', 'so', 'it follows that' or something similar. However, this isn't always the case. Often these words are left out because the structure of the argument is fairly obvious and doesn't need to be signposted. Similarly, in some contexts you can leave out a premise that is strictly necessary for the argument. For instance, if I say:

> Grasshoppers are insects.
> So they have six legs.

it is fairly obvious that I intended you to realize that I believe the unstated premise

> All insects have six legs.

even though I hadn't spelt that out. With more complicated arguments, it is often a good idea to make explicit any such unstated premises so that the underlying structure of the argument becomes clear. To make sure you've grasped the idea of implicit premises, try the following exercise.

EXERCISE A.1

What is the unstated premise in each of 1–5 below? For each one, write out your answers in the following form:

> Unstated premise:
> Stated premise:
> Conclusion:

1   Fred is a cat, so of course he likes tuna fish.
2   Your car tyres are bald, so your car will never pass the MOT.
3   George Eliot was a woman, so she was mortal.
4   Studying philosophy helps to improve your thinking skills. So you should study philosophy.
5   I think, therefore I exist.

Now check your answers against those at the end of this appendix.

TRUTH AND VALIDITY

We looked earlier at the following argument:

> If God did exist, then children wouldn't ever die of incurable diseases.
> Some children do die of incurable diseases.
> So God doesn't exist.

This is a valid argument. If the premises are true, then the conclusion must be true. Philosophers use the words 'valid' and 'invalid' only to refer to the structure of *arguments*. An argument cannot be true or false; it can only be valid or invalid. On the other hand, statements, conclusions, assertions, assumptions and premises may be true or false. This use of language differs from everyday uses of the words 'valid' and 'invalid': you will quite often hear people say 'that's a valid point' or 'that view is invalid'. What the speaker means in each case (using the terms as a philosopher would use them) is 'what you said is true' and 'that view is false'. There is a great difference between validity and truth.

A valid argument has a structure that guarantees a true conclusion provided you feed in true premises. It is 'truth-preserving'. You could visualize it as a kind of ticket machine, like the machine that gives you tickets for the Underground. Its machinery is such that (assuming that it is working properly), if you insert genuine coins (= true premises), then you are guaranteed to get a ticket (= a true conclusion). If, however, you use counterfeit money (= false premises), you may or may not get a ticket (= true conclusion); you certainly couldn't be certain of getting a ticket.

For instance, in the argument we've been examining, if the premises are true, then the conclusion that God doesn't exist must be true. If you said that the assumption and premises were true and also that the conclusion was false, you would be contradicting yourself. It would be like saying, 'London is the capital city of England; but London isn't the capital city of England.' However, if one or both of the premises are false, there is no guarantee that the conclusion is true, despite the argument's validity. The question of whether or not an argument is valid can be addressed separately from the question of whether or not its premises and conclusion are true. The question of validity is about the form of the argument; the question of the truth of premises and conclusion is about its content.

Philosophers are particularly keen to present valid arguments with true premises since that's the best way of guaranteeing true conclusions. They use the word 'sound' to describe any valid argument with true premises (and therefore, also, a true conclusion).

EXERCISE A.2

At this point it is worth pausing to revise some of the key terms introduced so far. The following exercise is meant to give you feedback on your understanding of the material and to give you a chance to put into practice what you've learnt. Don't be discouraged if you don't get the right answers first time around: use the answers and explanations at the end of the appendix to help you revise the material covered.

1   Underline the conclusion in each of the following arguments.

   (a)   Vegetarians don't eat animals. Prawns are animals. I eat prawns. I'm not a vegetarian.
   (b)   Your party cannot win the next election. The only way to win an election is to reduce taxation. Your party won't reduce taxation.

2   Which of the following are valid arguments?

   (a)   Vegetarians don't eat animals. Peanuts are animals. So vegetarians don't eat peanuts.
   (b)   All humans are mortal. Flamingos are birds. So flamingos are mortal.
   (c)   Anyone who buys a lottery ticket has a small chance of winning. My sister has bought a lottery ticket. So she has a small chance of winning.
   (d)   All forms of killing are morally wrong. Capital punishment is a form of killing. Therefore capital punishment is morally wrong.

3   Match the following terms with the appropriate definitions (a)–(h).

   argument
   assertion
   prejudice
   conclusion
   implicit assumption
   sound argument
   premise
   valid argument
   (a) an unstated premise
   (b) a structure that guarantees a true conclusion if the premises are true
   (c) a statement from which an argument's conclusion is derived
   (d) a statement given without providing any reasons or supporting evidence
   (e) a belief that is formed without considering evidence for or against it
   (f) a statement derived from premises and from which it follows
   (g) reasons leading to a conclusion
   (h) a valid argument with true premises.

A FORMAL FALLACY

Like the word 'valid', 'fallacy' is used in a technical way by philosophers. In ordinary conversation you often hear people say 'That's a fallacy', meaning simply that what someone has just said is untrue. However, when philosophers use the word 'fallacy' they usually mean that an argument is invalid. A fallacy in the strict sense, usually known as a formal fallacy, is an invalid argument. An example should clarify this.

Consider the following argument:

All punks wear safety-pins.
Johnny Rotten wears safety-pins.
So Johnny Rotten must be a punk.

Is this a valid argument? Well, at first glance you might take it to be so. One reason for this is that the structure seems quite close to a well-worn example of a valid argument:

All men are mortal.
Socrates was a man.
So Socrates was mortal.

However, if the punk example had precisely the same form, then it would look like this:

All punks wear safety-pins.
Johnny Rotten is a punk.
So Johnny Rotten wears safety-pins.

In fact the argument

All punks wear safety-pins.
Johnny Rotten wears safety-pins.
So Johnny Rotten must be a punk.

is an *invalid* one: it is an example of a fallacy. The conclusion does not follow logically from the premises, regardless of whether or not the conclusion happens to be true. The conclusion is a *non sequitur* (Latin for 'it does not follow'). This is because the way the supposed argument is structured allows for the fact that someone can wear safety-pins and yet not be a punk. One way of understanding this is by thinking in terms of a diagram (Figure A.1).

Circle A stands for the class of punks and circle B for the class of all safety-pin wearers. As you can see, circle A is within circle B, but there is still the possibility of being in circle B without being in circle A. So you cannot conclude from the fact that you are in circle B that you *must* also be in circle A. That's why it is a fallacy: the structure of the argument doesn't reliably give true conclusions, even if you always feed in true premises. The argument is invalid.

Here is a second example of the same fallacy:

All witches keep black cats.
My neighbour keeps a black cat.
So my neighbour must be a witch.

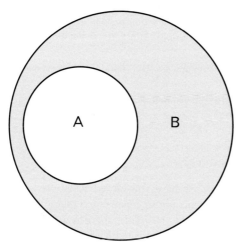

Figure A.1

Again you can see that the conclusion would only follow if the first premise read 'All *and only* witches keep black cats.' But it doesn't say that. So regardless of whether or not it is true that my neighbour is a witch, the argument is fallacious: it is an invalid structure, one which is not truth-preserving. Even if the two premises are true, there can still be people who keep black cats who are not witches. This is precisely the kind of faulty reasoning that has fuelled witch-hunts of various kinds in the past. Such witch-hunts, in addition to using faulty reasoning, were based on the (possibly false) premise that witches actually existed. However, more recent 'witch-hunts', such as the anti-Communist campaign implemented by Senator McCarthy in the 1950s in the United States, often committed the fallacy outlined above. The fact that an individual shared some characteristic with known Communists, such as being interested in workers' rights, was taken as conclusive evidence that this person was a Communist. However, just as having a black cat doesn't make you a witch, being interested in workers' rights doesn't make you a Communist, even if all Communists are interested in workers' rights.

EXERCISE A.3

Which of the following are formal fallacies?

1   All great artists have been slightly crazy. I'm slightly crazy, so I'll end up being a great artist.
2   All babies cry. You're a former baby. So you must have cried.

3   If you break the speed limit, you'll get stopped by the police. You've been stopped by the police. So you must have been speeding.

4   Some philosophers are terrible writers. You're not a philosopher. So you must be a good writer.

5   All fish have gills. Dolphins are fish. Therefore dolphins have gills.

The answers are given at the end of this appendix.

DEDUCTION AND INDUCTION

The examples of arguments we have considered so far have all been deductive arguments. Deductive arguments are so constructed that if the premises are true, then the conclusion must be true. However, there is another important type of argument which does not guarantee the truth of the conclusion even if all the premises are true. Inductive arguments are usually based on evidence which by its nature cannot be conclusive: their conclusions can only ever be *probable*, never certain. For instance, the following is an inductive argument:

All the flamingos I have ever seen were pink.
Therefore all flamingos are pink.

The fact that I have seen quite a few flamingos, and they were all pink, seems to support the conclusion that all flamingos are pink. However, as it only takes one non-pink flamingo to undermine the generalization that all flamingos are pink, I cannot be absolutely sure that every flamingo in the world is pink. For all I know, there are some albino flamingos. If naturalists who have watched flamingos for decades report that they have never seen a flamingo that wasn't pink, this lends further support to my conclusion. Yet even then the slight possibility would remain that a non-pink flamingo might show up. This inductive argument is very different from a deductive one since with a deductive argument, provided that the premises are true, you can be absolutely certain that the conclusion is true. This is not to say that induction is to be despised for its unreliability: we happily rely on inductive reasoning every day of our lives.

EXERCISE A.4

Which of the following are examples of deduction? Which of induction?

1   All gods are immortal. Zeus is a god. So Zeus is immortal.

2   The sun has always risen in the past. So it will rise tomorrow.

3   All the students I have ever met enjoyed studying philosophy. So all students enjoy studying philosophy.

4   If you add the milk too quickly, the sauce will go lumpy. You added the milk too quickly. So the sauce will go lumpy.

5   All mammals are sensitive to pain. Rats are mammals. Therefore rats are sensitive to pain.

The answers are given at the end of this appendix.

EXERCISE A.5

You've now been studying philosophy for some while, but do you have a clear idea what the subject is? Stop and jot down a few notes in answer to the question: *What is philosophy?* It's not an easy question to answer, but try to identify several distinctive features of the subject.

DISCUSSION

When you've written down your own answer, read Extracts 1–4 at the end of this appendix where you will find a range of responses. There is no single right answer to the question: philosophers have at various times disagreed profoundly about the nature of their subject. Thinking about the question yourself, before looking at other people's answers, should have helped to focus your reading.

EXTRACT 1: BRYAN MAGEE, 'WHAT MAKES A THINKER A PHILOSOPHER?'[1]

Any philosopher of any significance must hold at least some beliefs which differentiate him from everyone else, otherwise he would not be significant. Over the millennia almost every imaginable variety of philosophical belief has been held by some philosopher or other. What differentiates a reputable philosopher from disreputable ones is not that there is some 'correct' canonical set of beliefs which he holds but that, whatever his beliefs, he is prepared to put up reasons for them and to see those reasons subjected to scrutiny of the utmost rigour, and to abide by the outcome. He subjects his concepts *and* his arguments *and* his methods to critical analysis, not only on the part of others but on his own part, and lives with the consequences. Provided he does this with full intellectual honesty he can be a Christian or a Hindu or an atheist or anything and be a proper philosopher. Of course, there are some beliefs which have been shown by analysis to be so flawed – incoherent, perhaps, or self-contradictory – that it is now no longer possible, as it might once have been, for someone who is both intelligent and intellectually honest to hold them. The abandonment of such beliefs is part of what constitutes intellectual advance.

EXTRACT 2: WHAT CAN PHILOSOPHY CONTRIBUTE TO PUBLIC DEBATE?[2]

What philosophy can do is to bring to the surface what is already implicit in different arguments or more general positions in a debate. It makes explicit the implications of particular positions and, often just as importantly, it illustrates what those assertions or positions do *not* entail. It demands that any assertion or position should be backed up by arguments, in the form of reasons, for holding the beliefs and commitments which underpin it. And, finally, philosophical investigation can help us to develop criteria for evaluating the arguments that we put forward to substantiate our positions.

EXTRACT 3: MARY WARNOCK, 'WHAT IS THE VALUE OF STUDYING PHILOSOPHY?'[3]

It's very difficult for me to answer the question what the value of studying philosophy is because I've always enjoyed it so much. I do think that, among other things, it's an exceptionally interesting subject because it relates directly to a lot of things that we take for granted, like the way we talk, what we mean when we say things, and presuppositions that we have that we've never looked at before. [...] It's a wonderful subject to teach and learn because of the involvement of dialogue. Philosophers on the whole don't go off in their studies all by themselves: they tend to like to talk to people, and obviously talking is great fun. So it's an enjoyable subject. But I think, as well, that it probably has some effect in clarifying the way people think: being careful not to use words loosely; thinking 'hang on, what do I actually mean? what am I trying to say? and isn't there a better way of saying it?' Now those sorts of habits are very useful to all kinds of different people who are not philosophers at all.

EXTRACT 4: NIGEL WARBURTON, 'WHAT IS PHILOSOPHY?'[4]

What is philosophy? This is a notoriously difficult question. One of the easiest ways of answering it is to say that philosophy is what philosophers do, and then point to the writings of Plato, Aristotle, Descartes, Hume, Kant, Russell, Wittgenstein, Sartre, and other famous philosophers. However, this answer is unlikely to be of much use to you if you are just beginning the subject, as you probably won't have read anything by these writers. Even if you have, it may still be difficult to say what they have in common, if indeed there is a relevant characteristic which they all share. Another approach to the question is to point out that philosophy is derived from the Greek word meaning 'love of wisdom'. However, this is rather vague and even less helpful than saying that philosophy is what philosophers do. So some very general comments about what philosophy is are needed.

Philosophy is an activity: it is a way of thinking about certain sorts of question. Its distinctive feature is its use of logical argument. Philosophers typically deal in arguments: they either invent them, criticize other people's, or do both. They also analyse and clarify concepts. The word 'philosophy' is often used in a much broader sense than this to mean one's general outlook on life, or else to refer to some forms of mysticism. I will not be using the word in this broader sense here: my aim is to illuminate some of the key areas of discussion in a tradition of thought which began with the Ancient Greeks and has flourished in the twentieth century, predominantly in Europe and America.

What kind of things do philosophers working in this tradition argue about? They often examine beliefs that most of us take for granted most of the time. They are concerned with questions about what could loosely be called 'the meaning of life': questions about religion, right and wrong, politics, the nature of the external world, the mind, science, art, and numerous other topics. For instance, most people live their lives without questioning their fundamental beliefs, such as that killing is wrong. But why is it wrong? What justification is there for saying that killing is wrong? Is it wrong in every circumstance? And what do I mean by 'wrong' anyway? These are philosophical questions. Many of our beliefs, when examined, turn out to have firm foundations; but some do not. The study of philosophy not only helps us to think clearly about our prejudices, but also helps to clarify precisely what we do believe. In the process it develops an ability to argue coherently on a wide range of issues – a useful transferable skill.

PHILOSOPHY AND ITS HISTORY

Since the time of Socrates there have been many great philosophers. I named a few of these in my opening paragraph. An introductory book on philosophy could approach the subject historically, analysing the contributions of these philosophers in chronological order. This is not what I shall do here. Instead I will use a topic-based approach: one focusing on particular philosophical questions rather than on history. The history of philosophy is a fascinating and important subject in its own right, and many of the classic philosophical texts are also great works of literature: Plato's Socratic dialogues, René Descartes' *Meditations*, David Hume's *Enquiry Concerning Human Understanding*, and Friedrich Nietzsche's *Thus Spake Zarathustra*, to take just a few examples, all stand out as compelling pieces of writing by any standards. Whilst there is great value in the study of the history of philosophy, my aim here is to give you the tools to think about philosophical issues yourselves rather than simply to explain what certain great figures have thought about them. These issues are not just of interest to philosophers: they arise naturally out of the human situation and many people who have never opened a philosophy book spontaneously think about them.

Any serious study of philosophy will involve a mixture of historical and topic-based study, since if we don't know about the arguments and errors of earlier philosophers, we cannot hope to make a substantial contribution to the subject. Without some knowledge of history philosophers would never progress: they would keep making the same mistakes, unaware that they had been made before. And many philosophers develop their own theories by seeing what is wrong with the work of earlier philosophers. [...]

WHY STUDY PHILOSOPHY?

It is sometimes argued that there is no point in studying philosophy as all philosophers ever do is sit around quibbling over the meaning of words. They never seem to reach any conclusions of any importance and their contribution to society is virtually non-existent. They are still arguing about the same problems that interested the Ancient Greeks. Philosophy does not seem to change anything; philosophy leaves everything as it is.

What is the value of studying philosophy at all? Starting to question the fundamental assumptions of our lives could even be dangerous: we might end up feeling unable to do anything, paralysed by questioning too much. Indeed, the caricature of a philosopher is of someone who is brilliant at dealing with very abstract thought in the comfort of an armchair in an Oxford or Cambridge common room, but is hopeless at dealing with the practicalities of life: someone who can explain the most complicated passages of Hegel's philosophy, but can't work out how to boil an egg.

THE EXAMINED LIFE

One important reason for studying philosophy is that it deals with fundamental questions about the meaning of our existence. Most of us at some time in our lives ask ourselves basic philosophical questions. Why are we here? Is there any proof that God exists? Is there any purpose to our lives? What makes anything right or wrong? Could we ever be justified in breaking the law? Could our lives be just a dream? Is mind different from body, or are we simply physical beings? How does science progress? What is art? And so on.

Most people who study philosophy believe that it is important that each of us examines such questions. Some even argue that an unexamined life is not worth living. To carry on a routine existence without ever examining the principles on which it is based may be like driving a car which has never been serviced. You may be justified in trusting the brakes, the steering, the engine, since they have always worked well enough up until now; but you may be completely unjustified in this trust: the brake pads may be faulty and fail you when you most need them. Similarly the principles on which your life is based may be entirely sound, but until you've examined them, you cannot be certain of this.

However, even if you do not seriously doubt the soundness of the assumptions on which your life is based, you may be impoverishing your life by not exercising your power of thought. Many people find it either too much of an effort, or too disturbing to ask themselves such fundamental questions: they may be happy and comfortable with their prejudices. But others have a strong desire to find answers to challenging philosophical questions.

LEARNING TO THINK

Another reason for studying philosophy is that it provides a good way of learning to think more clearly about a wide range of issues. The methods of philosophical thought can be useful in a wide variety of situations, since by analysing the arguments for and against any position we learn skills which can be transferred to other areas of life. Many people who study philosophy go on to apply their philosophical skills in jobs as diverse as the law, computer programming, management consultancy, the civil service, and journalism — all areas in which clarity of thought is a great asset. Philosophers also use the insights they gain about the nature of human existence when they turn to the arts: a number of philosophers have also been successful as novelists, critics, poets, film-makers and playwrights.

PLEASURE

A further justification for the study of philosophy is that for many people it can be a very pleasurable activity. There is something to be said for this defence of philosophy. Its danger is that it could be taken to be reducing philosophical activity to the equivalent of solving crossword puzzles. At times some philosophers' approach to the subject can seem very like this: some professional philosophers become obsessed with solving obscure logical puzzles as an end in itself, publishing their solutions in esoteric journals. At another extreme, some philosophers working in universities see themselves as part of a 'business', and publish what is often mediocre work simply because it will allow them to 'get on' and achieve promotion (quantity of publications being a factor in determining who is promoted). They experience pleasure from seeing their name in print, and from the increased salary and prestige that go with promotion. Fortunately, however, much philosophy rises above this level.

IS PHILOSOPHY DIFFICULT?

Philosophy is often described as a difficult subject. There are various kinds of difficulty associated with it, some avoidable.

In the first place it is true that many of the problems with which professional philosophers deal do require quite a high level of abstract thought. However, the same is true of almost any intellectual pursuit: philosophy is no different in this respect from physics, literary criticism, computer programming, geology, mathematics, or history. As with these and other areas of study, the difficulty of making substantial original contributions to the subject should not be used as an excuse for denying ordinary people knowledge of advances made in it, nor for preventing them learning their basic methods.

However, there is a second kind of difficulty associated with philosophy which can be avoided. Philosophers are not always good writers. Many of them are extremely poor communicators of their ideas. Sometimes this is because they are only interested in reaching a very small audience of specialist readers; sometimes it is because they use unnecessarily complicated jargon which simply confuses those unfamiliar with it. Specialist terms can be helpful to avoid having to explain particular concepts every time they are used. However, among professional philosophers there is an unfortunate tendency to use specialist terms for their own sake; many of them use Latin phrases even though there are perfectly good English equivalents. A paragraph peppered with unfamiliar words and familiar words used in unfamiliar ways can be intimidating. Some philosophers seem to speak and write in a language they have invented themselves. This can make philosophy appear to be a much more difficult subject than it really is. [...]

THE LIMITS OF WHAT PHILOSOPHY CAN DO

Some students of philosophy have unreasonably high expectations of the subject. They expect it to provide them with a complete and detailed picture of the human predicament. They think that philosophy will reveal to them the meaning of life, and explain to them every facet of our complex existences. Now, although studying philosophy can illuminate fundamental questions about our lives, it does not provide anything like a complete picture, if indeed there could be such a thing. Studying philosophy isn't an alternative to studying art, literature, history, psychology, anthropology, sociology, politics, and science. These different subjects concentrate on different aspects of human life and provide different sorts of insight. Some aspects of anyone's life will defy philosophical analysis, and perhaps analysis of any other kind too. It is important, then, not to expect too much of philosophy.

ANSWERS TO APPENDIX EXERCISES

EXERCISE A.1

1   Unstated premise: All cats like tuna fish.
    Stated premise: Fred is a cat.
    Conclusion: So of course he likes tuna fish.

2   Unstated premise: If your car tyres are bald, your car will never pass the MOT.
    Stated premise: Your car tyres are bald.
    Conclusion: So your car will never pass the MOT.

3   Unstated premise: All women are mortal.
    Stated premise: George Eliot was a woman.
    Conclusion: So she was mortal.

4   Unstated premise: You should study subjects which help to improve your thinking skills.
    Stated premise: Studying philosophy helps to improve your thinking skills.
    Conclusion: So you should study philosophy.

5   Unstated premise: Everything that thinks exists.
    Stated premise: I think.
    Conclusion: Therefore I exist.

EXERCISE A.2

1   (a) I'm not a vegetarian; (b) Your party cannot win the next election.
2   (a) valid (even though one of the premises and the conclusion are false); (b) invalid; (c) valid; (d) valid.
3   a = implicit assumption; b = valid argument; c = premise; d = assertion; e = prejudice; f = conclusion; g = argument; h = sound argument.

EXERCISE A.3

1   Formal fallacy. From the premise 'All great artists have been slightly crazy', it doesn't follow that anyone who is slightly crazy will end up being a great artist.
2   Valid argument.
3   Formal fallacy. Speeding is not the only possible explanation of why you have been stopped by the police. So the conclusion cannot be deduced from the premises.
4   Formal fallacy. The first premise doesn't state that *only* philosophers are terrible writers. So the conclusion does not follow from the premises, since you could still be a terrible writer even though you weren't a philosopher (and, incidentally, you could still be an excellent writer even though you were a philosopher).
5   Valid argument (despite its false premise: dolphins *aren't* fish).

EXERCISE A.4

1   deduction
2   induction
3   induction (provided that I haven't met every student)
4   deduction
5   deduction

NOTES

1   From Bryan Magee, *The Great Philosophers*, Oxford University Press, 1987, p. 66.
2   From Law Commission Consultation Paper 139, *Consent in the Criminal Law*, HMSO Publications, 1995, Appendix C, 'Consent and the criminal law: philosophical foundations', paragraph C4, p. 246.
3   From an interview with Mary Warnock for A103 TV4, recorded February 1996.
4   From Nigel Warburton, *Philosophy: The Basics,* Routledge, revised 3rd edn,1999, pp. 1–7.

Answers to exercises

EXERCISE 1.1

1 murder.
2 beasts of burden, evil, master.
3 obstinate, pig-headed.
4 philistines.
5 never, never, never, slaves.

EXERCISE 1.2

Bear in mind that the answers to this exercise are not all completely clear-cut. (1), (5), (6), (8), (9) and (10) are all straightforward restrictions of negative freedom. (2) almost certainly isn't (unless someone has somehow restricted your growth. (7) probably isn't, unless you are an outstanding footballer whom someone has deliberately prevented from playing football for your country. (4) and (12) could involve restrictions on negative liberty if someone else's actions were making you poor (or at least not rich enough to do the things described).

EXERCISE 1.3

1 positive.
2 negative.
3 positive.
4 negative.
5 negative.
6 positive.

EXERCISE 1.4

1 (a) positive; (b) negative.

2   The metaphor of being master over one's own life, no one's slave, still leaves open the possibility of being a slave to one's own passions. The idea of a higher and rational self (the master), which should keep in check the lower irrational self (the unruly slave), comes from this.

3   Berlin put these words within inverted commas to indicate that he does not necessarily accept that such a nature is *real* or that such a self, if it exists, is *higher*. He is reporting how other people use these words rather than endorsing this way of speaking himself.

4   Berlin claims that some advocates of positive liberty have gone so far as to insist that other people don't necessarily know what they really want, what their higher selves seek. Such advocates of positive liberty may ignore what other people say they want and bully, oppress or torture them on the grounds that that is what their 'real' selves would want. This, they claim, is not coercion, since it is what their victims' 'real' selves wish for. It is not a case of forcing people to do what would be good for them because they can't appreciate what is good for them; it is a matter of forcing people to do what at a level unavailable to them they, allegedly, wish to do.

5   The paradox is that people are forced to do what they say they don't want to do on the grounds that they really do want to do it. What they really want to do, on this analysis, is what they really don't want to do.

EXERCISE 1.5

1   logically necessary.
2   contingent.
3   contingent.
4   contingent.
5   logically necessary.
6   logically necessary.
7   contingent.

EXERCISE 1.6

(2), (4) and (5) consist of a generalization followed by a counter-example.

EXERCISE 2.1

(1) and (3) involve a contradiction. The others do not.

EXERCISE 2.2

1   Yes.
2   No.
3   No.
4   No.

EXERCISE 2.3

(1) and (2) are examples of the companions in guilt move.

EXERCISE 3.1

Answers are included in the main text.

EXERCISE 3.2

Mill would probably count (2), (4), (6), (7) and (11) as unacceptable infringements of liberty.

EXERCISE 3.3

1   necessary, sufficient.
2   sufficient, sufficient, necessary.
3   necessary, sufficient.

EXERCISE 3.4

1   ambiguous: in the context 'bank' could mean the margin of the river or the financial institution you find in a high street.
2   vague: 'east of here' doesn't give precise enough information in the context.
3   vague: a precise age would usually be required.
4   neither vague nor ambiguous: it is possible to make out a case for this being ambiguous since 'small' could refer either to 'business' or to the size of the person offering the service; however, it is hard to imagine that this would be genuinely ambiguous, since the former meaning is much more plausible than the latter.
5   ambiguous: 'on my account' could mean either 'on my behalf' or 'on my bank account'.
6   ambiguous: 'fair' could mean either just or having light coloured hair.

EXERCISE 4.1

Answers are included in the main text.

EXERCISE 4.2

(4) is the best definition of 'playing devil's advocate'.

EXERCISE 4.3

Answers are included in the main text.

EXERCISE 4.4

Answers are included in the main text.

EXERCISE 4.5

1   In order to be virtuous you need to know something about vice. What safer way is there to learn about sin and falsehood than by wide reading? This is the benefit of such reading.

Like Mill, Milton saw value in the expression of false views.

2   How can we trust the censors unless they are incapable of making mistakes and beyond corruption?

Milton's clear implication is that human beings are fallible, and perhaps rarely completely immune from corruption. The first of these points relates closely to Mill's Infallibility Argument: the argument that anyone who censors free expression assumes their own infallibility (which is an unreasonable assumption to make for a human being).

3   Truth becomes stagnant if people believe what they believe simply on the grounds that some figure in authority has told them that this is what they ought to believe. Even if the belief is true, it is not held in the appropriate way.

Here Milton is using the Dead Dogma Argument that Mill also uses.

4   Censorship is a cowardly way out when we should be concerned to refute, not simply silence, wrong opinions.

This point is quite similar to Mill's notion that truth will emerge from a collision with error.

5   We will very likely censor truth by mistake since new truths can look very much like falsehoods when we aren't used to them.

This relates to Mill's Infallibility Argument. Mill gives a number of examples of cases where new and important truths have been stifled by censorship because they had the appearance of falsehood.

EXERCISE 4.6

Answers are included in the main text.

EXERCISE 5.1

The three reasons Mill gives are:

1   the people who have formed the customs may have done so on the basis of too narrow a range of experience, or may have misinterpreted that experience.
2   the customs may simply be unsuitable for the person in question.

3   pursuing a way of life simply because it is the customary way of going about things doesn't help to develop our distinctively human attributes.

EXERCISE 5.2

Answers are included in the main text.

EXERCISE 5.3

Answers are included in the main text.

EXERCISE 5.4

Answers are included in the main text.

EXERCISE 5.5

(2) and (4) are examples of vicious circularity, the others are not.

EXERCISE 5.6

Answers are included in the main text.

EXERCISE 5.7

Answers are included in the main text.

EXERCISE 6.1

1   False. Adding together everyone's particular will gives you the will of all.
2   False. The will of all is that everyone should receive £1 million.
3   True.
4   False. The will of all could not be put into practice in this example.
5   False. The whole point of the quoted passage is to distinguish the general will from the will of all.

EXERCISE 6.2

(1), (4) and (5) are first-order desires; (2) and (3) are second-order desires because they are desires about desires.

Revision test

This test is intended to help you revise some of the main points covered in this book. Try working through the questions without using your notes or referring back to the text. Then compare your answers with those at the back of the book.

1 Negative liberty is:

(a) Freedom from psychological blocks which prevent you from doing what you really want to do.
(b) The opposite of freedom, namely imprisonment.
(c) Toleration of different approaches to living.
(d) The absence of obstacles, including natural ones, to what you want to do.
(e) Freedom from constraints imposed by other people's actions.

2 Positive liberty is:

(a) Freedom from all constraints.
(b) The freedom to live as you please without state interference.
(c) Freedom to act, self-mastery, or self-realization.
(d) The kind of freedom that Locke advocates in relation to religious belief.
(e) Freedom which you are certain you have.

3 According to Isaiah Berlin:

(i) Negative freedom has never been achieved.
(ii) Negative freedom is the only type of freedom worth pursuing.

(iii) Positive freedom has in every case led to totalitarianism.

(a) (i) only.
(b) (ii) only.
(c) (iii) only.
(d) (ii) and (iii) only.
(e) None of (a) – (d) above.

4   According to Berlin, those who believe in a 'final solution' believe that:

(a) There is a huge diversity in the ends people seek, and consequently the only way to resolve differences is to force minorities to comply with the majority.
(b) We should always be tolerant of individual differences, because everything will work out for the best in the end.
(c) All worthwhile goals in life are ultimately compatible.
(d) We should never tolerate groups which threaten a society from within.
(e) Whatever solutions to social problems are selected should be final; we should never revise our opinions on their suitability.

5   According to Berlin:

(i)   The concept of negative freedom has never been abused.
(ii) Historically the concept of positive freedom has often been abused.
(iii) Those who abuse the concept of positive freedom sometimes have justified oppression on the grounds that it may be necessary to force people to be free.

(a) (i) only.
(b) (ii) only.
(c) (iii) only.
(d) (ii) and (iii) only.
(e) None of (a) – (d) above.

6   Which of the following statements are true?

(i)   'Freedom' is never an emotive word.
(ii) The meaning of 'freedom' is fixed and doesn't vary according to the context in which it is used.
(iii) The words 'freedom' and 'liberty' are often used interchangeably in the context of political philosophy.

(a) (i) only.
(b) (ii) only.
(c) (iii) only.
(d) (ii) and (iii) only.
(e) None of (a) – (d) above.

7   Locke argued that:

(i)   Those who were themselves intolerant deserved to be persecuted.
(ii) Some forms of religious intolerance were irrational.
(iii) Atheists should not be tolerated.

(a) (i) only.
(b) (ii) only.
(c) (iii) only.
(d) (ii) and (iii) only.
(e) None of (a)–(d) above.

8   Premise 1: Magistrates' only sanction is physical force.
    Premise 2: Physical force never changes religious belief.

    What conclusion did Locke draw from these premises?

(a) Magistrates ought to use psychological torture if they want to alter people's religious beliefs.
(b) Intolerance of any kind whatsoever is always wrong.
(c) Magistrates who try to change people's beliefs by using physical force rarely succeed.
(d) Magistrates can't alter people's religious beliefs.
(e) Magistrates who persecute people on religious grounds can't really want to change their victims' minds.

9   Which for the following are contingent facts?

(i)   If you believe something then you believe that it is true.
(ii) Locke's *Second Letter concerning Toleration* was originally written in Latin but subsequently translated into English.
(iii) You are attempting to answer this question now.

(a) (i) only.
(b) (ii) only.
(c) (iii) only.
(d) (ii) and (iii) only.
(e) None of (a)–(d) above.

10 Which of the following best describes Locke's Unchristian Argument?

(a) No Christian should ever be persecuted for his or her beliefs.
(b) It is unchristian to question the nature of religious belief.
(c) It is unchristian to be hypocritical.
(d) Christians ought not to persecute atheists.
(e) It is unchristian to persecute others.

11 Mill believed that:

(a) Utilitarianism was a false philosophy.
(b) The state should intervene to force adults to lead worthwhile lives, even when they risked no harm to others by their choices.
(c) Paternalism is appropriate towards children but not towards adults.
(d) The Harm Principle should be applied to all societies, no matter what their state of social development.
(e) Harriet Taylor made no significant contribution to *On Liberty*.

12 Fitzjames Stephen

(i)   Was basically in agreement with Mill's conclusions in *On Liberty*, and just wanted to suggest minor amendments.
(ii) Suggested that Mill's division between acts which only affected the person concerned and those which had the potential to affect others, was untenable.
(iii) Believed that coercion was always morally wrong and should never be used.

(a) (i) only.
(b) (ii) only.
(c) (iii) only.
(d) (ii) and (iii) only.
(e) None of (a)–(d) above.

13 According to Mill's Harm Principle:

(a) It is permissible to harm someone else if they harm you first.
(b) Governments shouldn't ever do anything which harms their subjects.
(c) Freedom is not worth anything unless it includes the freedom to cause minor harms to people who get on your nerves.
(d) Taking offence is a paradigm case of being harmed.
(e) People can be forcibly prevented from harming others.

14 Those who think Mill fails to provide a utilitarian justification for the conclusions of *On Liberty* argue that:

(i)   A consistent utilitarian would have to be prepared to use coercion when this would maximize aggregate utility, even if no one risked being harmed if coercion was not used.
(ii) Mill had already publicly rejected all the major utilitarian beliefs by the time he came to write *On Liberty*, and no longer saw himself as connected with utilitarianism in any way.
(iii) Mill provides insufficient guidelines for the successful application of the Harm Principle.

(a) (i) only.
(b) (ii) only.
(c) (iii) only.
(d) (ii) and (iii) only.
(e) None of (a)–(d) above.

15 Which of the following arguments does Mill use in support of freedom of speech?

(i)   Unless a view is allowed to be challenged and discussed it is likely to be held as a dead dogma.
(ii) Geniuses have only ever emerged in societies which set no restrictions on freedom of speech.
(iii) Those who censor other people's views are usually hypocritical.

(a) (i) only.
(b) (ii) only.
(c) (iii) only.
(d) (ii) and (iii) only.
(e) None of (a)–(d) above.

16 Mill argues in favour of:

(a) Complete licence as to how you live your life.
(b) Treating geniuses as reliable authorities on how best to live.
(c) Following the customs of the society in which you find yourself, thereby building on accumulated wisdom.
(d) Encouraging eccentrics to tone down their eccentricities for the greater good of society.
(e) Paternalism towards those incapable of making responsible decisions for themselves.

17 For Rousseau the general will is:

(i)   Synonymous with the will of all.
(ii) What any rational member of society should choose.
(iii) The general consensus.

(a) (i) only.
(b) (ii) only.
(c) (iii) only.
(d) (ii) and (iii) only.
(e) None of (a)–(d) above.

18 Marcuse argues that:

   (i)   In advanced industrial societies everyone recognizes their real needs.
   (ii) Affluence is the most straightforward path to genuine freedom.
   (iii) It is never right to censor a sincerely held opinion.

   (a) (i) only.
   (b) (ii) only.
   (c) (iii) only.
   (d) (ii) and (iii) only.
   (e) None of (a) – (d) above.

19 Taylor argues that:

   (i)   The pursuit of increased negative freedom is the best route to self-real-
         ization.
   (ii) Positive freedom is an unachievable goal.
   (iii) We can have internal obstacles to achieving freedom.

   (a) (i) only.
   (b) (ii) only.
   (c) (iii) only.
   (d) (ii) and (iii) only.
   (e) None of (a) – (d) above.

20 Which of the following were *not* objectives of this book?

   (a) To give you practice in a range of reasoning techniques.
   (b) To help you understand and think critically about some important argu-
         ments about freedom.
   (c) To provide a detailed examination of Mill's arguments in *On Liberty*.
   (d) To explain the history for the word 'freedom' from the time of the
         Ancient Greeks to the present day.
   (e) To broaden your philosophical vocabulary.

Answers to revision test

1 (e)
2 (c)
3 (e)
4 (c)
5 (d)
6 (c)
7 (d)
8 (d)
9 (d)
10 (e)
11 (c)
12 (b)
13 (e)
14 (a)
15 (a)
16 (e)
17 (b)
18 (e)
19 (c)
20 (d)

Bibliography

Ashley, Chris, *et al.* (eds) (1994) *OU Open Teaching Toolkit: Tutoring and Counselling Students in Prison*, Open University.

Barry, Norman P. (1989) *An Introduction to Modern Political Theory*, 2nd edn, Macmillan.

Berlin, Isaiah (1969) *Four Essays on Liberty*, Oxford University Press.

—— (1998) *The Proper Study of Mankind*, Pimlico.

Boswell, James (1992 edn) *The Journals of James Boswell 1762–1795*, John Wain (ed.), Mandarin.

Dent, N.J. (1992) *A Rousseau Dictionary*, Blackwell.

Devlin, Patrick (1963/1983) *The Enforcement of Morals*, Oxford University Press.

Dworkin, Ronald (ed.) (1977) *The Philosophy of Law*, Oxford University Press.

——(1985) *A Matter of Principle*, Harvard University Press.

Fitzjames Stephen, James (1967 edn) *Liberty, Equality, Fraternity*, R.J. White (ed.), Cambridge University Press (first published 1873).

Glover, Jonathan (ed.) (1990) *Utilitarianism and its Critics*, Macmillan.

Gray, John (1995) *Isaiah Berlin*, Fontana Modern Masters.

——(1996) *Mill, On Liberty: A Defence*, 2nd edn, Routledge.

Hart, H.L.A. (1963) *Law, Liberty and Morality*, Oxford University Press.

HMSO (1995) *Consent in the Criminal Law*, Law Commission Consultation Paper no. 139.

Horton, J. and Mendus, S. (eds) (1991) *John Locke:* A Letter Concerning Toleration *in Focus*, Routledge.

Jahanbegloo, Ramin (1993) *Conversations with Isaiah Berlin*, Phoenix.

Koestler, Arthur (1959) *Sleepwalkers*, Hutchinson.

MacCallum, Gerald C. jnr (1991) 'Negative and Positive Freedom', in Miller (1991).

MacIntyre, Alasdair (1970) *Marcuse*, Fontana Modern Masters.

Magee, Bryan (1987) *The Great Philosophers*, Oxford University Press.

Marcuse, Herbert (1969) 'Repressive Tolerance', in R.P. Wolff, Barrington Moore jnr and Herbert Marcuse (1969).

——(1991, 2nd edn) *One-Dimensional Man*, Routledge.

Mendus, Susan (1989) *Toleration and the Limits of Liberalism*, Macmillan.

Mill, J.S. (1962 edn) *On Liberty*, in *Utilitarianism and other Writings*, Mary Warnock (ed.), Collins.

——(1985 edn) *On Liberty*, Gertrude Himmelfarb (ed.), Penguin.

——(1989 edn) *Autobiography*, John M. Robson (ed.), Penguin.

——(1991 edn) *On Liberty and other Essays*, John Gray (ed.), Oxford World's Classics, Oxford University Press.

Miller, David (ed.) (1991) *Liberty*, Oxford University Press, Oxford Readings in Politics and Government.

Milton, John (1993 edn) *Complete English Poems, Of Education, Areopagitica*, Gordon Campbell (ed.), Dent, Everyman, updated 4th edn.

Oates, Joyce Carol (1994) *On Boxing*, The Ecco Press.

Orwell, George (1949) *Nineteen Eighty-Four*, Penguin, 1989 edn.

Phillips, Miles (1987) 'Prisoners of the Inquisition, 1568–75', in John Carey (ed.), *The Faber Book of Reportage*, Faber.

Rousseau, Jean-Jacques (1973 edn) *Discourse on the Arts and Sciences*, in *The Social Contract and Discourses*, G.D.H. Cole, J.H. Brumfitt and John C. Hall (eds), Everyman, Dent.
——(1994 edn) *The Social Contract*, Christopher Betts (trans.), Oxford University Press, World Classics.
Sherry, Norman (1994) *The Life of Graham Greene. Volume Two: 1939–1955*, Jonathan Cape.
Swift, Jonathan (1726) *Gulliver's Travels*, Penguin Classics edn, 1985.
Taylor, Charles (1991) 'What's wrong with negative liberty', in Miller (1991).
Warburton, Nigel (1998) 'Freedom to Box', *Journal of Medical Ethics*, 1998, vol. 24, pp. 56–60, reprinted in Warburton (ed.) (1999).
——(1998) *Philosophy: The Classics*, Routledge.
——(1999) *Philosophy: The Basics*, revised 3rd edn, Routledge.
——(ed.) (1999) *Philosophy: Basic Readings*, Routledge.
——(2000) *Thinking from A to Z*, revised 2nd edn, Routledge.
Wasserstrom, Richard A. (ed.) (1971) *Morality and the Law*, Wadsworth.
Williams, Bernard (1973) 'Deciding to Believe', in *Problems of the Self*, Cambridge University Press.
——(ed.) (1979) *Obscenity and Film Censorship*, Cambridge University Press.
Wolff, Jonathan (1996) *An Introduction to Political Philosophy*, Oxford University Press.
Wolff, Robert Paul (1969) 'Beyond Tolerance', in R.P. Wolff, J.R. Barrington Moore and H. Marcuse (1969).
Wolff, R.P., Barrington Moore, J.R. and Marcuse, H. (1969) *A Critique of Pure Tolerance*, Jonathan Cape.

Index